God=mc²?

God = mc²?

God=mc²?

Getting Spirituality Down to a Science!

So that you can create the life of your dreams by tapping the power of Divine Energy!

PRASANN V. THAKRAR

Copyright © 2010 by Prasann Thakrar

Published in India for Om Enterprise Group, LLC, and available via the website, www.GodEqualsmcSquared.com and other fine online and offline retail outlets.

God=mc^2 is a Trademark of Om Enterprise Group, LLC.

Edited by: Debra Weigert * Cover concept by: Prasann Thakrar

Cover design by: Dharmesh and Kalpa Joshi, www.kalpart.com

All rights reserved. No part of this book may be reproduced by any mechanical, photographic, or electronic process, or in the form of an audio recording; nor may it be stored in a retrieval system, transmitted, or otherwise be copied for public or private use - other than for "fair use" as brief quotations embodied in articles and reviews - without prior written permission from the author and/or the publisher.

Medical Disclaimer: The author of this book is not a medical doctor and does not dispense any medical advice or prescribe the use of any principle or technique mentioned in this book as a form of diagnosis, treatment or cure for any medical problem - physical, emotional or mental - or for that matter any problem that could have a medical or clinical nature to it. If you think or know that you may be suffering from any such medical condition(s), please seek the advice of a physician or another medical professional. You may use the information in this book for your spiritual advancement and well-being or you may use it for any purpose at all. However, regardless of the reason for your use of any of this material, neither does the author, nor does the publisher assume any responsibility for your actions. By purchasing or reading this book in any form, whether that may be in print, electronically, i.e., via an e-book download, or listening to it in an audio format, you implicitly release the author and the publisher of this book of any liability, whatsoever.

**To order a copy of this book, please visit:
www.GodEqualsmcSquared.com
Or
www.AllYourWishesFulfilled.com**

ISBN-13: 978-0-9841947-9-7
ISBN-10: 0-9841947-9-7

First Printing - October 2009, Limited Quantities (Advance Reading Copies)
Second Printing - July 2010

Printed in India

Aksharatit Offset Printers, Pvt. Ltd.
Gujarat, India

Dedicated to my son Krish,
the apple of my eye!

I love you!

TABLE OF CONTENTS

FOREWORD - By Dr. Vipul Chitalia, M.D., Ph.D. xi

PREFACE xv

SECTION I: Introduction 1

Chapter 1   : Goodbye! 3

Chapter 2   : Huh? "Goodbye??!!" What kind of a nonsensical way to *start* a book? 5

Chapter 3   : My own existential crisis 21

Chapter 4   : Coming to America (Not quite Eddie Murphy-style!) and what has happened since then 33

SECTION II: Query - What Is "It" All About, Anyway? 43

Chapter 5   : Can *you* handle the truth? 45

Chapter 6   : Mission: Impossible? (Or at least, very, very difficult!) 53

Chapter 7   : We are all One! (Really? That's such a platitude, or is it?) 61

Chapter 8   : Elementary, my dear human 67

Chapter 9   : "My Karma ran over your dogma!" 75

Chapter 10   : *Dharma & Greg*? No, Dharma and....you! 81

Chapter 11   : Greed *is* good! 87

Chapter 12	:	Definitions - Spirituality Defined, Religion Understood, God Decoded, Science Demystified, Faith Fathomed, Conscience Comprehended 93
Chapter 13	:	Know Thyself! (What does that even mean?) 113
Chapter 14	:	Are you a (*The*) *Secret* admirer? 117
Chapter 15	:	Question: The one of Life, the Universe, and Everything; Answer: 42 125

SECTION III: Phenomena - Spiritual Phenomena On The Verge Of And Now Explicable By Science; And Vice Versa! 129

Chapter 16	:	The red shoe on the roof: Near Death Experiences examined; you guessed it; for science's sake.. 131
Chapter 17	:	From *near* death to death *actually*! Is it so morbid that we shouldn't talk about it? Naaaah!... 135
Chapter 18	:	Are you a Sinner or a Saint? 141
Chapter 19	:	You got ghosts? Whoyagonna call? 145
Chapter 20	:	Conversations with a *real* psychic: My 11-year old niece! 149
Chapter 21	:	E.T.'s and UFO's - Science "fiction" or science "fact?" 161

Chapter 22 : Time would be on your side in your travels if you could Teleport or Bilocate 167

Chapter 23 : Quantum Possibilities! A very "real" possibility of a "new" you?! 171

SECTION IV: Action - What Should We Do, Exactly, To Lead The Life Of Our Dreams - The Kind That We Are Meant To Lead? 183

Chapter 24 : "Science is truth!" 185

Chapter 25 : You want to change your life for the better? Then practice spirituality scientifically and apply science religiously 193

Chapter 26 : Specific applications for specific situations 231

Chapter 27 : Meditate; don't medicate! (Well, medicate to heal your body; meditate to heal your soul) 255

Chapter 28 : Kundalini Rising! How you can use the power of this evolutionary energy to change yourself and the world 261

Chapter 29 : Pro Bono (Hint: This does *not* mean "being in favor of the band U2's lead singer") 265

Chapter 30 : Can we *ever* afford to *not* be nice? 273

Chapter 31 : Leggo my ego! 277

Chapter 32	: Do you think that the world would be *any* different if *you* did not exist?	287
Chapter 33	: How will you see yourself and everybody else after this?	293
Chapter 34	: "God wants spiritual fruit, not religious nuts!"	297
Chapter 35	: Closing time!	303
Chapter 36	: Goodbye! (For real now, I mean it!)	307

ADDENDUM 309

RECOMMENDATIONS AND SOURCES 311

ACKNOWLEDGMENTS 317

ABOUT THE AUTHOR 323

FOREWORD
By
Dr. Vipul Chitalia, M.D., PhD

Science is ever-evolving, while spirituality is eternal. Many attempts have been made to substantiate one on the basis of the other. However, as it happens in kidney transplants where the body finds it difficult to accept an external kidney, psychologically, the rejection of any concept is easier than its acceptance. This could explain why the acceptance of the idea of God or "Supreme Consciousness" is not a natural phenomenon, and why, most of the time, a book with an Atheistic message hits the New York Times bestseller list.

If you talk to growing kids, especially teenagers, you would realize that they would say "I hate you!" or "I hate this," before they learn to love someone or something. Hatred and rejection, thus, are sort of immature instincts, whereas learning to love and being accepting requires a lot of practice and maturity. Similarly, when someone says "I don't believe," they have a lot of growing-up to do. They would need to embark on the journey "inward." Since we all are spirits at the core of our being, it should be easy, or at least, easier, to accept something we are born with already or something which is internal or which lurks within us throughout our lives. Why then, even if we try hard to understand, we fail to see it? This begs the fundamental question, have we honestly dissociated ourselves from our souls which are within us, or have we chosen not to feel and see them?

Look at a ruler. On one side, the distance is depicted in centimeters and on the other side in terms of inches. Both run parallel and in perfect congruence! One would wish that science and God were so simple that they would have such a relationship. Neither has science perfected itself nor has God decided to fit Himself entirely in the "box" of human intelligence and scientific understanding.

It seems He loves playing Hide and Seek, especially with our inner "Einstein"; the inquisitiveness within all of us. And in playing that game of Hide and Seek, the Supreme reveals to us a few aspects of His whole truth, via science and the scientific method. So, even though science is moving *towards* being able to explain God, and it will remain ever-approaching that state of fully being able to explain All That He Is, we can still know and experience God in the meantime, however, through spiritual means.

Any discipline ought to be studied in its own terms and rules. Physicians undergo training for almost a decade before they can even prescribe an aspirin. The greater the depth of a discipline, the longer it takes to fathom. In that vein, the journey to imbibe the Eternal Truth usually spans over many births. One of the pivotal aspects of science is its reproducibility. If the experiment is done under the same conditions and using the same parameters, the result yielded ought to be similar. A game of chess played over and over again, following the rules would achieve the same result every time, thus the reproducibility. Similarly, many souls with an open and enthusiastic yet patient and loving attitude have had an experience of God with the same sort of reproducibility. In other words, the process of reaching the level where one can experience God is scientific because it is reproducible. Thus, God is scientific!

Over centuries, many institutions have come into existence and humongous volumes of text have been written to explain Him. We still have not evolved ourselves to experience or relish Him in a spontaneous way such as enjoying an ice cream cone or taking an evening stroll. However, He comes like a cool breeze or a heart beat; so simple and spontaneous. We have to train our senses to experience God everywhere, be it in a talk show or a movie.

In this book, Prasann Thakrar has provided a fundamental understanding regarding the different scientific and spiritual facets of God in an uncomplicated and easy-to-understand fashion. They say that "a mother is born in labor"; I feel Prasann was "born" in the process of writing this book! I have seen a metamorphosis of Prasann during this period from a habituated, worldly person to a cool and calm "surfer" on the "Innernet" of his soul.

In today's world, we have a lot of information readily available everywhere and in every form, but still this does not treat loneliness or depression. While taking care of patients who may be suffering from loss of memory, Dementia, or are otherwise disoriented or delusional, I realize the value of a simple conversation or some form of human interaction. As you read this work, you will realize that this casual and conversational style is an unconventional one, as far as normal written prose is concerned; however, via this style of writing, Prasann has effectively delivered "the goods." He has perfected the fine art of combining scientific and spiritual writing, and has done it in a uniquely fun way. Prasann covers these topics of science and spirit in a way that would be practical and usable to you. Based on that, I am of the opinion that the "conversation" that he engages you in would be appreciated very much in today's environment where people have little to no time to interact with one another, let alone to engage someone in a conversation that could be potentially life-transforming. So, I know that you will enjoy this "talk" with him, and it just may change your life for the better.

In conclusion, on the overall subject of science versus spirit, I would like to say that God is and has always been all-encompassing; infinite and eternal; and therefore, science will remain ever-approaching Him!

Vipul Chitalia, M.D., PhD
Harvard-MIT Division of Science and Technology
Massachusetts Institute of Technology, Cambridge, MA

PREFACE

I want you to be happy. Not just the regular ol' happy; I want you to be blissfully, completely, totally, infinitely and eternally happy! In other words, I want you to experience the state of being which is known as *Ananda* in the ancient Indian language of Sanskrit – Bliss!

I want you to know that not only is it possible, but that you came here to do just that. And that you; yes, *you*, the person reading these words; already possess all that you need or could *ever* need to accomplish that goal. And my job is, simply, to help you realize that knowledge, first, so that you would reach a point of believing that you do, in fact, possess all that you could ever need. And once you are there, it is my job to help you actually realize that goal; although, you will already be on your way to doing that on your own once you are aware of the infinite supernatural powers that you wield. But before I can do anything to get that process started, I have one very fundamental question to ask you:

Do you believe in God?

If you do believe in God's existence, then think about the reason *why* you believe. If you don't believe or are not sure, then think about why that is the case with you.

Please pause, and think about the answer to this question before you read any further. You could also answer this question: Are you an Atheist, an Agnostic, a Believer, a member of the Clergy, or a Layman, or a Scientist?

Your answer to the question above is moot, as far as *I* am concerned. I only asked it to get *you* to think about where you are on the Spectrum of Belief.

Regardless of whether you believe in God's existence or not, or if you are unsure, I know one thing to be absolutely true: You *want* to believe! Why?

The reason I know that you want to believe is because by believing, life does get easier. Or at the very least, we *think* that life *should* get easier if we believe in God. Well, why would life get easier if we believed? It would get easier because we could ask for God's help when we are in need of help, couldn't we? And if we do believe in God's existence, and ask for His help, we would also believe that He would, as a matter of fact, come to our aid. This would be a logical conclusion because if God does exist, and if we pray for His help, then how could He ignore our prayers?

I have a heartfelt request for you: Please do bear with me here because I know that you might have heard these questions - the question that I asked you about your belief in God, and the ones that I am *about* to ask - being asked of you before. Maybe you might have even heard them asked in the same way as I am asking them. And based on that you might start to think that you have read, and heard and even seen all of this before. That what is to follow after this series of questions is going to be the "same ol', same ol'."

I promise you that it will not! So, having made that solemn request and also the subsequent solemn promise, I have a few more questions for you. This time around, the answers to these questions do matter to me as well, and are not just of importance to you alone. Here are the other questions:

Do you want to have lots of money? I mean lots and lots of it? Do you want to find your "soul mate" and be madly and deeply in love with that person, forever? Do you want all your other relationships to be great also? Do you want to be at the peak of your health always, and have a great-looking body to go along with that? Do you want a great job or business that you absolutely love and enjoy working at every single day? Do you want fabulous friends with whom you can laugh and enjoy your life?

Well, of course you do! We all want all of those things, without exception. The questions in the paragraph above were not meant to be "trick" questions at all. However, they *were* meant to be rhetorical ones to get you to think about what are the things that you want in your life. And now, I have yet another set of rhetorical questions for you.

Do you want to be happy? I mean, really, really happy? Do you want peace in your life? Do you want to lead a stress-free life? And do you want to experience these states of being *all* the time?

Again, please do bear with me here because you may have also heard the correlation being made - a correlation that I am about to make - between the "material" things; i.e., the ones that I mentioned a few paragraphs ago, and the "feeling" states of being; the ones that I mentioned in the paragraph above.

We all know this to be true; it is not *new* knowledge that we all want all of these physical and material things in our life - the wealth, the relationships, the career, the health, the friends and anything and everything else we can imagine - for one ultimate reason or purpose, and that is….to be happy!

Happiness is the *why* of wanting all the material wealth, isn't it?

(Again, this is not news to us, however, it may surely be the case that we seem to forget why, exactly, we might be striving to achieve some kind of a material success in our lives. And in our dogged pursuit of the *means* to the happiness, we forget the real why, the *end* to those means! That realization or remembrance may seem like new knowledge or news to us, however.)

The reason for wanting the ultimate end - happiness - is, simply, because we are *meant* to be happy. We all have a gut instinct of this being true, don't we? In fact, not only are we meant to be happy, we are meant to be happy *all the time*! We are meant to be in a state called "bliss," which means being in a state of happiness, contentment, peace and always experiencing and being filled with love.

Some religious and spiritual traditions have been quoted (erroneously, in my opinion) as saying that the material things are not important. The only thing that is important is the "inner" happiness. I would only partially agree with that. I do agree that inner happiness is extremely important, and I would even go as far as saying that the attainment of the ultimate inner happiness, this bliss that I just talked about, *is* the *ultimate* goal of life, and therefore not just an "extremely important" thing, but that it is *the most* important thing.

However, the problem that we, as humans, encounter is that we are *both*, physical and spiritual - body and soul - and therefore it becomes imperative that we achieve both, the physical *and* the spiritual goals, in order to be truly happy, and therefore experience the bliss that we are supposed to experience.

All material things exist for one and only one reason - to serve the spiritual being. In my opinion, if somebody were to say that they can teach us how to achieve spiritual enlightenment, but they *will not*, or worse, *cannot* teach us how we can achieve material wealth, they are simply not capable of doing either of those things. So, *both* are *equally* important in the context of humanity, and the human experience.

This book is about exactly that - how to achieve *all* of these goals - the physical and the spiritual, as you will see.

Now, switching gears or really only seeming to switch gears, I would like to ask you a few more questions.

Have you ever wondered about or asked yourself these questions: *Who am I? Why am I here? What is the meaning or purpose of life? Does God really exist? And if He does exist, then why aren't all my prayers answered? Why do "bad" things happen to "good" people?*

And if you are *really* analytical, *Why do "good" things happen to "bad" people?* (Because you *know* that they *do* happen - you see some really "horrible" people seemingly enjoying their lives thoroughly and without a care, and all the while doing all the "bad" things, even criminal things, imaginable - and it just does not make sense to you. You might wonder, "How could *that* be?")

You might have wondered about any of the combinations of *good* and *bad*, *things* and *people* that you could come up with. You might have pondered many other such seemingly unanswerable questions.

I know that I have pondered them. My having pondered these questions led me to doing extensive studies of some hard scientific research out there, and doing some spiritual analysis of the circumstances and events that have transpired in my own life. Moreover, it led to some scientific and spiritual "experimentation" in my life.

From my research, I have uncovered *scientific* evidence of God's existence! Yes, you did read it correctly, there is scientific evidence of the existence of the thing, being, or entity we call God. The *spiritual* evidence, if you will, already existed. It exists in terms of what religion preaches and from what is said in the holy books of all religious and spiritual traditions. However, I had to prove it to myself that the spiritual evidence was also real and valid. And so I was also provided with the *spiritual* evidence of God's existence, along with the *scientific* evidence that I sought.

From all of my research and experimentation, I have found evidence that not only does God exist, but that He (or She or It) *wants* to answer *all* our prayers!

Well, as long as we "pray" the "right" way. (Here when I say "pray," it does not mean religiously. It could simply be a wish that you might have or it might have been a request. In other words, it might simply be something you want or desire in your life.)

And when we learn to "pray" the "right" way, we *can* have all the material wealth, *and* all the spiritual bliss, *and* also have all our "unanswerable" questions answered - all in one fell swoop!

Please know that I write about non-denominational spirituality, based on science. I do not preach any particular religion, and I write very little about the overall subject of religion. If this book is taken in the right context, and I have faith and a knowing that it will be, the information that is revealed here will only serve to *strengthen* a reader's faith in whatever religion one believes in, and at the same time, paradoxically, make them stronger believers in science. And the reason I believe that this will happen is because my book reveals the scientific evidence of God's existence. So, now, science will be backing up the faith of Believers. Interestingly enough, if Atheists or Agnostics are open to seeing and accepting the evidence presented here, it will make them believers of God.

Another note of importance: I have used a very conversational and colloquial style of writing in this book, with mixed-in narration. For the most part, I have written it the way I would speak; the way I would talk to you, if you were my friend or acquaintance. It will "sound" to you like we are sitting across from each other and having an informal conversation. You will find that this style of writing is unlike traditional prose you might find elsewhere and that I don't always follow the rules of grammar. For example, I start many sentences with "And." I also use capitals for the initial letters of many words which may not be proper nouns, and thus do not require capital letters; however, I have done so for specific effect or emphasis. My hopes are that you all will really like this unique approach that I have chosen as a way to express my thoughts.

Also, to make these complex and "heavy" topics of science and spirituality seem simple and "light" and therefore, very easy to understand, I have used all kinds of pop-culture references; viz., movies and movie quotes, lyrics from popular songs, TV shows, commercials, bumper stickers, church signs, popular books, spiritual texts, my personal experiences, and quite frankly, anything and everything that I found which could help get the message across more effectively, and even humorously and entertainingly. I hope that this will also make these topics easy to relate to. And if they become easy to understand and relate to, it will be a breeze to apply the related practical principles in your life.

In other words, it will make these goals of life-transformation, and of creating and leading one's dream life very easy to achieve. (As they surely can be, and should be!)

Having said that, I beg of you to know that you need not have experienced any of these "pop-culture" things that I refer to in order to really understand what I am talking about. In other words, you need not have seen the movies, heard the songs, watched the TV shows or commercials, have come across the same bumper sticker, seen the particular church sign, read the particular books, or otherwise have known about the particular person, place, event or thing that I am referring to, for you to "get" what I am trying to convey.

Of course, it surely can only help if you have, but it is not entirely necessary because I do try to provide proper context of the particular pop-culture reference, and therefore, even if you may not know of the one I am referring to, the concept behind it should still be understandable to you. As an exception to this rule, if there is something that will be extremely important for you to know about or experience - for example, read a particular book or watch a particular movie - I will say so expressly.

Also, I would like to reiterate that this book will, if anything, reinforce the faith that one may have in one's own religion. It will make that faith stronger. And if some Believers have had their faith questioned lately, it will serve to remove those questions, once and for all. This book is not meant to sway Believers into becoming Non-Believers, and it is also not meant to promote one specific religion or spiritual tradition over another. It may, however, without intention, make Believers out of Non-Believers. It is also not meant to undermine science; it merely points out that science is approaching that point where it will be able to march in lock-step with spirituality; however, that it is not quite there yet.

I would also like to add that even though this is not a "peer-reviewed scientific work," it does have a lot of scientific material, examples, experiments, and conclusions - all of which are based on sound scientific principles and the scientific method. At the very least, that is my own opinion.

So, that was all about the overall concept of the book. Now, I will give you a breakdown of the physical layout of its content. And after that, I will end the Preface with the ultimate intent of this book.

It is broken down into four different sections, and I have presented a more detailed description of each section right before it begins, so you will know what that section entails. However, here's a brief description of those sections so you will have an idea of what to expect.

The first section is a more detailed introduction of the book. It has a description of the circumstances that led to my writing it and the several reasons for my having done so. It has more of my personal information than any other section or chapters. Personal information such as my life-crises and the struggles that I have had in my life. It also elaborates on my intention for the readers of this book, more so than I have done here.

The second section is a Query Section, in which I delve deeply into the question and answer of what "it" is all about, "it" being Life, God, the Universe, Spirituality, etc.

In the third section, the Phenomena Section, I hone in on various "spooky" or "mysterious" phenomena which, up until very recently, most scientists were simply not willing to do research on.

In this section, I also reveal what these phenomena have to do with science or spirituality, and ultimately, what they have to do with you.

The fourth section is what I call the Action Section of the book. In this section, I suggest the actions that one can take; and if taken step-by-step, and methodically, actions which will guarantee success in transforming one's life. So, those are the four sections of the book and that describes the physical lay-out of the book.

Lastly, I would like to disclose the overall intent of the book by taking immense pride in saying that this is the second Self-Empowerment book in print. Of course, this "fact" is self-proclaimed because there is only one other book of its nature that I have come across.

The first one in the "new" genre of Self-Empowerment books is entitled *The Biology of Belief*. In the Preface of the book, the author, Dr. Bruce Lipton, says that his book is not a Self-Help book, it is a Self-Empowerment book. I loved that! In that same vein, I could truly say that mine is also the same. So, instead of being the umpteenth in a genre of "Self-Help" books, this is the second entry in this new genre of Self-Empowerment books.

By virtue of it being so, my intention for it is to be the facilitator or purveyor of the knowledge that is going to help create the life of their dreams for billions of people worldwide. To empower them with the knowledge - the knowledge that is encoded in their souls, but that they have temporarily forgotten how to access - that they *already* possess the power to bring bliss to themselves. And by being thus empowered, they will then be inspired to start using that power to create and lead the life of their dreams.

So, I truly wish you all the best that life has to offer, and I have faith that in your being empowered and inspired to create and lead the life of your dreams, you will also empower and inspire others you may come into contact with to do the same.

Now, that's what I call a truly virtuous cycle!

SECTION I : Introduction

In this Introductory Section, I start with the mention of the nuances of the English language by talking about the meaning of some words in common use that we will find is not exactly what we originally thought it might have been. The close examination of these words of everyday-usage will, quite literally, change the English language, if I may say so without sounding boastful. Or, at the very least, change that small part of the English language that pertains to the usage of those specific words. Of course, we will also examine what the usage or meaning of those words has to do with science or spirituality, exactly.

Apart from that, in the first two chapters, I mention the several reasons why I decided to write this book, and also explain why I think this may be relevant to you.

I would like to say, here, that after about five pages or so into Chapter 2, you *may* choose to, temporarily, skip the rest of that chapter and fast-forward to Chapter 3, because although the rest of Chapter 2 *is* important, it is more of a personal rant and rave from me. I am not asking you to ignore and not read what I have written in the rest of Chapter 2 because that would be completely absurd, coming from an author. (But then again, this *is* a unique book, so maybe even that is not so absurd.) I am just saying that you *may* want to *come back to it*, later on. I just don't want it to stop you from moving ahead in your reading, and if you do find that it is stalling you, you can simply skip ahead, but *only after* having read the first five pages of that chapter.

God=mc²?

In Chapter 3, I discuss my most major life-crisis, among other crises; I write about my struggle with Depression, Obsessive-Compulsive Disorder, and my hunger-strike against God in my early teenage years - the deepest, darkest and most frightening and hopeless times of my life - and my subsequent encounter with a person who, to this very day, I cannot be sure was a human being. In Chapter 4, I talk about how and why that encounter led to my deciding to immigrate to the United States. I briefly mention my struggle with a second major bout of Depression later on in my late twenties, and how I, eventually, ended up on my current path.

The reason I go into these details about how and why I was inspired to write this book, and what I went through in my life, is because I think that once you know these details, I truly believe that you will find them to be relevant to your own life, or to some issue or problem that you may have been dealing with in your own life. I trust that you will find this information invaluable in helping you figure out what it is that *you* want to change in *your* life, and why. And not only that, I have faith that you will come to a place of knowing that you *can* truly change anything in your life, also.

You know, the much corny and clichéd "If I can do it, so can you!" message is what I am trying to convey by briefly divulging my "boring" life-story in this section.

And thereby, I hope to successfully segue into what my intention is for you, which is to have a permanent, *positive* impact on your life - a total change or transformation in every aspect imaginable - so that you can create and lead a life of your dreams, which is what we all are meant to do.

Chapter 1
Goodbye!

Goodbye! (Yup, that's it - "Goodbye" - I am going for the shortest chapter in history - one word, well, of course, not counting these words within the parentheses here!)

Chapter 2
Huh? "Goodbye??!!"
What kind of a nonsensical way to *start* a book?

Yes. *Goodbye!* We have all used this word all our lives, haven't we? We have all used it regardless of whether we are at one end of the spectrum of religious belief, as the most devout believers or as members of the clergy; or if we are agnostics, scientists, laymen or are at the other end of the spectrum as complete atheists. (You might be wondering what the word *Goodbye* has to do with one's religious beliefs. As you will see just a little bit later on, it has a *lot* to do with it.)

Despite having used this word all our lives, most of us have no idea as to what it means. Okay, maybe we do, but we think it means something like "Hasta La Vista, baby!" as my favorite movie star and Governor, Arnold Schwarzenegger, has so famously said and immortalized in *The Terminator* franchise, basically meaning "See you later," or "See you tomorrow," or something to that effect. Have a "good" bye as opposed to having a "bad" bye; whatever *bye* is

God=mc²?

supposed to mean. Why would we ever wish anything bad to anybody; so it *had* to be a good bye, right?

I had thought the same thing too until I was exposed to its true meaning. Here's how it happened:

A few years ago, one evening, on my way back from work on my commute from South Station (Boston) back to Attleboro (a small city located in the southern part of Massachusetts), I had picked up the Boston Herald and was reading it on the commuter train, as had been my routine for the previous few years. After having read some news stories, I read the puzzle or trivia question of the day, which was a daily feature of the Paper. The question for that day was, "What does the word *Goodbye* mean?"

And I never forgot the answer to it! I was awestruck at the fact that it was a word that I had used, pretty much, *all* my life and never really had any idea, whatsoever, as to what it *really* meant. In fact, it had been one of the very first words that I ever spoke when I learned to talk, as it is for almost all children. One of the very first words that children learn to speak is, in fact, *Bye*.

Before moving on, I have to give credit where credit is due for this "new" knowledge that I had gained. And it is due the Boston Herald, one of the two biggest newspapers in the Boston metro area.

So, you might ask impatiently, "*What* is the real meaning of the word *Goodbye*?" The meaning is "God be with you!"

Shocked? Surprised?! I know that *I* was definitely surprised! And quite frankly, I was even more surprised to find out that it is not even a word - it is actually a shortened Middle English *phrase* - "Good be with ye," i.e., "May the Good be with you." In other words, may *God* be with you. As *Good* and *God* are synonymous, and this fact will be evident when we discuss, in detail, the definitions of both of those words, later on in the book. Also, the actual word *God* originated from the word *Good*.

Huh? "Goodbye??!!"

So, technically, now knowing this, the atheists and/or agnostics of the world would, or at least, *should*, stop using this word to bid somebody adieu, shouldn't they? The reason that non-believers would stop using the word, in my humble opinion, is because they would be wishing that may God be with that somebody that they are saying Bye to. (*Goodbye* further contracted is *Bye*, as it may be evident to us now.)

Incidentally, another Middle English version of the same is *Goodspeed*, or *Godspeed*, again, meaning pretty much the same thing - "May God speed you." In other words, "May God accelerate your progress." (This reminds me of a scene from the 1996 hit action flick, *The Rock*. The legendary Sean Connery, who plays a former British intelligence agent named John Patrick Mason, makes a comment about Nicolas Cage's character who is a biochemist and an expert on chemical weapons and works for the FBI in this capacity. His name in the movie is Dr. Stanley Goodspeed. If memory serves me well, Connery says to Cage that *Godspeed* and *Goodspeed* are the same, or mean the same thing.)

Anyhow, regardless of which one of these you use, you are acknowledging not *just* the *existence* of God, but also the *presence and the active involvement* of God in everybody's life, or at the very least, in the life of the person to whom you are wishing the same. That by simply "wishing" or "praying" that it would be so, God would actually *be* with somebody; that is what you are saying when you utter that word. But here's the problem, *if* it is a problem: You can only truly believe that God is actually *with* somebody, if you *first* believe in the *existence* of God Himself (or Herself); that goes without saying but I am saying it anyway.

(Note: For simplicity's sake, I will often refer to God as a "He," or a "She," or an "It," because I don't want to give an indication one way or another. I am neither asserting nor denying that God is a being like us, and that God is a male or a female entity. Please know that

God=mc²?

I will use any one of those pronouns at any given time and that I am referring to the *same* God, no matter what pronoun I may use.)

Regardless of how we may choose to or choose not to use this word in the future, *Bye* does have a new meaning to us; or I should say we are now being exposed to its true meaning, which is new to us.

This realization just stuck with me like a few other things that have stuck with me, and I will also share those other things with you later on. Anyhow, that realization made me think about the fact that there are so many more words and phrases and idioms and clichés we use on a regular basis and only have a *vague idea* of their etymology and therefore the meaning of the same because, for the most part, when you learn how and from what source a word originated, you also learn its original and true meaning - its *real* meaning - the meaning that the person who coined it wanted to convey. The same applies to a phrase, or an idiom or a cliché. (As far as *Goodbye* is concerned, for simplicity's sake, I will just call it a "word," instead of a word formerly known as a phrase.)

The word *Goodbye* is truly a perfect example of an actual English word that we all use - all over the world, regardless of the native language. It may not be news to you (or it *may* be news to you) that even in a lot of countries where English is not the primary language, people say the word *Bye* to each other when leaving each other's presence or company. And now we know that it has huge religious implications, doesn't it? (As I had mentioned in the first paragraph of this chapter, we will see that it does.)

Wars have been fought and countless lives have been lost over the meaning of words! Millions - many, many millions, if not billions have been needlessly sacrificed over the meaning of the words *Life*, and that of *God* and *Religion* and for that matter, even *Science*.

Some people might argue that it is not the *meaning* of the words that people fight over, but rather the *ideas* represented *by* those words. And again, I would say that, ultimately, it is still the meaning of the words that make up the concept or the idea of what it is that the word is describing. And that is precisely why one word has a different meaning for one person and another meaning for another person (and thus, the resulting fights over it).

And for that reason, I found it completely, totally, and utterly necessary that I write this book. I had to do it to honor the lives of the people who tried to convey the right meaning of these words to us. I had to do it as a sign of respect and homage to them.

Now, it may sound petty, but despite, and especially because of what I *just* conveyed, that is *not* the primary reason for my writing this book.

My primary reason or aim is to get us thinking about how it is that these ideas or concepts represented *by* these words - *God, Religion, Science, Spirituality, Life* - actually interact with one another and how they compare and contrast with one another. In turn, causing us to see these words in a new light, while and as we really understand their true meaning. And thus, truly getting enlightened about all of these subjects - because, deep down in our hearts and minds, we all really *do* want to be enlightened, don't we?

And when this aim is realized, we all will see that, really, Science and Spirituality simply don't have to be in the diagonally opposite corners of the Cosmic Boxing Ring. They simply are on the same exact team, and just passing the baton onto another member of the team for this lap of the track - this "lap" being whatever you want to choose - this decade, century or millennium.

I know, I know - I just mixed two sporting metaphors, but you get the point, don't you? Or to use a non-sports metaphor - that they are two sides of the same exact coin. Oh, wait - that could be the coin toss in a sporting event - ok, so now I have used three sporting metaphors.

God=mc^2?

Regardless, when that happens; i.e., when we will see that Science and Spirituality are on the same team, we will be able to see the "practical" side of Spirituality as never before explored and explained. We will learn the "How's" and the "Why's" of practicing Spirituality scientifically, and of applying Science religiously, in our lives. And this "technology" or "know-how" will help us lead a more happy, peaceful and joyous life - which is what we all want - *regardless* of where we fall on the Spectrum of Belief or which Spiritual/Religious tradition we subscribe to (*or even if we subscribe to none*).

Of course, we *can* have all the other things that we all want too; all the "juicy" stuff; the stuff of our dreams - to have a lot of money, better relationships, better health and a better body than ever before, a beautiful home, a fancy car, or a *few* fancy cars, great friends, and anything else that we can think of - all of which only *add* to our happiness, peace and joy in life. At least, all of these things are *supposed* to add to our happiness, peace and joy in life. And if we find that they are *not* doing so, we will learn how to allow for that to happen, and at the same time, bring *more* of these things into our lives.

Thus, the practice of applying this knowledge will allow us to do exactly that - create and lead a life of our dreams - in every possible way and even in ways that we may have previously thought to be impossible.

(As I had mentioned in the explanation of this Section, this is the part from where you could choose to hit the "fast-forward" button to the beginning of Chapter 3 for now, and come back to the rest of this chapter later on. If you are a brave soul, and wish to continue reading this chapter and want to read my rant, I do commend you on that, but please don't say I did not warn you.)

To reiterate what I had mentioned in the Preface, please know that I write about *non-denominational* spirituality, based on science.

Huh? "Goodbye??!!"

I do this because it is my opinion that spirituality is *more* important than any specific religion, and that, ultimately, religion teaches spirituality anyway; i.e., how to become spiritual; in other words, how to connect to Originating Spirit – God. So, if you can connect to God, or want to do so *with* or *without* subscribing to any particular religion or spiritual tradition, then you are following what religion teaches anyway. (Well, religion is *supposed* to teach that; whether it really does that or not would be a subject that would require a whole other book.) That's why I neither follow any particular religion, nor "preach" it, and that's also why I write very little about the overall subject of religion.

However, *only* for a *few* moments, why don't we discuss *one* of the *two* most controversial subjects of our time - Religion, and the other being Politics – as in "Don't talk about Religion or Politics!" Well, since I was told, more than once or twice, to *not* talk about either of these subjects because they are "controversial," "sensitive," or even "offensive," I am not only going to *talk* about them - I am going to write a whole flipping book about a subject related to *both* of them.

(Pun most definitely intended in terms of it being a "flipping book," and also notice that I did not use the obvious offensive "f" words - either of them - a la *What the BLEEP do we (k)now!?* Which, by the way, is one of my favorite movies - a hybrid film - a combination of a documentary and a feature film. It is a favorite because it changed my life and it also happens to be *one* of the *several* reasons for my writing this book.)

And of course, I have already done that; i.e., write the book; you are holding it in your hands right now, flipping through it, scanning it, or reading it.

But before I go on, I would like to, if I may, opine a little bit more on the sensitive or controversial subjects of Religion and

God=mc²?

Politics as to the reason why they are so. Here's the fact that the reason people find it difficult, if not impossible, to have a "civil" discussion about Religion and/or Politics is that they are just downright intolerant of another person's belief about *either* or *both* of these controversial topics. (In my "opinion" this is a "fact"; I say that tongue-in-cheek because how can an *opinion* be a *fact*!?)

There, I said it! Better yet, I *wrote* it - it is in print - that I think that people are not as tolerant as they may think they are. People might think and even genuinely feel that they are *not* intolerant (please pardon the double-negative here) and that they are really open-minded and are, in fact, open to new ideas and suggestions. That they are more than willing to change their mind if presented with a good argument from somebody that would make them reconsider their position on *anything*.

But they are simply not that way. (At least, most of them are not. Again, these folks may be good-natured and good-hearted people, and they may really believe that they are open-minded and very tolerant. However, they don't know that they aren't that way because their mind-set and thought processes have just not been challenged enough to make them realize that.) *Some* are truly so, and indeed, those "some" make the world a better place in which to live, and thankfully, many more are moving towards a more open-minded attitude, and that makes me very hopeful about our future.

I am looking forward to a time, very soon, when we *can* have a "civil" discourse and a discussion; a healthy debate about these things. I truly do believe that this will transpire in a not-so-distant future.

Hopefully, my endeavors here help do just that - allow many more minds to be open to the ideas presented in this book and, at the very least, generate intelligent debate about them, if not an acceptance and application of the principles presented here.

Huh? "Goodbye??!!"

Throughout the book, I do tend to digress a little (really, *a lot*) and those segues and detours may not seem related to the subject at hand, but mostly, they are. It may be some additional information, say, about a particular word, or a place or something quirky about the topic at hand. I do hope that you will really find these little "detours" and digressions as amusing, entertaining, educational, or even enlightening as I think and hope they are.

I am totally and thoroughly ready for the fact that some of you may not agree with some, or even a lot, of what I have to say in this book and that is perfectly okay with me as long as you *do* see what my primary intent behind it is. Which is, after all is said and done - or in this case, after all is *written* and done - to have a permanent, positive impact on *you*. I hope to change *your* life for the *better*, once and for all. And if this book does that even for *one person* on this whole planet, then I would have done my job, and I would have done it very well.

Anyway, as Jay Severin, a host of a "controversial" radio talk program that focuses on Politics and political issues which is aired on the Boston Talks radio station on the WTKK, Greater Boston Radio, Inc. network, would always say, "We should be able to disagree without being disagreeable." (President Obama used to say that a lot on the campaign trail when he was still a candidate in the last Presidential election. I have also heard him say the same after he was elected to the highest office in the Land. However, the first person that *I* have ever heard make that statement is Jay.)

So, in that vein, I don't agree with a lot of things that Jay says on-air, and then there are a few things that I do agree with him on. However, now, after having learnt to *really* think for myself, and also having adopted Jay's motto, I *try* not to allow any disagreements I have with anybody let me become disagreeable with them, and if that does happen in a rare case, I apologize as soon as I can.

God=mc²?

(Sidebar: I am an advocate of free speech, controversial or otherwise. Any wonder why I, myself, am writing this book which could, very easily, be categorized as "controversial." However, having said that, just because one has the right to express oneself freely doesn't mean that one is also exempt from the consequences, whether they may be good or bad, resulting from the exercise of that right. There is still a responsibility that comes along with the right to freedom of expression.)

By the way, if you *really* want to have your thinking challenged and can see through; rather, *hear* through, the controversy (regardless of political persuasion, and *only if* you are a strong individual who can take potentially belief-changing metaphorical "punches" to the head), other than reading this book, I would suggest that you tune-in to Jay's show - every weekday - from 2:00 PM to 6:00 PM. By the way, in comparison to Jay's show, my book represents potentially belief-changing, and therefore, life-transforming metaphorical "gentle taps" to the noggin. (Not quite the punches that Jay throws, but still pretty potent in their effects!)

And did I just hear somebody ask, "What's the frequency, Kenneth?" 96.9 FM - in the Boston-Metro area, if you are in range of the transmitted frequency and can tune in.

(Note: I have no affiliation, whatsoever, with Jay Severin or with the 96.9 FM Boston Talks radio station, as a whole, and any opinions expressed by Jay are solely his opinions, and are not related to mine and make no reflection on my book, either positive or negative; well, with the exception of the one point I mentioned above about "disagreeing without becoming disagreeable.")

So anyway, I will now step off the Political Soap Box - that's all from me on that subject and believe me, that was not much at all - I could have gone on for hundreds of pages (maybe Jay will invite me to co-author a book with him about Politics, if I may be so lucky

Huh? "Goodbye??!!"

and deemed qualified enough to do so) however, for now, *that* was enough.

We have other very controversial subjects to tackle here. The point in mentioning Jay's show was (and still is) that we don't *have* to agree on *everything*. In fact, it really would be pretty boring if we actually did agree on everything. A lot of you might agree with me on that, I reckon, and the irony of *that* agreement is not lost on me.

If there were no disagreements over anything, there would be no new ideas created or discussed. No progress, in the *real* sense of the word, would be made! So, we *do* want opposing and challenging ideas and philosophies and schools of thought interacting with each other all the time - the only caveat being, we don't allow ourselves to get disagreeable in the process.

That, my friends, is the way to be a part of and to encourage the evolution of humankind, and yes, we *are* evolving - in every possible way - physically, mentally, intellectually, emotionally and spiritually!

Incidentally, Jay's show or for that matter, the 96.9 FM Boston Talks radio station, as a whole, has (or *used* to have) a tag-line - it is "Boston's Talk Evolution." Coincidence? I think not. (That may have changed, recently – maybe only a few months before this book goes to print. However, that only reiterates and signifies the importance of this talk about evolution and change.)

And that, among several other reasons, is the dialogue and discourse that I want to generate by writing this book. To get *all* of us to think about *God, Religion, Science* and *Spirituality* - the *meaning* of those words - in the true sense - in the way they were originally *meant* to be understood, and I really do mean *all* of us - regardless of whether we are Believers, Atheists, Scientists, Agnostics, Clergy or Layman. And yes, even if we think that we really know the meaning of those words already.

God=mc²?

Of course, what good is knowing, intellectually, the real meaning of these words if we don't start applying the practical principles behind them in order to create and lead the life of our dreams? For you to learn how to apply the principles mentioned herein *is* the ultimate goal or intention of mine, and we will surely realize that intention together.

At the very real danger of sounding like I am bragging (and I beg for your forgiveness if I do sound like that because I am not doing so), another one of the several reasons that I am writing this book is because I think that I have received a blessing. I am so very thankful for having received this blessing which is, in my opinion, this ability to write. And not just the ability to write, I am also thankful for the inspiration, hopefully, to write *well*. I am talking about an ability to express oneself in an articulate manner, and to write in such a way that the true intents and meanings of the words written are clear to the reader. When the reader understands what the writer is trying to convey, that, in my opinion, is good writing, regardless of whether the reader agrees with the presented ideas or not.

Of course, I *think* that I *do* have that talent; otherwise I would not subject my readers to a sub-par piece of work. (I wanted to use another word that started with a "c" and ended with a "p" instead of the word *work*, but you get the idea.)

Only *you* - my readers - can truly and honestly judge whether I possess this talent or not, and I am sure that you all will judge me fairly and accurately. I had originally written that it was a "God-given talent," but that sentence had me making a positive statement - right here - in the introduction of the book that not only does God exist, He also imparts these gifts. So I removed that statement. Regardless of the source, I am utterly grateful for this "gift," "blessing," natural talent, or ability.

As I mentioned before, at the risk of sounding boastful, I brought up this topic of possessing natural talents or gifts in my hopes

Huh? "Goodbye??!!"

of motivating or even inspiring you to look within yourselves to find your own unique natural talent. To find that *something* that only you can do. Or something that *only you* can do *in* the way you do it, in your own unique way. Something that you are passionate about but have not yet pursued. Whatever "it" may be. Whether it is painting, making music, writing prose or poetry, sculpting etc., it does not matter. It does not have to be just the arts. You could have the talent to be an exceptional carpenter or an exceptional doctor. You could be very talented in the field of providing customer service because you happen to be a "people person," or you could have the skills to be a lawyer, or you could be great at public speaking, or being an engineer, or being an inventor might be a passion of yours. It can be the sciences - or it can be anything at all.

My dear friend, Dr. Vipul Chitalia, M.D., PhD, who is also my scientific and spiritual guru, always says to me that "It is a gross sin against God to not use the talent one possesses." I have come to agree with him; if there does exist such a thing as a "sin," *this* would be it!

(We will discuss this in much greater detail in Chapters 25 and 26, which deal with specific details of how to create and lead the life of one's dreams. For now, suffice it to say, one should try to endeavor to discover that "gift," and try to be grateful for it, and of course, try to use it for the good of humanity, along with the good of oneself. Also, in Chapter 18, we will discuss whether "sins" truly exist or not.)

While growing up in India, I attended schools where the medium of teaching was English, and somehow, I have always had an affinity for the English language from ever since I can remember learning my first words. No wonder that I had known and felt that I should have been writing and trying to explore the possibility of writing professionally, now, for over 17 years - since my first days in college. This was right after the time when I first arrived in the United States, which was in 1993. After feeling this initial nudge from

God=mc²?

within to write, I got distracted by other things and, consequently, the urge to make writing my passion and profession subsided to the point where I ignored it. Besides, I also did not know *what* to write about, back then. All I knew was that I would have loved to have been writing, and so it was an "aimless passion," and therefore it did not take me anywhere. Now, that dormant urge has re-ignited and knowing what I now know, I feel that I *must* put that urge to good use. Now, I also have a subject that I feel very passionate about; i.e., the one of bridging science and spirituality to create and lead the life of one's dreams, and so I wrote this book.

Hammer, the rap artist formerly known as M.C. Hammer, made famous by his mega-hit album from the early 90's, *Please Hammer, Don't Hurt 'Em*, rapped in *U Can't Touch This*, the uber-famous song from that album, "Oh my Lord, thank you for blessing me with a mind to rhyme and two hype feet; it feels good….," and thus expressed - by those words - his gratitude for the rapping and dancing talent that he possessed. In the same way that he was grateful, so am I - for *my* mind and the experiences that I have had and for every single person that I have ever interacted with, on *any* level - because all I am is the result of *all* of those interactions.

So, thank you - to *all* of you - to every single one of you that I have ever come into contact with, because *you* helped shape the person that I am today. And so, obviously, without you all - I would not have learnt what I have learnt. I simply would not be the person that I am today. That is, the person who has written this book and who hopes that it will change the lives of its readers.

And every one of you is God's creation just like I am. (Ooops, did I just let the proverbial "cat out of the bag" again? Did I already answer, in some way, the question that I raised as the title of this book?)

Huh? "Goodbye??!!"

Nope. Sorry! I am claiming all of these events as a fact, which they absolutely are; i.e., that I am a result of all of my interactions, and that I am truly thankful to all of you for who I am now, and what I have become.

But who, or what created the Universe, and everything - every living and non-living thing - in it and who, or what is God, exactly, is still up for debate. At least, up until the very end of this book, or somewhere in the middle - you are just going to have to find it for yourselves. Sorry to be such a tease! But if I told you what happens in the "end" now, why would you read the rest of the book?! This isn't the *Titanic*, and we all don't already *know* what happens in the end. (By the way, I am a self-proclaimed "movie buff" and "expert," however, I have yet to see one of the biggest grossing movies of all time - you guessed it – *Titanic*.)

So, after what Chapter 1 was, i.e., the *shortest* chapter in history, followed by Chapter 2, which may have seemed to be the *longest* introduction to a book.......finally, here goes nothing!

Chapter 3
My own existential crisis

Well, *that* is an ongoing process; i.e., to feel the crisis of my existence and to rise above or to overcome it every single day, and if possible, to rise above it ever so slightly higher than the day before. The goal, in this process of rising above the crisis, is to reach a progressively higher place every day. To make a "new high" every day. And I am *not* talking about a substance-induced high here.

"This stock has been making *higher* lows, and *higher* highs." This is what some Wall Street professionals, known as Technicians or Technical Analysts, would say when looking at the chart of a stock's price movement - one that has been on a generally steady uptrend. And even on days that the price of the stock is down, it is still higher than the price it was at before it made the latest move upwards. It is akin to taking two steps forward, and one step back, and continuing with that kind of a movement, progressively forward, or higher, to keep the metaphor consistent. (Normally, taking two

God=mc²?

steps forward and one step back would be considered to be a negative thing; however, here, in the context of rising above one's crisis of existence, and, apparently, also in terms of the Technical Analysis of a stock's price movement, it is surely a positive occurrence.)

Anyhow, there is a *single event*, or even a *single moment* in time, that completely and totally turned my life around, and ultimately, set me in motion towards reaching the goal of the path that I am on – the goal of Higher Consciousness. (Although, it did take several more years for me to even realize that it had been such a monumental moment in my life.)

It is the very reason that I even ended up coming to these United States of America, leaving behind my life, my friends, my home in a small city in the State (Province) of Gujarat, which is located in the Western part of India. The name of my city is Baroda, or as they now call it, Vadodara, which was its original name before the British anglicized it in their pronunciations during their rule over India. By the way, in a similar fashion the city of Bombay is now, again, called Mumbai, which was its original name.

Vadodara is about 300 miles northwest of Mumbai, to give you an idea of the geography of where I grew up. (And now, with the super success of the movie *Slumdog Millionaire*, it is ever more important to satisfy the curiosity of my readers who may want to know where, exactly, I am from.)

I, *most certainly*, would not have been writing this book if I had not had the inexplicable experience that I had about 19 years ago because I would have been dead otherwise.

I had initially fought with the idea of including this "chapter" of my life, so to speak, in this book as an actual chapter in it. I really thought that I did not want to bore you with my "tale of woe," and quite frankly, it was, and still is, a very *personal* matter for me. It was also a very *private* matter for me, well, up until now, of course, since I will be sharing it with you here.

My own existential crisis

I finally did convince myself that I should include it, but I was going to put it near the end of the book because I thought that it was not consequential to whether or not my readers "got anything" out of this book; however, I did think that it may be important enough to be included *somewhere* to provide *some* context of the circumstances and situations that I had been through in my life. And then someone close to me told me that I *had* to include it in the book, and right in the beginning.

The reason, they told me I needed to do so, was that they thought my story was truly powerful, and that by sharing it, I would be able to help a lot more people than I could have without sharing it. And as you will see, contrary to my initial belief, it really is very consequential to what I am trying to do here. Which is, hopefully, to get you to see that you can totally transform your life, if you choose to do so, and that you really do have the power to do just that.

So, here I am, about to tell you my story with the faith that even if it gives hope to one single person on the verge of ending their life, or suffering from Depression, or from Depression *and* OCD, or is in some hopeless situation otherwise, then having told it would be well worth any embarrassment that it could quite possibly bring me.

Of course, please note that you *don't need* to be suffering from *any* of the above mentioned maladies in order to have any benefit from this story, or for that matter, from this book. You could have some minor problems in your life, or even have no problems at all, and still gain a lot from the material here. If your life is going fairly well, and all you want to do is simply improve things in one or more aspects of your life, you will still be able to benefit from the subject matter and the principles in this book, and still change your life for the better, because *life can always be better*, even if it is already pretty good.

(OCD stands for Obsessive-Compulsive Disorder - as most of us may very well know what that is, thanks to the "Defective

God=mc²?

Detective" named Adrian Monk, played by the extremely talented Tony Shalhoub in the series named after and based on this title character, which used to be on the USA network. Another very famous character who suffers from OCD onscreen was in the name of Melvin Udall, played by the incredibly amazing Jack Nicholson in the movie *As Good As It Gets*.)

So, as I hinted above, but did not directly admit it, I suffered from clinical Depression and OCD, well before it may have been considered even remotely "cool" to have OCD. In my late to mid teenage-years, I had all kinds of things going on in my life, and I had just come to the end of the road. Divulging all the details of my 1/8th - life crisis would require a memoir by itself. So, for now, it should suffice to say that because of the situation I was in, I had been very sad and depressed, and as the situation persisted, this condition of chronic sadness changed into a serious Depression of a clinical nature. I had developed obsessive-compulsive tendencies from a few years before that; however, they had not much affected the quality of my life. But now, combined with my Depression, the whole thing just put me over the edge! I had a few good friends, but I did not trust any of them with the gravity of my situation. I did not truly believe that they could have helped me (maybe they *could have* helped me, but I did not believe, at that time, that they could have). And family, well, they would just not have understood me, or so I thought.

So, one day in 1990 or 1991, I don't remember exactly what year it was, I left a note for my parents and ran away from home. The note said this:

Dear Mom and Dad,

I am going through some things that I know you won't understand or be able to help me with. I am badly addicted to drugs and so I need to be away from home right now, and I am going to a place where I hope to get better and to become free of this addiction. Please do not try to find me because I won't be found.

My own existential crisis

If all things go well, I will be back. If not, then I won't be coming back home ever again.

Prasann.

Of course, I made up the story about the drug addiction just so that I would have a reason to tell them about why I was running away from home. I placed the note in an envelope, and sealed it. I handed the envelope to Murthy, the security/elevator attendant of the building that I lived in. I told him, "Please deliver this to my home in about an hour."

Then I hired a small cab, an auto-rickshaw - a vehicle that looks a lot like the very cute and diminutive Smart "for two" car - and went straight to the Vadodara S.T. (State Transportation) bus station. I boarded an S.T. bus headed to a place about 220 miles from my city, a village called Veerpur (also spelled alternatively as "Virpur").

Veerpur is very sacred place. It is the birthplace of a Saint called Jalaram. Saint Jalaram was born in 1799 and he dedicated his life to serving people and to feeding the hungry. There are legendary stories of how this Saint, long after his departure from Earth in 1881, helps any and all who ask for his help.

Normally, one does a pilgrimage to Veerpur, his birthplace. People often promise to sacrifice enjoying a beloved delicacy that they simply cannot live without; others perform extremely unpleasant acts such as walking barefoot for hundreds of miles to reach Veerpur; many others partake in other similar austerities in order to "please" Jalaram and thus, to receive his blessings and divine grace.

What I had in mind was something a little bit different. I decided that I would not eat any food, nor drink anything, not even water, until Saint Jalaram fixed my problems. In other words, I went on a hunger-strike against Jalaram! This meant that the hunger-strike was indirectly against God, because he was a great follower and devotee of Lord Rama, and the Hindus believe Lord Rama to be one of the ten "avatars" or incarnations of the Almighty.

God=mc²?

I had brought prayer beads with me to Veerpur. This set of prayer beads had 108 beads, and one would recite the name of God as one would move the beads through one's fingers, one by one. This is like a Rosary. Basically, it is a method of counting without actually paying attention to the actual number of times one would have repeated God's (or a Saint's) name or recited a particular "mantra." So, one would start the count at the "head bead," a bigger bead than all the rest, and there is also this fuzzy little thing on the head bead, to differentiate it from the rest of the beads. So, one would start there, on the "mala," meaning "garland" or "necklace" of beads, and that would indicate the first bead or count, and when the head bead was reached again, one would know that one had repeated the "mantra" 108 times.

So, I had that mala, or prayer beads with me, and I carried them wherever I went while I was in Veerpur. After getting off the bus, I had walked into the center of the village, where Jalaram's temple was located. I went into the temple and prayed in front of Saint Jalaram's picture (there is no statue of Jalaram there; there is only his picture, the only real photograph of him). Then I went to this little yard near the entrance of the temple and sat down and started to recite Jalaram's name, going through the beads, over and over again. I was there until the temple closed, which was at about 8 or 9 PM.

I stayed at a small motel for the first night that I was there. While in the motel room, I even remember thinking and contemplating a much faster end to my life, but then coming to a conclusion about sticking to one that I had already chosen. Besides, I did not really *want* to die; I just wanted my problems solved! So, I remember getting down on the floor, on my hands and toes, and banging out as many push-ups as I could.

Now, when I recall this scene, I can't help but laugh - because there I was, a person on a hunger-strike against God, trying to burn off as many calories as possible in order to hasten the arrival of the "end moment." The logic was that Saint Jalaram would not let me

My own existential crisis

die, especially since I had been a believer and devotee of his all my life, which I had truly been. The preferred outcome would be that he would miraculously materialize and fix everything before I died or was even close to dying. Conversely, if the worst-case scenario were to transpire, Jalaram would not show up, meaning that he would have abandoned me, and I would die of starvation and dehydration. Of course, that being the farthest from the preferred outcome.

Anyhow, I must have fallen asleep after doing a lot of push-ups. The next day, I went to the temple and, again, prayed all day for Jalaram's intervention, which, of course, would be considered "divine" by its very nature.

Late in the evening, the temple was closed for the night and I realized that I had no place to stay for the night because I had brought only enough money to get back home by bus. If I stayed in the motel another night, I would not have enough cash to get back (if, by the grace of Saint Jalaram, that were to happen, and that was, in fact, what I was counting on).

So, that night, I walked back to the Veerpur bus station, which was located on the outskirts of the village, if my memory serves me right, and found a bench there and made myself as comfortable as possible. I had a back-pack with me with a change of clothes, and I remember using it as a pillow, at times. And then, later on that night, as the mercury dropped, I found that I was cold, and I remember converting my "pillow" into a "blanket." I stuck my arms into the back-pack at the openings of the zippers. My back-pack had those double zippers instead of just the solitary one, and so, I created two openings just large enough to slide my arms into it. Then I held the back-pack close to my chest, with my arms completely in it, to keep me warm.

The next morning I walked back into the village and stayed at the temple, praying hard and begging Jalaram to come to my aid. I continued to pray with the beads. But nothing happened! Neither did

God=mc²?

Jalaram materialize in front of me, nor did I even get a "vision" of him. No "miracles," no spontaneous resolution to my problems, nothing.

After a full day of praying; dejected, hungry, thirsty, exhausted, and emotionally drained, I walked back to the bus station that night also. At this point, it had been almost three full days since I had eaten or drank anything. And of course, an equal amount of time had elapsed since I had been "missing" from home.

(Now that I am a parent, I cannot believe how I could have put my parents through the agony and the ordeal of having their child go missing for days! My only excuse, if I even have one, would be that I was, obviously, out of my mind with misery at that time, and that I was just not capable of thinking about anybody else.)

So, I approached my "bed," the same bench that I had slept on the night before, and laid down, and put my head on my "pillow." Somewhere in between bouts of crying and praying, I somehow fell asleep. Then suddenly, at least that's how it seemed to me, somebody tapped on my shoulder and woke me up! It must have been 3:00 AM or so as it was still very dark outside. It was an older looking man, dressed in a brown uniform (kind of like the UPS guys). That uniform happens to be the standard uniform of the drivers and conductors of the S.T. buses of the State of Gujarat.

So, it made sense to me that he was a bus driver and this was, after all, a bus station. I was still a bit groggy and attempting to get my bearings when he asked me a question. "What are you doing here at this time, son?" I hesitated in answering and even before I could say anything, he asked me, "You have run away from home, haven't you?" I nodded sheepishly to indicate that I had.

Then he asked me, "Where are you from?" I replied convincingly, "Ahmedabad." Now that I was fully awake, and had my defenses up, I lied and told him that I was from another big city in my State. I did not want to give him the opportunity of contacting my parents

My own existential crisis

and letting them know of my whereabouts and have them come get me because that would have defeated the whole purpose of my having run away from home.

Then he said in a firm, yet gentle tone, "Your parents must be worried sick about your being missing and so you should return home as soon as possible." He added calmly, "Whatever your issue or problem may be, it will surely be resolved soon after you get home safely."

I lied again, and said, "You are right. My parents must really be very worried. I will take the first available bus back home." Of course, I had no intentions of leaving that place alive unless my problems had been solved. He said "I am very glad that you have made the right decision. You just get home, and then you will see that all will be well." Then he was gone as mysteriously as he had appeared. I didn't know where he went, I was just glad that he was gone because I felt guilty about lying to him and did not want to keep doing so.

Despite having already made up my mind about what I was going to do, the bus driver's words gave me a glimmer of a hope. I don't know what it was; the tone of his voice, or maybe the glint in his eyes; but I believed him. I got a feeling that, somehow, things were going to be alright. I just did not know how.

I could not go back to sleep after that, and before I realized it, a couple of hours must have gone by and the sun was already starting to rise. It was getting brighter and brighter. It must have been six o'clock or so when I made my way back to the village and to Jalabapa's temple and started to pray with the beads. (Devotees of Saint Jalaram also call him Jalabapa - "Father Jalaram." *Bapa* or *Bapu* means "father," just like Mahatma Gandhi was also lovingly known as *"Bapu."* The language to which I am referring is Gujarati, my native tongue.)

God=mc²?

After an hour or two, I got this sudden feeling that things were, as a matter of fact, going to be better if I returned home. I did not hear any words in my head or anything like that, I just got a feeling that Jalaram had or, at the very least, was going to, solve all my problems. At that moment, I felt no need to stay there any longer. It was as if my prayers had been answered!

I still did not break my fast and end my hunger-strike, though. I just cannot seem to remember why I would have done that. It couldn't have been the fact that I had only enough money for the bus ride back home, and that I did not have money for food because there is food served all day at the temple, completely free of charge. Jalabapa had dedicated his life to feeding hungry people, and the temple built in honor of celebrating his service and divinity also has been doing the same now for over 124 years or so.

Anyhow, I said a prayer of "thank you" to Saint Jalaram by going inside the temple and closing my eyes and bowing my head in front of his picture. His walking cane and a make-shift back-pack of sorts - a bag made by taking a rectangular piece of sturdy cloth and tying the opposite corners to each other - are also in display at the temple. I said a prayer of "thank you" to these two belongings of Saint Jalaram. And then, I started to walk back to the bus station. Once I got there, I went up to the ticket window to inquire about the timing of the departure of the next bus headed back home, and to buy the ticket for the same. There was a bus departing later on that afternoon or early evening, but I would have had to take another connecting bus from the destination of that one, because it did not go all the way to Vadodara. Even though it meant that I would get home at around three or four the next morning, it was fine with me because I wanted to get home as soon as possible, and that would have been the fastest way.

So, after having bought my ticket, I was just hanging around the bus stop contemplating whether I should go back into the village again, and spend some more time in Jalaram's temple when I thought

My own existential crisis

about the bus driver whose words had given me hope. So, I went back to the ticket window and asked the employee minding the window about this bus driver. I explained that it was an older gentleman, who, it seemed, may have lived in Veerpur, and was present at the bus station at around 3:00 AM. I speculated that maybe he must have just gotten done with his shift or that he may have been ready to start it.

The person at the window said that he did not know a bus driver with that description, and not only that, there would have been no reason for anybody, let alone a bus driver, to be at the bus station at 3:00 AM. There were no buses coming in or leaving for a few hours before that time, and for a few hours after that time.

That made me think about the whole scenario again. He was right! I recalled that when the bus driver had woken me up, there were no buses there at all, in fact. None! And in fact, there were no other people around at that time, either. Neither passengers waiting to board a bus, nor any who might have just gotten off an arriving bus.

And since the bus station was on the outskirts of town, there was really nobody else around either.

I got some major goosebumps right then. Who was that person? Was it even a person?! Was it an angel?!! Was it Saint Jalaram himself?!!!

Well, I did not have a definite answer then, and I don't have one still. However, I do know that it was the miracle that I needed!

(As a dear friend of mine, Michelle Kurcina, said to me, "It gives a whole new meaning to the UPS slogan, 'What can Brown do for you?'" And considering the fact that the "bus driver" had been dressed in a brown uniform, it surely does!)

Chapter 4
Coming to America (Not quite Eddie Murphy-style!) and what has happened since then

On my ride home from Veerpur, I had begun contemplating a situation that had been presented to me by my parents almost a year ago, from that day.

I contemplated the extremely important, and life-changing, decision to immigrate to the United States of America, which had been left up to me. You see, a few years back from that time period (maybe in the 1980's) my uncle - my father's brother, Anil Thakrar - and his family had been living here in the U.S. for a decade and a half. My uncle had become a Naturalized U.S. citizen with the help of his employers at that time. After becoming a citizen, he had filed petitions with the INS, the Immigration and Naturalization Service (which is now called the USCIS), to have his blood-relatives be able to immigrate to the U.S. This, by the way, is one of the very important and most coveted privileges of being a U.S. citizen; i.e., to be able to file petitions with the INS in order to have relatives come to America legally.

God=mc²?

Among many other relatives, one of those petitions was for my father and our whole immediate family. However, by the time it was our turn in the long queue of pending files to be processed, it had been almost a decade from the time since my uncle had filed his petitions. Years or decades for one's file to be the next for processing was normal and quite routine for these types of Visas, the Permanent Resident kind. These Visas grant the "Resident Alien" status to a foreign national; the famous or infamous, depending on how you look at it, "Green Card." (On a related note, every time I saw the phrase "Resident Alien" on my Green Card, it made me feel like I was actually an alien, you know, an E.T. And that, inexplicably, always made me nostalgic and want to phone home!)

Anyhow, by the time it was our turn to have our files processed, my three sisters were already married, and would not have been able to immigrate to the U.S. because they were no longer single, and also were over the age of 21 years. My brother was still single, but unfortunately, he was over 21, and therefore ineligible for the Green Card.

I, the "baby" among the five of us, was still eligible to tag along with my parents, as a qualified dependent child under the age of 21 years. I was around 14 or 15 years old at the time of our turn to have our file processed.

My parents were in their early 50's, and were not very keen on uprooting themselves from their native place at that age and starting their lives over in a "strange place," half the way around the world, unless they felt that by doing so, they would be ensuring a very bright future for me.

So, they asked me what I wanted to do and left the decision up to me. I had been against the whole idea from the beginning! I had my life, my friends, and my school as I wanted them to be; at least, for the most part things were the way I wanted them to be. I could see myself taking over my dad's oil business in the future. By the way, in case if you are wondering, that was edible or cooking oil,

Coming to America

and not the crude kind. If my dad had been in the crude oil business, I most definitely would not have left! Regardless, even if that were to not work out, I would have found some decent job, and did not doubt that I would have had any trouble making a good living. So, I did not feel that I absolutely *needed* to come to the U.S. I had no good reasons to do so. Overall, my life was great, well, other than the few issues that I was facing, but it did not seem that something huge was about to go wrong in my life. And so I had said that I was not interested in coming to America.

My parents were okay with the decision; however, they were still going ahead with the formalities of getting the paperwork done, and actually were going ahead with things as if we were still immigrating to the U.S. They just wanted to get the Green Cards which would have allowed us to come to America if and when we were to choose to do so thereafter and decide to become legal residents of the U.S. In the meantime, we would still be able to live in India, just as we had been doing all along.

If they had turned down the petition or just not responded to the request for follow-up paperwork and the request to complete the appropriate procedures from the United States Consulate, which is the entity in charge of processing the application on the Indian side of things, the file would have been closed, and our right to immigrate to the U.S. would have been taken away from us. Two of my uncles and other relatives did do exactly that. They simply were not interested in moving to America because they had been quite happy where they were.

So, fast-forwarding about a year, and coming back to that moment on the bus back from Veerpur, I decided that I did, in fact, want to come to America now. Not to immigrate to the U.S. and make it my permanent home, necessarily, but to simply come here to get a good college education. I had decided that once I was done with getting an education, I would go back to India because I really did like my native country.

God=mc²?

I had been attending college in India. I was going to a Polytechnic school which granted the equivalent of what would be considered an Associate's Degree here, in various engineering principles. I was enrolled in the Civil Engineering program, and had already attended a semester of it, or even a full year of it at that time; I don't remember exactly.

However, I had really been interested in the Mechanical and/or the Automobile Engineering Degree, but since my grades were not good enough to qualify for enrollment in that program, I had settled for the program that I did qualify for - Civil Engineering.

So, obviously, I was unhappy about not being able to pursue the career path that I had wanted to. Well, at least that's what I had thought at that time regarding what I wanted to do "when I grew up," and the resulting unhappiness ended up being the rationale behind deciding to explore other, more favorable possibilities on the other side of the Earth. Also, I felt that I needed a fresh start, overall, considering all that I had just gone through. That I needed to hit the "Reset" button of my life.

And that's exactly what I did!

February 2, Groundhog Day, 1993, is when I, along with my parents, first set foot on American Soil, or I should say American Snow! It was the middle of winter and it must have been snowing in New York City before I landed there since there was some accumulation of the "white stuff" on the ground.

I stepped out of the airport, and since I had never seen snow before, said, "Oh, Snow!!!! Cool!" And then immediately thereafter, I said, "Brrrrr. Cold!"

(I am sure that the much-revered citizen of Punxsutawney, Pennsylvania, and our friend, "Phil" the Groundhog, would not have seen his shadow that day because the sky was cloudy and overcast in New York City after the snowfall. Of course, we all know what *not* seeing his shadow would have meant - four more weeks of winter!

Coming to America

However, since Phil was not a co-passenger of mine on that flight from India, I am assuming that he was chillin' at his "crib," literally and figuratively, on the Gobbler's Knob area of his well-known hometown in PA, and probably making his famous prediction from there, as he normally does.)

After a couple of days in New York State, visiting a few of my dad's friends and acquaintances, we made our way to Waltham, Massachusetts, where my dad's best friend, from back in India, resided.

Even though my uncle lived in Pennsylvania, since I wanted to go to school and because I had heard so much about MIT and Harvard, even if I were not going to be able to attend those, I still wanted to attend a college in the same State as these world-famous institutions of higher learning were located. And so we decided to make Massachusetts our new home State.

(By the way, being interested in Engineering, getting accepted at MIT would have been a dream come true for me, and I did try, unsuccessfully, to get in, after my first year at MBCC - Massachusetts Bay Community College.)

Anyhow, I slowly started getting settled into the life here in these United States. In September of 1993, I enrolled at the community college for the Fall Semester, while working two jobs - working at a supermarket named Star Markets (now called Shaw's), bagging groceries, which was my first job ever, and bussing tables at an Indian restaurant called Bombay Mahal, located in downtown Waltham, MA.

At the beginning of my second semester there, I met my first "real" girlfriend. I fell deeply in love with her. Seven months later, I was left heart-broken and all alone after a nasty break-up with the love of my life! A few months after that, I started smoking, and after I turned 21, I started drinking (yes, I actually did not really drink much before I turned 21; sure I had a beer or two, here and there, before that). In retrospect, I can attribute these addictions to my not being

God=mc²?

able to get over her at that time. In other words, on my inability to move on.

I did move on, eventually, but I was really sad and heart-broken from the whole episode. Despite that, I did not fall into a clinical depression. However, my addictions, the ones that I had taken on because I had felt that I "needed something" to help me cope with all this, were "welcome guests" in my life after that, and therefore, they stuck around gladly.

After that I did not even finish my two-year degree. I dropped out of college and just focused on working for a few months or maybe even a year or so. And then, I decided to go back to school, and this time, I decided to enroll for the Computer Science program at the UMass Lowell campus. I attended a year of that, and promptly dropped out.

After a couple of years of aimlessness, I went back to MBCC and decided that I needed to have *some* kind of a Degree in my hand, and so I ended up getting my Associate's in General Business, finally, in 1998.

I was extremely efficient with my time; I took five years to get my two-year Degree. At this point, I was a super-duper, major underachiever of an Indian. And I was darn proud of it, too!

Fast-forwarding to 2001; I met Meera, the girl who would become my wife. It was an "arranged introduction." That is, it was the first step in an Arranged Marriage. Via a mutual acquaintance, I was given her email address, and my parents suggested that I start communicating with her via email. After a few months of that, we started talking on the phone regularly.

She lived in India, and I went to visit her, and to meet her for the first time in October of 2001. Yes, right after 9/11! I almost decided against going, but I had already bought my tickets, and it was, in my opinion, the safest time to fly, ever. So, I did not cancel the plans. On that trip to India, we got engaged to get married.

Coming to America

A few months after getting back, I suffered from my second major bout of Depression. After about three or four months of suffering, this time, mild anti-depressants and a little bit of "talk therapy," - nothing formal, just from my Primary Care physician - did the trick. Within a few weeks, I was back to being myself. In retrospect, I think the Depression may have been triggered by my feelings of not being mentally ready to get married at that time.

(Now, I have a *knowing* that I will never suffer from Depression - of the clinical kind - ever again and even if I do end up getting a mild case of "the blues," I have the capability of curing myself of them *without* the help of anti-depressants. I have that confidence because of the fact that I have learnt that there is a spiritual remedy to this problem. And for that matter, there is a spiritual solution to *any* problem, as my spiritual *guru*, whose name I will reveal shortly, often says.)

Anyway, in June of 2002, I went back to India, and got married. Thereafter, married life, and life, in general, was pretty routine.

Then, on May 19, 2006, I had been flipping through the channels on the "boob-tube" when I saw a familiar face flip by, and so I went back to that particular channel. It was a gentleman talking about his book and CD set, on QVC, the home shopping channel. A few months or weeks before that moment, I had been similarly flipping through the channels, as we guys tend to do, and had caught a part of a "Special" show on PBS with this same gentleman. It was Dr. Wayne W. Dyer! I had never known or heard about Dr. Dyer before that show on PBS. At that time, I had watched a little bit of his program entitled *The Power of Intention*. I had even recorded the remainder of the program on my DVR (Digital Video Recorder). However, since I had not deliberately changed the "Save" setting for this specific program, it automatically got deleted when the available storage space on the DVR hard-drive got to a point of 20% or less. I was really bummed out about that!

Anyhow, I had liked what I had heard on the PBS Special, and had made a mental note to get his book or his material because it surely sounded like something that I could use in my own life to make a positive change in it.

God=mc²?

However, I had never gotten around to getting his book or CDs. So, on that life-changing day in May of 2006, after watching and listening to him talk about making a positive change in one's life, I ordered Dr. Wayne Dyer's *Being in Balance*, a set that had his book and 6 CDs, entitled the same, from that QVC program.

(By the way, in admitting that I actually ordered something from QVC, I am neither ashamed of having done so, nor insecure about my "manhood" in admitting the same.)

The rest, as the cliché goes, is history! I will share a few more of the ensuing details with you in Chapters 14 and 25. For now, it should suffice to say that my life changed dramatically after reading and listening to Dr. Dyer's material. The change was surely very dramatic and drastic, but it was not instantaneous. It was gradual; however, the initial realization that I needed to change my life, and also the one of knowing that I had the power to do so, well, *that* was instantaneous.

Epilogue to this chapter

As it may be obvious, Dr. Wayne Dyer is my idol, and my self-proclaimed spiritual *guru*. His book and CDs, mentioned here, and others that I have not mentioned, have absolutely changed my life! I, wholeheartedly and vehemently, recommend all of his material - his books, CDs, and seminars. However, after reading this chapter, you could make an argument that maybe you should just read Dr. Dyer's material only. Of course, I am in agreement with making him your spiritual "Teacher," but I think that you will not want to stop there.

If you do genuinely feel that all you want or need are his teachings, then of course, you can or should stop and not explore any further.

However, having said that, I would also say that if you are new to practical spirituality or to metaphysical thinking, or to writings or teachings that bridge science and spirituality, you will experience or may have already experienced this odd phenomenon: You become a

Coming to America

voracious reader of any and all books or material on these subjects that you can get your hands on! At least, that is exactly what happened to me. And when that happens (or if it has already happened to you), you should read not only my book, as you already are doing, and not only Dr. Dyer's book(s), you should also try and read as many other books of this nature as tickles your fancy.

The reason I say so is because you will see some very different ways of conveying some of the same information. It may be that the particular language, style and "voice" of a particular author or expert may not always convey a particular spiritual or scientific idea or concept and it may result in you simply not "getting" that specific idea. And not only that, there will also be, almost always, something new that you will find when you explore new books by new authors, and also new books by the "veterans." The reason for this is that there are always advances going on in Metaphysics *and* Physics. Both, Science and Spirituality are perpetually evolving! (Well, to be precise, our *understanding* of the *principle* or *practice* of spirituality is evolving, whereas Spirit, Itself, is not. On the other hand, it is the very nature of Science to be evolutionary.)

Regardless, you will want to stay abreast of that evolution. However, again, you absolutely need not take my word for it. I am just very sure that you will feel that way on your own.

Another reason to read several different books from several different authors is because you can get corroboration from their life stories and from what they have learned and shared with you in their books. Corroboration about the facts of how the Universe really works, and what life is really all about. You will get this corroboration because Universal Truths are, well, universal, by nature.

This corroboration, in turn, will strengthen the beliefs that you may want to strengthen so that you can advance on your path to achieving higher consciousness, and therefore, the resulting life of your dreams.

SECTION II: Query - What Is "It" All About, Anyway?

This is the Query Section of the book. I am not going to provide a detailed breakdown, chapter by chapter, as I did in the explanation of the first Section. However, I will still provide a general synopsis of the covered topics. (I will continue this type of an outline description for Sections III and IV; however, I won't go into the details of each chapter, for the sake of brevity.)

In this Section, we will examine some questions; the questions of what "it" is all about - "it" being any of these - life, God, the Universe, science, spirituality and religion, etc. We will discuss, in great detail, the definitions of some very crucial words; however, we won't just examine their dictionary meanings, we will hone in on the real concepts of those words. Similarly, we will discuss ideas of the Law of Cause and Effect, also known as the Law of Karma, and other spiritual laws such as the Law of Attraction, the Law of Dharma, etc.

And together, we will come up with the answers to some of life's most vexing questions!

Do keep in mind that this section is dedicated more to the *theory* of these concepts; however there is some practical, usable material here also. In the Action Section, which is section IV, we will delve more deeply into the very specific, practical, step-by-step action we can take to create the life of our dreams. In other words, the Action Section is where we will *practically apply* the theory we learn here in the Query Section.

Chapter 5
Can *you* handle the truth?

"You can't handle the truth!"
Jack Nicholson, as Colonel Nathan Jessep,
A Few Good Men

As in the line from the movie *A Few Good Men*, the character played by Jack Nicholson exclaimed, "You can't handle the truth!" Which, by the way, is one of the top ten famous and most quoted lines from a movie, and you will see more of those famous movie quotes from me in this book. Anyway, I agree with that line, at least, partially, even though what Colonel Nathan Jessep was talking about in the movie has nothing at all to do with what we are talking about here.

We, human beings, are *more* spiritual than physical! And *that* is the truth that we, at the present moment in time, are simply not capable of handling. However, we are surely getting there, because that *is* our purpose; not just to *handle* that truth, but to actually *realize* that truth.

Many religious and spiritual traditions and schools of thought have said that this physical existence and the Physical Plane are simply

God=mc²?

not real. The only thing that *is* real is the Field of Spirituality. I do disagree with that.

The "Physical" is normally defined as all the things that we perceive physically - i.e., with our five physical senses - what we can see, touch, taste, smell and hear. That being said, the Physical is definitely real. But it is only a *part* of Reality! Not the whole, but a part, and it could be an infinitesimally *small* part of Reality, but the fact is that the Physical *is* real. And it is also the case that the Physical emanates *from* the Spiritual, but again, that does not make it non-real or unreal.

However, on the other extreme of thinking about it, as opposed to thinking that the Spiritual Field is the *only* field or plane of Reality, it would *also* be equally unfair to think that the Physical is the *only* thing that is real. The reason that I do point that distinction out is because in the present day and age, the Physical is treated as the one and only plane there is in existence. It is treated as the *most* important aspect of life (again, because of the false assumption that it is the *only* Reality).

The Materialists do, in fact, see the world as such - purely physical, and nothing else. As Madonna so famously sang, "We are living in a material world, and I am a material girl," most scientists would view themselves as Materialists, in the same vein.

(Materialists, as mentioned above, think that everything is made up of physical matter, i.e., "material," alone. That all things are made up of material, and not only all *things*, but even all *phenomena*, inclusive of consciousness, can be explained via material causes; i.e., via the interaction of two or more materials. On the other hand, Mystics believe that the higher truth is of a spiritual nature, and they encourage the direct experience of this reality, and ultimately, one of God. The Mystic engages in practices that create or enhance the awareness of these spiritual experiences. I guess, in that sense, I could be considered a Mystic. However, at the same time, I do not deny the importance of the Material world. So, am I really a Mystic or a Materialist? The answer to that is "Yes!")

And again, on the other extreme, we have the Spiritual/Religious and Mystical traditions saying that the Physical is simply not real. That it is simply "an illusion." A mirage!

To deny the physical part of Reality, *however much* a *small* part of Reality it may be, is to deny our own physical existence, isn't it?

Let's assume that what I have written, and is printed by my publisher onto this piece of paper making the page of the book that you are holding, and you are doing so with the physical hands that you possess, while you are lounging in a chair right outside the pool in your backyard - all of these things are not real. Okay. Assumed.

Now what?

The question to ask would be, then, "How do we *really* know what is really, really *real*?" I mean, really?!?! How?

Why, then, are we even experiencing this "life," if I may even call it that now? Should I ask, more appropriately, a "dream-like state?" And not just why, but why *in* this particular *way*, why in *this* manner? What is the purpose of *that*?

We all have a physical body, but does that mean, necessarily, that we do *not* possess a spiritual body (or self) also? Why do both of these things *have* to be mutually exclusive? Why can't we be physical *while* being spiritual beings? Like Dr. Dyer always says, "We are not Human beings having a Spiritual experience; we are Spiritual beings having a Human experience!"

I want something to be clear - the fact that we *are* spiritual beings does not nullify the fact, and it *is* a fact, that we are also physical beings at the same time. And just because we are physical beings also does not, necessarily, nullify the fact that we are spiritual beings. And that is the conundrum. That is the dilemma. That is the problem. That is the human condition. And that is what Dr. Wayne

God=mc²?

Dyer talks about in his book, *Being in Balance* - we simply have to learn to balance what is important to us in the physical plane against what is important to us in the spiritual plane. We have to live our lives while being in balance - being *as much* in balance as possible, because true and complete balance is not possible while we are *in* this physical body, as Dr. Dyer has said so poignantly. (Please note that this "balance" that I am talking about here is not a balance between any two other ideas or concepts; e.g., I am not talking about "Work-Life Balance" here. I am talking about a balance between what is important to us in respect to our physical being and existence versus what is important to us with regards to our spiritual goals. So, this idea of balance *can* apply to Work-Life, but just not necessarily.)

Either we have to be dead, meaning our spirit has to be out of the body because of physical death; or we have to learn to *leave* our body, at will, while being alive, in order to experience that state of Oneness. In that state of Oneness, there is a complete balance - where there is nothing *to* balance against something else - we are physically *one* with everybody and everything else in the Universe!

There is really no way to *intellectually explain* how that would feel or be like; one simply has to experience it for oneself. I will talk more about what that feeling of Oneness may feel like, later. I will *try* to describe it in Chapter 7, again, knowing that it can really only be felt; words cannot really express what that is going to be like. That feeling of Oneness is also called Unity Consciousness. That state of consciousness is one of the *beginning stages* of what is called Nirvana, Enlightenment, Self-Realization or God-Realization.

(*Ineffable* is a word that describes something that cannot be described with any of the words that we have in all of our languages. It, literally, does mean "indescribable." Oneness is ineffable!)

Anyway, back to this current world of Separateness as we now know it. While in it, we have to learn to come to terms with the fact that we are *both* of those things, at the *same* time. And when we can

Can *you* handle the truth?

learn to transcend the physical, we *can* be at two different and distinct places "in space" at the same exact moment or instance "in time."

Quantum Mechanics - a branch of Physics that deals with how little particles, I mean very little particles, act and interact with one another - says that a particle - an electron or a photon, for example, *can* be at two distinct places at the same time. Not two *different* particles, but the *same* exact particle!

How is that possible? Quantum Bilocation! Isn't that miraculous? And Science - modern, empirical Science - is talking about "miracles?" Isn't that, in and of itself, a miracle?!

By the way, the term *Quantum Physics* or *Quantum Mechanics* is derived from the fact that the smallest individually and discretely existing, and measurable "pieces" or "packets" of energy are called *Quanta* – which is the plural of the single packet of energy, the *Quantum* of energy. (Not to be confused with the *Quantum of Solace*, which is the latest installment in the series of movies featuring the most famous fictional spy of all time, whose name is, of course, Bond, James Bond.)

Anyhow, these Quanta, meaning packets of energy, are released via sub-atomic particles; viz., electrons or photons, as electrical charges or light radiation which ranges from Radio waves, to Visible light, to X-rays and, ultimately, to Gamma rays, respectively. In other words, electrons represent an *electrical charge*, whereas photons carry electromagnetic radiation in the form of *light*.

Anyway, it surely has taken Science a long, long time to come to a conclusion. And it is not even quite there yet - just like every single human being, and for that matter, even "Matter" - *everything* in the Universe - and *even* Science *itself* is evolving towards God - which, by the way, *is* the purpose of all life, and of existence itself. That is the conclusion that Science *must* arrive at, sooner or later!

Soon, there will be some kind of an upheaval from the masses – the enlightened masses, among which will be scientifically

God=mc²?

"enlightened" folk - and they will say, unequivocally, that there *must* be a God or Spirit or something of that sort. A Force or a Source that creates the Universe and everything in it. Like we all have always known and felt that there really *is* something bigger than us. (You could always ask what President Bill Clinton meant when he said, "It depends upon what your definition of 'is' is.") That there is something greater than us that creates us; there simply *has* to be something like that, shouldn't there?

(Note: Einstein's theory of General Relativity, Newtonian/Classical Physics, and Quantum Mechanics - all of these three theories put together explain how and why things happen or operate at different levels of the Universe. General Relativity explains how the mass and energy, and therefore the gravity, of celestial bodies such as planets, stars and galaxies affect each other and the combined "fabric" of time-space. Newton's laws of physics dictate how objects such as billiard balls and automobiles are supposed to behave when forces such as gravity and friction are acting on them. Quantum Mechanics tells the story of how atomic and sub-atomic particles interact with each other to create the experience of reality at that level. In other words, there are three very different theories that can explain phenomena at three different levels of existence, but none is capable of successfully doing so at all levels of reality. Therefore, there is this search for a single theory that combines all the principles and laws of nature so as to be able to explain phenomena at all levels of existence. This theory can truly be described by the highly "scientific" and very "technical" name for it: The Theory of Everything!)

And now Science is starting to talk about the Unified Field Theory, and "The Theory of Everything," as mentioned in the Note above, and things like that - theories that claim that there is this "Field" which permeates all of Space - it is *even* in the space where there is *nothing*; i.e., where there is supposed to be a total vacuum. So, there is *nowhere* that it is not. It is everywhere that you can imagine it to be, *and* it is even there where you cannot imagine it to

Can *you* handle the truth?

be. And that all things emanate *from* it. So, this Field creates everything in the Universe, and maybe even the Universe itself. It holds all the raw data, all the usable information that can be derived from that data, and all the knowledge that could possibly exist about *everything* there is to know. It also has the record of all *events* in the Universe – past, present and future!

Well, that sure sounds a lot like God, now, doesn't it? The Omnipresent, the Omnipotent, the Omniscient. (The One that is present everywhere, is all powerful, and is all knowing.)

It is!

Modern or empirical Science is *just* now coming to a point where Spiritual Science was eons ago! (That is what I am going to call it - Spiritual Science - and therefore, officially coin a new phrase by doing so, if it already hasn't been coined.)

We, as in humanity, *knew* what life was all about back then, and how, and more importantly, why, everything existed and operated. It wasn't an exercise in futility as life has become nowadays, at least in some cases. It had a purpose. And that purpose was clear as crystal! And that purpose still does exist; we simply have to acknowledge that it does, and try to find it, and try to live up to it.

And what is this purpose; this mission? The next chapter tells us exactly what it is.

Chapter 6
Mission: Impossible?
(Or at least, very, very difficult!)

Cue the *Mission: Impossible* theme music, mentally, before you start to read this chapter. Okay……..do you have it "playing" yet? If so, you are ready!

It is your mission, if you should choose to accept it, to become one with the rest of the Universe. Not just to *know* intellectually that you are one with it, but to actually *experience* it, and after having experienced that Oneness, to experience full and perpetual happiness – Bliss. *That* is your mission! This message will self-destruct *never*! It will always remain in your consciousness and known to your soul forever. If you fail to fulfill this mission or somehow forget about it or get distracted by something in this lifetime, God *won't* disavow all knowledge of you and of your soul's existence. He will come to your aid to guide you back onto the path where you can fulfill this mission in this lifetime, or maybe in another one, if need be.

God=mc²?

That is the difference between the IMF - the Impossible Mission Force - and God. God is there by your side *all* the time. Never does God say that you are not one of His creatures, and thus undeserving of His mercy, grace, forgiveness, or love. Therefore, God does not need "plausible deniability." He (or It) *always* remembers and acknowledges your existence simply because He created you and me! And as I said before, He comes to your aid, as needed. You just have to be aware that the aid could come in *any* form. People, things, events, or circumstances are created or used by God to help you to complete your mission. But you do have to ask. Even God does not help unless His help is requested, because He assumes that if you do not ask for help, you are doing fine and don't actually *need* the help. (And there is a very specific way to ask for His help, in other words, to pray. This is not a religious prayer, per se. You could consider it a wish, or a request even. And we will discuss that in much more detail later on.)

As described above, the mission is very simple, isn't it? Or at least it *sounds* very simple. But for most people, if not all, it does seem to be a very, very difficult task, if not downright impossible. (Any wonder why I picked this as the title of the chapter.)

However, it is an absolute fact that this mission is really as easy or as difficult as we may *think* it is. Therefore, if we think that it is easy to accomplish this mission, it will actually become easy to do so, and conversely, if we think that it is difficult, then it will end up becoming so.

And how we perceive this mission to be comes back to the choice of accepting the fact that we are not just physical beings alone, we are spiritual beings also. And that at the time of the physical death of our body, our soul remains completely intact and it returns to being just that - 100 % pure, unadulterated spirit.

Our physical body is, in essence, science, whereas our soul is spiritual, isn't it?

Mission: Impossible?

We can all accept this as being true (or not, since it is always a matter of choice). In fact, it almost is a way to get some solace to know that "this is not all there is to life," and that does do wonders for my own self. My hope is that it would help you too.

Despite how consoling or soothing this belief may be that "there is more after this," let's not settle for that consolation. And here's why: After finishing this book, we will all know that first and foremost, there really *is* a *lot more* to life here - *as it already is* - and we will find out what that "more" is. Then, secondly, that there really is more to it *after* this life, also! By the way, there was more to it *before* physical life began, also.

Anyhow, accomplishing the mission of experiencing Oneness with the Universe, and the resulting Bliss is our ultimate goal in life, as we have determined. However, there are objectives that need to be met or achieved in order for us to accomplish this overall goal.

So, for example, in Business, the singular goal could be achieving maximum profitability. The objective(s) via which that goal could be achieved, may be all or any one of these: Cutting costs of operating the business; increasing efficiency of the work-force and of the equipment; increasing productivity; innovating new products or services, thus leading to an increase in sales, and therefore in revenue; marketing the products or services more effectively, again leading to increased sales; etc., etc. All of these objectives would lead to the overall goal of achieving maximum profitability, which, in turn, is the very reason and purpose of the existence of a business.

Similarly, the overall goal of life is to attain Self-Realization or God-Realization by experiencing Oneness, and from and by this experience, live in a state of constant joy - which is called Bliss. When this word, *Bliss,* is used to try to explain that elusive (or *supposedly* elusive) state of being where one lives in a never-ending state of happiness and joy, most people think that it is only meant for the very few who might dare to undertake such an endeavor.

God=mc²?

Most people cannot even fathom what Bliss might be like, let alone want to experience it. It's not that some of us simply don't want to experience it; it's just that I don't think we truly believe that it is really possible to exist in, or experience, such a state. Again, ideally, it sounds fabulous, doesn't it - no sadness, no anger, no stress, no negative emotion? Just pure, positive Bliss!

Makes me want to say, "Sure! I want that! Where do I sign-up?"

However, we only truly believe that we can have *moments* of joy, and peace and happiness, and not an actual *state of being* where we experience those positive states *all* the time. And therefore, the erroneous rush to all things physical and towards *only* things physical, at the neglect of the spiritual. Why? Because we have been programmed to believe that only physical things will bring us those moments of joy, however fleeting, temporary or short-lived they may be.

Again, please do not get me wrong - I am not saying that the physical is not important. It surely is! *All* good things in life are there for us to enjoy. That is absolutely the only reason for them to exist. That is why they came into being. They were put here - in the physical plane of existence - for that exact purpose. (And we will, most definitely, talk about how we can get all the things that we want, later on in this book.)

However, I implore you to understand the difference here that our *only* reason to exist is not *just* to enjoy them. As you might have heard many a times, "We eat to live, and not live to eat." Or something to that effect.

So, in relation to the example of the goals and the objectives in the field of Business, what are the so-called objectives that we need to achieve in order to achieve the final and overall goal of life? The objectives could be to learn to be more patient; learn to be more loving; more generous; learn to control the ego; learn to be fearless; learn to be more kind. (These are just *few* of the examples.)

Mission: Impossible?

Those things that I just mentioned are *spiritual objectives* that need to be met in order to meet the highest *spiritual goal* of Self-Realization, also known as Enlightenment, or God-Realization. In other words, ultimately, to learn to be like God!

The attainment of physical objectives is supposed to *add* to the joy and pleasure of attaining (and in certain cases, *assist in attaining*) the spiritual goals. Ultimately, there is no other separate physical goal. The overall physical goal and the spiritual goal is the same exact thing: Self-Realization and the resulting Bliss.

As you will find out, there is not just *one* singular path to Enlightenment, there are *many*. One of the paths is, in fact, doing so via the process of leaving all physical and worldly things behind and going into a forest or some uninhabited place and doing meditation and *tapasya* (penance) for years and years. Like the Buddha did. The Path of Renunciation, and deep meditation, which is also known as, ironically, the Royal Road; and as it is referred to in Sanskrit, *Raja Yoga*.

(By the way, the word *Yoga* means "union." The word *union*, in this context of Yoga, would have no meaning by itself. The question would be, "The union of what and what?" So, specifically, it is the union of our consciousness with Divine Consciousness or God. Generally, Yoga is synonymous with meditation, as far as a Hindu is concerned, because one can achieve the experience of Enlightenment via meditation. Here in the West, and quite frankly, even in the East, lately, we have been conditioned to simply think of the specific "Yogic" exercises and postures *as* Yoga; however, those exercises are only a method to get the body ready to experience the actual Yoga; the *union* with God-Consciousness.)

Jnana Yoga is the Path of Knowledge via which one seeks and gains the true knowledge of the Self, and how the Universe operates and that we are all one, and thus attains Enlightenment.

God=mc²?

But again, those are just *two* of *several* paths! Another is the Path of Action; *Karma Yoga*. This is the one that you can follow by simply living in the world as a normal human being and enjoying all that life has to offer and all the while offering your actions to God.

Then there is the Path of Love or *Bhakti Yoga*. One can attain Enlightenment by loving God.

Now, I have always asked "How, exactly, does one love God?" How can anybody express love to something that *is* love, itself? It is like saying "We should each give a dollar to the wealthiest person in the Universe; to the one who has infinite wealth." A single dollar, or for that matter, *any* amount of money would not mean much to the person who has infinite wealth, right?

So, then what do you give somebody who *has* and *is* everything?

Coming back full circle, how do you love *Love* itself? Well, one loves God by *seeing* God in every person that one encounters, and by loving them as they would love God. For example, you can love your child and see your child as God, and therefore, indirectly, love God (*as* your child). Anything you do to take care of your child would be considered service and the expression of love towards God.

I will try to answer those types of questions; like the one of how does one love Love itself, in more detail, and others as well, later on in this book.

(Before I go any further, I do want to clarify that none of these paths are "religious" paths, per se. However, they can be classified as "spiritual," which they surely are. What I am trying to say is that you can practice following any of these paths, if you would like to do so, while maintaining your own Faith.)

Anyhow, in short, the mission or purpose of life is to attain Self-Realization *while* living life and enjoying all the *good* things in life, and at the same time realizing or accomplishing the physical and spiritual goals that we set for ourselves.

Mission: Impossible?

At least, that is what *I* endeavor to do, and if you see the benefits, then to share the ways to do the same with you.

As I mentioned in the Preface, we *can* have all the material wealth, *and* all the spiritual bliss, *and* also have all our "unanswerable" questions answered - all in one fell swoop. However, why do these *seem* to be such difficult tasks? I think the answer is that we all look to only the *physical* realm for the answers to *all* of our questions and since a lot of the problems we face did not originate in the physical realm, the solutions to them cannot be found there either.

We have to look for the answers in the spiritual realm. We will discuss, in detail, how to do that, exactly.

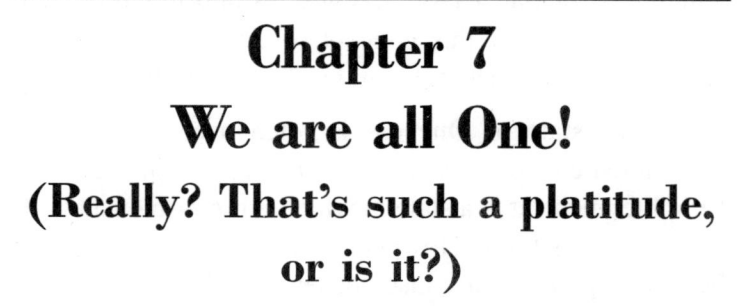

Chapter 7
We are all One!
(Really? That's such a platitude, or is it?)

You might have heard this phrase a lot, "We are all One!" Or as I mentioned in the previous chapter that it is our goal to, experientially, become one with the rest of the Universe. Upon reading that, you might have rolled your eyes and thought, "Here we go again, this concept of 'Oneness,' what does that even mean?"

I do have to agree that it has become somewhat of a cliché, or even a platitude; however, I assure you that it is really significant to our study and practice of spirituality.

(Platitude, not to be confused with a Platypus, which is a duck-billed, beaver-tailed, otter-footed, semi-aquatic mammal generally only found in Eastern Australia, and in the State of Tasmania. By the way, a Platypus is the only *mammal* that lays eggs instead of giving birth to its young ones. Anyway, so a *platitude* is not a mammal of any sort. It is an often quoted saying - a statement, phrase, or a word - which has lost its meaning through over-use. The word *platitude*

God=mc²?

is also often used to describe a seemingly profound statement, that which a particular person may use, as unoriginal or shallow. In that sense, *Oneness*, or this concept of everybody really being one or connected, is a perfect example of a platitude.)

This state of Oneness is often used to describe a state of consciousness one will achieve in the process of achieving Enlightenment. It is a state in which our consciousness does not stay limited to our body. However, it is not an Out-of-body experience because a part of our consciousness is still within our body. It's just that it is not limited *to* the body. This happens when one may have been meditating on removing the energy blockages of the chakras in one's body, and finally, the spiritual energy called Kundalini breaks through from the Crown chakra. And as I had mentioned before, I will *try* to explain what that could be like.

(Please see Chapters 27 and 28 for detailed explanations of the process of meditation and about Kundalini and the Chakra system of the human body. However, right at this very moment, you don't need those details to understand this concept of Oneness. You can refer to those other Chapters later on.)

So, when this happens, suddenly, one finds that one starts to experience the *beingness* of the surrounding things and people! So, for example, if you had been sitting in your meditation room when you start to experience this feeling that you are now conscious of the walls of the room; that you *are* the walls of the room, then you can be sure that this process is beginning. And then you realize that you *are* also the whole building that you are in. You can "see through" the eyes of the other people in the building, and you can hear their thoughts as if they were your own. And this process continues in an ever-expanding radius - so you become or experience being (or having) the collective consciousness of the whole city, and then the country and then all of Earth, and then the solar system, and then the whole galaxy, and eventually, the whole Universe. (This is explained very nicely in a documentary that I recommend very highly, *The Voice*.)

We are all One!

All the while, you can also sense your consciousness in your own body - which is seated in the meditation room of your home.

The best way I can think of to try and explain what that could feel like is this: Right now, if somebody were to pinch you on your left arm, and at the same time pinch you on your right arm, would you feel both of those pinches or would you only feel one of them because you were pinched at the same time, and you are only *one* physical body? You would feel *both* of those pinches because both of your arms are part of and connected to you. Sure, there are two arms, but both of those arms belong to you. They *are* you, in a way; well, at least, physically.

In the same exact way, you would be able to experience everything that every living and non-living thing in the Universe was experiencing. All at the same time. You would feel as if you had the consciousness of the whole of the Universe. As if you *were* the Universe in its entirety!

(Mike Dooley, my favorite teacher from *The Secret*, might nod his head while reading this because he writes his famous *Notes from the Universe* as the Universe. By the way, I subscribe to these daily email "Notes" and they always have a very positive and uplifting overtone to them. I would suggest that you check them out also. For more information about how to receive these wonderful notes from the Universe, please see the Affiliates section of my website, **www.GodEqualsmcSquared.com**, or visit Mike's website directly, at **www.tut.com**.)

In reality, even when we may feel like we are only experiencing our own consciousness; it is a fact that there is really only *one* consciousness that is in existence. There is no separate consciousness for each of the almost seven billion human beings on planet Earth. It is all just one single consciousness. And for that matter, even in the entire Universe!

God=mc²?

Sure, through the context of our physical bodies we are, obviously, separate and distinct from another's body. And quite frankly, even though we are physically separate from one another, there is a Karmic element that reveals itself to us to show that we are, in fact, "connected" in the physical realm also. This is because we live in an interactive world. We are always interacting with somebody else, in one way or another.

As you might have heard a very famous line, "no man is an island," one from a work of prose, Meditation XVII, by English poet John Donne, meaning that no person is isolated from another person and that what happens to one has an effect on everybody else. What I say is that even if a man now lives *on* an isolated and otherwise uninhabited island, and therefore may be considered to *be* an island, he would have been born of a set of parents who are, obviously, related to him, and may not have been "islands" themselves. So, even if he was born on this isolated island and never came into contact with any other human being, maybe his parents were born in an interactive society with a lot more people around, and therefore, they had a lot more interaction with others. And through this constant interaction, the parents were connected to others. So, ultimately, even the lonely man on the island is connected to others that are not physically there or the ones that he has never directly interacted with. The others know him or know *of* him to be the child of this couple that they once knew. Maybe they are the grandparents of this child, and even though they have never seen him or maybe even don't know of his existence, they *yearn* for his existence.

No life or no death has ever been, or will ever be without profound purpose for everyone alive, for it only *adds* to all of humanity, regardless of whether it is a birth or a death of a human being. Forever! One may think that the birth of a life is an accretion to humanity, and therefore it can only add to it, and since death is the removal of a person from earthly existence, it can only subtract from all that the world is; however, that kind of thinking is not

We are all One!

accurate because of the interactive nature of the Universe. Think about what kind of a *positive* impact the lives *and* the deaths of Mahatma Gandhi, Mother Teresa, and Martin Luther King, Jr. have had on the whole world.

So, in fact, no man is an island!

We are connected to others through the Law of Karma, and therefore always forming Karmic-bonds with everybody else. And Karma comes into existence due to interaction, either direct or indirect. So, that was an example of how humanity is connected, *even* in the physical realm.

Anyhow, based on the *perception* and even the *physical reality* of bodily separateness, it may *seem* that even our individual consciousness is also separate and distinct from another person's consciousness. However, that is simply not the case! And one can only truly know and appreciate the profundity of this fact when one experiences, first-hand, the state of Oneness or Unity Consciousness.

In other words; i.e., the ones of spirituality, our individual spirits are really all part of the one and only Primary Spirit. That is, *we are*, in fact, all One!

Chapter 8
Elementary, my dear human

Sir Arthur Conan Doyle's venerable creation of fiction, Sherlock Holmes, is famously quoted as having said "Elementary, my dear Watson," however, it is a little known fact that the closest Sherlock Holmes has ever really been to saying that whole phrase is just "Elementary."

Just a tid-bit of information that my readers might find interesting. (This is an example of the totally useless information that I am filled with - like so many of us are - along with *some* useful information that I am sharing with you via this book.)

Anyway, pertaining to this word *elemental* or *elementary* - what does that mean? Well, a Chemist would say that something that is an "element" is something that occurs or exists "naturally" *in* the atmosphere, *on* the surface of the earth, or *beneath* the surface of the earth, etc.

God=mc²?

Elements are the things indicated on the Periodic Table via a chemical symbol (at the atomic level) - Metals, Liquids and Gases. An element, by itself; for example, Hydrogen, or a combination of two or more of these elements, form all the things that physically exist in the Universe. For example, Water, as we all know is - H_2O - which is the molecular formula for it; i.e., the combination of two atoms of Hydrogen, and one atom of Oxygen.

The word *elemental* also means *basic*, as in *Elementary School*, meaning *Basic school*. Meaning that it is, simply put, basic knowledge or basic substance.

By the way, I love the commercial by Dow Chemical which talks about how "the chemistry changes when we add the Human Element to the Periodic Table of the elements." And it shows the "new" element, Hu, the Human Element, as part of the Periodic Table. That is such a brilliant ad!

It is brilliant because it talks about the Physical and the Spiritual - the Periodic Table is physical in nature, isn't it? And when you add the Human Element, i.e., introduce consciousness, which is a spiritual element, the "chemistry" *does* change, doesn't it?

All things - all man-made things or invented by man - did not exist before man created them. (Duh, obviously - you must be thinking "What is your point?") The periodic table of elements existed *before* man created it by discovering one element after the other. Well, the *table* itself did *not* exist, but the elements which now make up the Periodic Table, of course, always did. Humans only created the Periodic Table by adding each element to it as they found them. But, again, those *elements* all existed *before* we actually found them, didn't they? And if we had not officially found or discovered them, they would have still existed. So, what changed?

We did!

We "became" conscious of our own existence! And *then* we started discovering these elements. We first discovered the four basic "elements" that existed in nature - Earth, Wind, Water and Fire - and

Elementary, my dear human

here, as described by the word "elements" - with quotes, is because they are not true elements, as in the chemical ones on the Periodic Table of elements.

(Note: There is a quirky phenomenon in Quantum Physics called "Tangled Hierarchy" that suggests that, in fact, those elements would *not* have come into existence if we had not become conscious, and so technically, they actually did not exist before we became conscious. What I would add to that is this: If they did, in fact, exist before we became conscious; well, then it was *in anticipation* of our becoming conscious. Like I said, it is a quirky phenomenon.)

Incidentally, I absolutely love the movie *The Fifth Element* starring Bruce Willis and Milla Jovovich and I watch it every single time I happen to catch it on TV. The movie conveyed the wonderful idea of how Love was the fifth "element" that existed in nature, other than the four physical "elements" that were in existence already; viz., Earth, Wind, Water and Fire, and that Love is the panacea, the only genuine cure-all, to all of humankind's problems. And Love is spiritual, isn't it? It can only be *felt* by the soul or the heart.

(By the way, there is now *scientific* evidence that love is, in fact, "felt" by the heart! Here I mean the actual physical organ that is the heart, not just the metaphorical symbol for what expresses and feels love; the kind that I always "wear on my sleeve." And as mentioned in *The Divine Matrix*, by Gregg Braden, "One of the most significant findings reported by HeartMath is the documentation of the doughnut-shaped field of [electromagnetic] energy that surrounds the heart and extends beyond the body." In other words, these findings seem to be pointing to the fact that the heart, *and not the brain*, is the most powerful transceiver, i.e., transmitter/receiver, of emotions and feelings. For more on this subject, please check out the website of the Institute of HeartMath at www.hearthmath.org.)

Anyhow, some might argue that there is also physical "love," and they would be right. However, that really is sexual attraction or lust.

God=mc²?

As the *10,000 Maniacs* sang, "Love is an Angel disguised as Lust....," well, I am not too sure that this claim is entirely true. I do agree that lust can morph into love, and often does. I even wrote an essay, and a subsequent article in the college newspaper at MBCC, entitled *Love: The Romantic Precipitation of Sexual Chemistry*. (This was one of the only two articles that I ever wrote for the Paper.) My disagreement with the lyrics above is that lust doesn't *always* turn into love! Lust can exist without there ever being love present, or it ever coming into the picture later on. This is because physical attraction is a very basic, even an "animalistic," drive implanted in us in order to ensure the propagation of our species, as we all might agree. And the lust that one can feel for another waxes and wanes, and eventually wanes after a long time or, as a matter of fact, even after a very short time. Incidentally, love that was based on and originated from lust could also very easily wane, unless it has evolved into a deeper, spiritual love based on more than just physical attraction.

So, love - true spiritual love, that is - only waxes, meaning it grows bigger and deeper with time, or at the very least, remains the same. And what about all the other types of love - *platonic* in nature - what about those? There was no lust present to morph into love. The love was *just there* or was felt, or developed over time - as in between friends - or as in the case of new parenthood - felt instantly. There could be an argument made that there were no "chemical," and therefore, *elemental* beginnings of platonic love.

However, scientists would present evidence to the contrary. They would mention Oxytocin, the bio-chemical (*not* Oxycontin, the pharmaceutical pain-relieving drug), as the reason why a mother feels the love that she feels for her new-born child. And then there will be all the other bio-chemical "explanations" of and for the different types of "love."

Romantic love produces different bio-chemicals in the brains of the people in love when compared to the ones present in the brain of a mother who has just given birth. Then there is the platonic and non-

Elementary, my dear human

familial love between friends, and that shows up as a different biochemical "signature" on images of the MRI scans of their brains. One could also argue that other family members (for example, siblings) don't necessarily feel biologically-induced love for each other just because they are born of the same parents. The love that they may feel is more of the same as friends feel for each other and is developed or felt over time, and not instantly. This, in my opinion, is true.

Here's an interesting observation that I had read about somewhere (I don't remember where, exactly): The images of the brain scans of the people in love were very much like, if not exactly like, the ones of the people suffering from Obsessive-Compulsive Disorder. In a way, it makes perfect sense! (It also explains why I am such a "loving" person.) All kidding aside, people experiencing romantic love for one another are obsessed with one another, and want to compulsively spend time with each other. They find themselves thinking about the other person all the time if they are not with them already, and they find themselves emotionally "stuck" - in kind of a sweet way - on that person of their desire, don't they?

Anyhow, as far as different types of love are concerned, there is also the love for all of humanity and for all sentient beings, called *Agape* love.

Regardless, chemical, whether biological or otherwise, means elemental, doesn't it? And therefore, all the different kinds of love are *all* elemental in nature, along with them also being spiritual.

But if God created *everything*, including Scientists and the Science that they practice, and all the elements that exist in the entire Universe, then technically, *all* of it *is* created by God, and thus, *intended* by Her!

All the elements and the bio-chemical processes present in the bodies of the modern human being also used to be present in ancient man, and still are present in animals. But what is different now? You guessed it, the "new" Human Element – Consciousness.

God=mc²?

The very thing that makes us "human," as opposed to an "animal," is *also* the very thing that makes us "god-like!" Having consciousness is what sets us apart from animals (*most* animals); I think we all can agree on that by now. And having this consciousness of the self, this knowledge of the fact that *we* exist, gives us the power to choose to do something or to refrain from that act.

The venerable and ubiquitous "Free Will to choose!" In other words, the free will to *choose* our thoughts, words and actions.

In the movie *Bruce Almighty*, the character played by the hilarious Jim Carrey was made the proxy for God who had gone on vacation and had left Carrey in charge of the Universe as God while He was vacationing. God, played by the amazing Morgan Freeman, decided to put Carrey's character as His proxy because he was complaining of the supposed poor job that God, in Carrey's opinion, had done with his life. While temporarily "playing" God, Carrey acknowledges the fact that *even* God does not, or rather *cannot*, "mess" with Free Will. In other words, the Almighty God has one and only one thing out of His control, and that is Free Will!

As a sidebar to the point here; I love the movie, however, I do have to disagree with one thing, and *only* one thing from the movie, and it is that they show God as being the "micro-manager" of everyone's life. (This may remind you of your boss at your job.) God answering prayers individually - and deciding on whether to grant them or not!? Is that what we believe God is and does?

Of course, the whole concept of God actually as a *Being* instead of *Divine Energy* or *Supreme Consciousness* is the very subject of this book, so we will definitely tackle that a little bit in this chapter, and a lot more in detail, throughout this book. (You might have heard the word *anthropomorphic* as describing what we believe God to be. In other words, a "human-like" being.)

And that is how a lot of us, if not *most* of us, see God. And He (or It) just isn't that way. God has given *us* the power to *be* god-

Elementary, my dear human

like by being able to create the life that we want for ourselves. God is like a CEO who has delegated most, if not all, of His authorities to us humans, so that we don't have to bother Him for every little thing and simply just take care of those things by ourselves. (However, ultimately, He is still the CEO of the Universe; the Head Honcho; the Grand Poobah!)

Anyway, I know, I know - I have digressed again - so getting back to the point I would say that this capability to create what we want for ourselves is like being God and that is Consciousness, the nth element, if you will, that I talk about, on the Periodic Table of elements.

In other words, *all* that we are and all that we can experience is Elemental; i.e., physical, and it *is* or *has* Consciousness; and therefore, is spiritual.

Chapter 9
"My Karma ran over your dogma!"
- A bumper sticker

Remember how I said that the meaning of "Goodbye" stuck with me since I first came across it? Here's another thing that I was never, ever able to forget, and now I know exactly why - so I could tell you guys about it - think I am exaggerating?

Well, this bumper sticker is another thing that just stuck with me (please pardon the pun about the bumper sticker "sticking" with me). Maybe it has something to do with the fact that I am a Hindu, and the word *Karma* has been in my vernacular since I could utter my first words. Anyway, the line from the bumper sticker is such a funny and clever pun that it is etched in my memory ever since I saw it a few years ago.

It talks about how *Karma* - a word that is thrown around, and I am sorry, but it really is "thrown around" and a lot of people are unaware of its true meaning - is more powerful than dogma. Karma means action or deed. Karma, whether good or bad, is "built up" and

God=mc²?

accounted for in the infinite and eternal records of our soul. And when one experiences the effects of Karma, they are called "Fal," directly translated to mean "Fruits." Meaning the fruits of one's actions. As Newton's Third Law of Motion suggests, every action has an equal and opposite reaction, right? In fact, the Law of Karma is the Law of Causality, in other words, of Cause and Effect. The action one takes is the Cause, and the fruit of that action is the Effect. Since this is a Law, there are also rules governing Karma, and its implications. You might have heard that much about Karma, but the following may be something you might not have heard before.

Did you know that there are actually different *types* of Karma?

A detailed discussion on the different types of Karma is something that I would like to engage in, however, not in this book, specifically. I will discuss the types, briefly, though. According to Hinduism, there are four different types of Karma. The first one is *Sanchit Karma* - all of the Karma that we have accumulated in all of our lifetimes until now. *Prarabdha Karma* is a small portion of that overall accumulated Karma which is now "ripened" and being experienced in this lifetime. Every single thing that is currently transpiring in our lives, good or bad, is doing so because of the ripening of that type of Karma. Thirdly, there is *Kriyaman Karma* - the Karma that we are creating right now. This type of Karma gets added to, or subtracted from, the balance of the *Sanchit Karma*, and this we will take into the next lifetime. And finally, there is *Agami Karma*, which is produced by our *intentions* to commit an action in the future. So, those are the different types of Karma.

Dogma, on the other hand, is simply "belief," or more specifically, religious belief. Don't get me wrong, please. I do think that dogma is good (*true* religious or spiritual belief, that is) as long as it is not imposed on others. The problem with dogma is that it almost always tends to try to convert. Or at least, that seems to be the intention of the dogmatic person.

"My Karma ran over your dogma!"

The fact is, no matter how dogmatic one may be, another's Karma will always trump the former's dogma, as suggested by the brilliant bumper sticker - kudos to whoever created it. Action, in accordance to the Golden Rule, will *always* be better than an idea or a belief, and for that matter, *any* idea or *any* belief.

(In case there is somebody who may not be familiar with it, here's the Golden Rule: Do unto others as you would have them do unto you! In other words, treat others as you would like to be treated. Anything that hurts or can potentially hurt you, will also hurt or potentially hurt another - whether it is physically, mentally, emotionally, spiritually, or in any other way. Acting in accordance to the Golden Rule would be to refrain from such a harmful or hurtful act - whether in word, thought or in deed.)

So, you might argue, then, that thoughts, well, more specifically beliefs - which are just thoughts held for a long time - which I just defined as dogma, are really, in fact, Karma. And hence, there is really no difference at all between Karma and dogma. And one cannot "run the other one over."

Not true! Good actions or deeds, just like good thoughts are simply put, good Karma. And thus result in a good Fal - good consequence. Thoughts are *potential* Karma which could result in *actual* Karma. So, in that sense, they are the "seeds" of Karma. However, action is potential Karma already actualized or manifested.

If the comparison was limited only to the thought realm; i.e., if we were comparing good *thoughts* to bad *thoughts*, then obviously, good thoughts are better and even stronger (scientifically proven to be so) than bad thoughts. However, in comparing action to thought, action (good or bad) will trump thought. In other words, actualized Karma trumps potential Karma.

(In this specific example, I am talking about good *actualized* Karma; i.e., good deeds or actions trumping bad *potential* Karma; i.e., bad or dogmatic thoughts.)

God=mc²?

To make it even a little bit *more* confusing, I would like to add that good *thoughts* do possess the possibility or potentiality of mitigating bad *deeds*. However, the mitigating good thoughts would have to be proportionally stronger and of a higher frequency of vibration than the vibrations represented by the bad deeds.

To give you an example of this, assume that there is a person who has committed an act of physical harm towards somebody, and thus, the perpetrator of the harm has now bad Karma to his name. In order to mitigate or lessen the bad effects of that bad Karma in his life (which would be the appropriate effects of his bad deed) he can think good thoughts and lessen some of the bad effects of that bad Karma by doing so.

Examples of the good thoughts in this case could be thoughts of good wishes to all people, even towards the ones that he knows to harbor hatred and ill-will towards him, and are not his well-wishers. Simply asking for forgiveness when the remorse is genuine, and not just felt because one got caught, is also an example of a good thought. Forgiveness of self and others mitigates bad Karma.

I do want to clarify that good Karma does not *directly* mitigate bad Karma. If a person has committed 27 bad deeds, and now commits 29 equally good deeds, then does the person now have a "net balance" of two good deeds?

No, it does not work that way; however, I used to hope that it did work that way. Since the Law of Karma is, well, a law, there are appropriate implications of both kinds of deeds, the good *and* the bad. One *must* suffer the consequences of the bad deeds committed, and one *will*, without fail, receive the rewards for the good deeds done, separately.

Believe it or not, the real end-goal is *not* to only have good Karma in our Karmic Account, but to actually be completely free of the chains of *any* kind of Karma. God-Realization is the way to do that. However, for the time being, we all can agree that since we are

"My Karma ran over your dogma!"

still in the process of "getting there," it is much better to earn and collect good Karma than its bad counterpart.

But again, we run into the problem of what really is "good?" Don't we?

All I am trying to say, without getting entangled in this web of words, is that if a person is good - whether or not one is "religious," and believes in God and performs any or all of the rituals that religious people are expected to perform - he or she *can* still accumulate good Karma. However, there is absolutely one Rule that simply *cannot* be violated by the "good" or at least, violated on purpose and repeatedly so, too. And of course, that is the Golden Rule! If they violate that - then no matter how dogmatic or religious they may be or may seem to be, they are not collecting good Karma. Period!

Chapter 10
Dharma & Greg?
No, Dharma and....you!

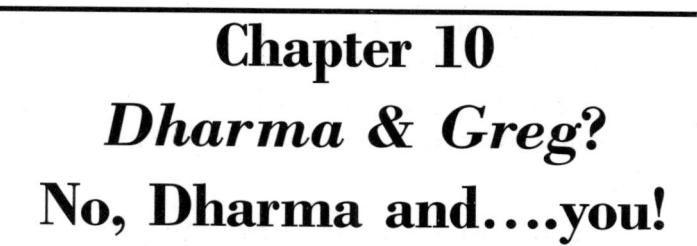

Dharma is a new word that you may or may not have heard yet. Well, maybe other than as the name of a title character on a TV show from a few years ago - *Dharma & Greg*.

(If it has not been abundantly clear by now, I love all things pop-culture; namely, movies, TV shows, songs, etc. Of course, I could be characterized as a "Pop-culture Geek" even! However, I would prefer the moniker "Pop-culture Spiritualist," if there is such a thing. Well, I guess there is now, and I am it! Regardless, this is one of the shows that I did not watch, but I remembered it because of its title being personal to me.)

Anyhow, *Dharma* is a Sanskrit word, just like *Karma* is. It has various meanings, but we will try to hone in on what the best one is and how it relates to our subject here, and especially, how it relates to Karma.

God=mc²?

In my opinion, it means duty or responsibility. Or more accurately, *universal* duty or responsibility. As I just mentioned, *Dharma* has several meanings, depending on the context it is used within. It can also mean "religion." As in, "Judaism is my Dharma," to give you an example. It also means what is right or the righteous path, or the good, as in Good vs. Evil - Dharma vs. Adharma. Universal destiny or purpose, what we all are meant to do, is another meaning.

We all do have a universal responsibility. In fact, we have one, and *only* one universal responsibility. And that is also towards one and only one person. Ourselves! And the responsibility that we have is to seek our own bliss. That's it. It is really as simple as that. And it is also as easy as that.

You might have heard about something "being simple, but not easy," well, this is simple *and* easy. It's just that others have told us, erroneously, that we are responsible for other people's bliss, and that other people are also responsible for our bliss. Bearing this false burden, and also loading it onto somebody else, is what makes this whole thing very complicated and very difficult, when it is supposed to be as simple and as easy as it really is or was meant to be.

And in my opinion, that is our Dharma. To be solely responsible for seeking, finding and living our own bliss. The actions that we may take or the paths that we may choose to walk on may be very different when compared to somebody else; however, ultimately, we all should seek our own bliss.

People also invoke the word dharma to remind somebody of their duties pertaining to a particular role that we play in society. For example, one would say that one has a particular dharma as a husband or as a wife. Or as a teacher, or a pupil, as a parent, and a specific and different dharma for a father versus the dharma of a mother, and so on and so forth. In my opinion, that description or meaning of dharma is related to the physical duties and responsibilities pertaining to that societal position or role. I do agree with that definition also.

***Dharma & Greg*? No, Dharma and....you!**

However that dharma, with a lower case "d" is at the physical level (and is also known as "Kartavya") and I will clarify more about the distinctions in the following paragraphs. Just know that we want to hone in on the greater meaning of Dharma, with a capital "D." To be solely responsible for seeking, finding and living our own bliss.

You know, there is only one exception to this rule, and it is not really an exception, if you really analyze the situation. And that is in the case of a parent. A parent of an infant or toddler or a young child is obligated to take care of the needs of that child because the child is incapable of doing so for itself.

So, now analyze this situation carefully. Is it the bliss of the child that the parent is really responsible for? Or is it just the basic needs that the parent is obligated to take care of?

If you have seen little children play; either with others or by themselves; you will come to a conclusion that even they don't obligate their parents or any other adults around them for ensuring their bliss. They take care of it themselves, don't they? They are in their own world, blissfully happy.

Basic necessities to sustain life and the ones necessary to create and sustain bliss are totally different things, aren't they? And here's an ironic observation - kids will find bliss in the things that also sustain their lives - for example, children playing with their food and having a grand ol' time in doing so. There is definitely a lesson in the wonderful example that these innocent, god-like beings provide us; that is, to really strive to find bliss in everything.

Other than that exception, of sorts, you could think about it this way: Do you really want to give that kind of a control over your bliss to somebody else? And for that matter, do you want to take on that kind of a responsibility for somebody else's bliss? As I mentioned before, do you want to load somebody else with this huge unbearable and undeliverable of a burden, and do you want to carry the same for somebody else?

God=mc²?

I know that for me, it is a big, fat emphatic "NO" as an answer for both of those questions! Regardless of what your answer for it may be, here's a fact: It is *impossible* to be able to create bliss for somebody else!

It is impossible because bliss does not result from the satisfaction of physical needs alone; it is a result of the satisfaction of spiritual needs also. You may be able to satisfy another's physical needs very well, but if you cannot satisfy their spiritual needs, you won't be able to bring bliss to them.

And from the very nature of spiritual needs, it is a necessity that the person who seeks the satisfaction actually has to seek to achieve it by doing the "inner work" necessary for it themselves. Nobody *else* can do that for another. (Unless it is God Herself, or a very highly advanced spiritual being who decides to impart that spiritual knowledge or satisfaction to a particular person.)

So, coming back full-circle, you should act to fulfill your dharma - with a lower-case "d" - which represents your physical responsibilities or duties as suggested by your role(s) in society. At the same time, you should also act to fulfill your Dharma, your universal spiritual duty.

In simpler words, we should do whatever it is that brings us bliss, while we fulfill our physical duties.

However, please note that I am *not* advocating leading a hedonistic lifestyle! By the very nature of this type of a lifestyle, it is one in which pleasure is sought, and pain is avoided, at all times and at all costs to self, and others.

I *am* advocating seeking a lifestyle, that in which, once you have achieved it, there is no need to seek pleasure because it *never* leaves you, and there is no need to avoid pain because you realize that there is *nothing* that can cause you pain ever again! This state of being is the very definition of bliss.

Dharma & Greg? No, Dharma and....you!

So, in a way, actually, I *am* advocating seeking and leading a hedonistic lifestyle, but raised to the nth power, but with a "minor" exception that it should be achieved with no cost to self or others. I just want to clarify, in other words, that we should not seek our bliss at *any* or even *some* cost to ourselves or others. That would be a blatant violation of the Golden Rule - the only Rule that we should *not* be violating, as I mentioned near the end of the last chapter. By violating this Rule, you may be able to *seek* your bliss, but you will *never* actually find it. So, it makes no sense to do that.

Not only that, the more your plan of action, method, or way to obtain your bliss involves the *betterment* or *improvement* of the lives of others – in *any* way possible – the faster and the easier you will achieve your bliss!

Could this "System" that we call *Life* be any more perfect than that?!

In conclusion, Karma; meaning action, in accordance with our Dharma; meaning our universal responsibility, is what we are here to do.

Chapter 11
Greed *is* good!

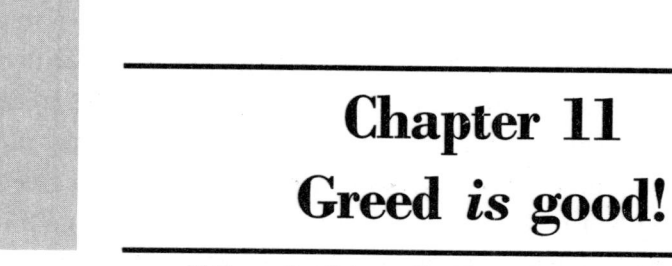

"Greed, for a lack of a better word, is good."
- Michael Douglas, as Gordon Gekko, *Wall Street*

I guess I simply must be crazy to even hint at something like this, especially in this economy, and considering the fact that we all put the blame on greed for the predicament we are in right now. We blame Wall Street's greed, and the greed of the Real Estate Investor, and of the Mortgage Company and so on and so forth, for the mess that we are in.

I absolutely agree with that. It was *all* of these *groups* of folks who were responsible for the economic predicament we are in right now (and not just one or two of them, because it would not have happened if it were only one or two of them). Anyway, I am not an Economist and I am not here to comment on why we were in this most recent recession, and I will stop after making the next point, which is the point that I *am* trying to make. I do agree that greed was the cause of the effect that we had been and still are experiencing - this economic downturn and the resulting joblessness.

God=mc²?

However, I would also like to add that the same greed was also the cause of the expansion and the growth of the economy. This expansion eventually and inevitably, led to the creation of a lot of the Real Estate and Stock Market wealth that was created in the last few years. This creation of wealth, in turn, led to the eventual and inevitable downturn and collapse of the economy because the greed got out of control. This is a fact that *nobody* can refute! We may not like it, but it is still the truth. It is just that we put the blame on greed when something bad or catastrophic happens, but we don't give it the proper credit when something good or great happens. It, rightfully, deserves *both*! At least, that is my opinion.

Anyhow, I told you that you would be seeing a lot of these famous movie quotes from me. "Greed, for a lack of a better word, is good!" That one, from the 1988 movie *Wall Street*, is definitely in the top 10 most quoted. (And you will probably hear it a lot more in pop-culture over the next few months because the sequel, *Wall Street: Money Never Sleeps* will be released later this year.)

So, greed, just the same as envy, is one of the Seven Deadly Sins; therefore, how can it be "good?" Especially after what I just said about it in terms of what is happening to our economy right now.

Well, to see if and why it would be good, let's examine - you guessed right - its meaning!

Greed is simply wanting more and more of something - especially money or material things or comforts that money can buy - and never being satisfied with what you get. Right?

Having defined *greed*, I would like to go back to that sequence from the aptly named movie, *Wall Street*, which is the source of this quote. There was a lot more to it than what Gordon Gekko, the character played so brilliantly by Michael Douglas, in an Oscar-winning performance, is so famously quoted as having said. I really

Greed *is* good!

do think it is extremely important for us to get the context in which he had said what he had said. I am not talking about the context in the movie, but in the context of life, and of spirituality and about the evolution of the spirit, which, as I said in Chapter 2 and elsewhere, is taking place always.

However, I will also provide a context in terms of the movie and the setting in which Gekko is making this famous speech:

It is a jam-packed room which is housing the shareholder meeting of a publicly-traded company called Teldar Paper. Gordon Gekko is one of the biggest shareholders in this particular company and has taken over the mic to voice his opinion about how the management of the company is doing.

And this is a few seconds into that speech: "The point is, ladies and gentleman, that greed, for a lack of a better word, is good! Greed is right. Greed works. Greed clarifies; cuts through and captures the essence of the evolutionary spirit! Greed, in all of its forms; greed for life; for money; for love; knowledge; has marked the upwards surge of mankind. And greed, you mark my words, will not only save Teldar Paper, but that other malfunctioning corporation called the U.S.A!"

Gives me goosebumps to read those words because it is true now as it was true then, and as it will be true forever. Greed *is* good! It truly is the reason why we, as human beings, have evolved, and it will continue to be the reason why we continue to evolve. In *every* way!

(By the way, the recession may be over, officially, since there was actual growth in the GDP, the Gross Domestic Product, in the third and the fourth Quarter of 2009, and the first quarter of 2010. Meaning that the U.S. Economy *grew* in the last few months. Do you think it had something, anything at all, to do with greed?)

God=mc²?

Well, what we are *really* experiencing when we feel greed, which is the endless need for more, is simply our soul, which is an *infinite* and *eternal* "thing," nudging us to attain something that is infinite and eternal, too. This is so that our soul can be satisfied also. So, in theory, and in practice too, one would *never* be truly and totally satisfied with the money, personal wealth or other materials things because only physical things can satisfy a need that is physical. But the soul is spiritual, and thus can *never* be satisfied (with the physical alone, that is), as I mentioned in the last chapter.

Now again, please don't get me wrong. It is absolutely *essential* to have our physical needs met and satisfied; as I have said before, and repeatedly. The personal wealth and other material and physically oriented things *will* satisfy the physical needs. Well, temporarily. Those physical needs can only be truly and permanently satisfied *while* satisfying the spiritual needs also. And as I had mentioned before - this situation brings up the conundrum - the dichotomy of our being both, physical and non-physical, at the same time.

Now, not all aspects of greed are good (just like not all aspects of *anything* are all good, no matter what the underlying act or emotion is). Like Barry White sang, "Too much of *anything* is not good for you, baby." You know, the ol' "Vice vs. Virtue" argument. Too much and also too little of something is an extreme, and therefore a Vice; anything in moderation is considered good and thus, a Virtue.

Anything in extreme is not good for you, right? Excessive physically-oriented greed often makes one lie to, steal from, or cheat another human being, doesn't it? It is what greed *makes* you do, if you don't really understand and/or can't control it, now, *that* is the bad part!

Also, greed causes this confusion of the human mind and even of the ego and makes it think that this endless need for more is actually a need for more *material* things. However, in reality, it is a

Greed *is* good!

need of the endless spiritual part of our being, and that's exactly why the need, itself, is endless.

Again, if we were to apply the Golden Rule, and treat others as we would like to be treated by them, then we would have no problem with greed, or for that matter, anything at all now, would we?

And not just that, guess what this book is all about? It is about satisfying the ultimate "greed" of the spirit, along with satisfying all of our physical needs. That is, achieving full and perpetual bliss, once and forever.

Could there be anything bigger or better than that? I think not!

Chapter 12
Definitions

Spirituality Defined

In the Summer of 2007, I had gone on a weekend trip to New Hampshire; the members of our *Satsang* group were all getting together for a fun weekend there. (The direct translation of the word *Satsang* is "the company of truth," or "to be in the presence of truth," however, in this context, it means a group of people who gather together regularly and discuss topics of spirituality.)

While I was driving to the house the Group had rented for the weekend, just as we crossed the border from Massachusetts and entered New Hampshire, I saw this sign on the side of the road, "Kindred Spirits," and it was the name of a liquor store.

And I remember laughing when I read that and remember thinking to myself, "What a perfect name for a liquor store!" Anyway, all kidding aside, I do hope that people know that "being spiritual"

God=mc²?

does not mean "being full of alcohol," i.e., being full of spirits. *That is a totally different kind of spirit!*

So, what is spirit? Simply put, it is the *essence* of who we *really* are. Like I said before, we are spiritual beings having a human experience. It is what people have called the Soul or as the Hindus call it - "Atman." It is what we were *before* we were incarnated in this human body, and it is what we will be *after* we leave this body when the body dies. It is the state our consciousness would be in if we could learn to leave the body, at will, and return to it, also at will. Of course, we are still spirit when we are in the body; it is just that we are *in* the body. We are *pure* spirit before and after life and death, respectively.

Anyway, you get the idea that spirit is the conscious, self-aware life-force within us. It is who we really are!

So, what does *being* spiritual mean, which is the natural question to have after defining *spirit*? Well, technically, we all *are* spiritual already, aren't we? Because if the essence of us is our spirit, then we all are spiritual, already. That just makes sense. I think what people mean when they say that they are "spiritual," is that they are *aware* of the fact that they are infinite and eternal because they are, primarily, a spirit. Also, often, folks refer to themselves as being "spiritual" in the context of not being "religious."

Spiritual people *know* that they are not *just* the body that will come to an end some day. They realize that they will continue to exist even after physical death. And that by being a spirit, they really are connected to everyone and everything else in existence. And of course, connected to, and an integral part of, the "Param Atman," or the Primary Spirit; Universal Consciousness, or the entity commonly known as God.

Therefore, spirituality is the practice of the above mentioned spiritual principles or beliefs.

Definitions

Of course, being spiritual also entails a lot of other things. It entails living a life in accordance with that particular understanding. And of course, it also entails reaping the rewards of a life lived thus; viz., material happiness, spiritual bliss, and having answers to all of our "unanswered" questions. All of which we have discussed, and will continue to discuss, throughout this book.

Religion Understood

I started the Definitions Chapter with spirituality because that would actually help understand the definition of religion better.

Religion is a collective, formal and organized way of practicing spirituality. It can also be defined as *"organized* spirituality." It tells us how to live our lives in order to truly "live" it. It tells us how to live, and it tells us what will happen if we do live according to the principles of spirituality and also what will happen if we don't. You could even call it the science of spirituality, or spiritual science, in a way.

(Religion is different from the Spiritual Science or Scientific Spirituality that I will talk about and define clearly, later on, and that which is actually backed by modern, empirical science, and also is scientific in its reproducibility. However, still, religion is a "science," in a way.)

It doesn't "poison everything" as Christopher Hitchens, the author of *God is not great*, would have us believe. In fact, it is the *antidote to* the poison *of* everything. Please don't get me wrong; as I said before in the chapter about greed, there is nothing wrong with anything - anything *positive*, that is - whether material or not - but the key being - it *has* to be *in moderation*. Anything in extreme quantities can and does poison one's life. So, everything has the potential of becoming poisonous, and the science of spirituality (religion) is supposed to protect us from that toxin.

God=mc²?

Now, if Mr. Hitchens had said, as the sub-title to his book, "How *Organized* Religion Poisons Everything," I would have agreed with him wholeheartedly in clarifying that Organized Religion can, and sometimes does, poison everything. I do, however, implicitly agree with Mr. Hitchens in that all religion that we are exposed to nowadays is, in fact, "organized," and he might make the case that it would be redundant to even mention the fact that it is so. And it would be doubly redundant if we were to take the meaning of religion to be "organized spirituality." (And it almost - and *almost* being the key word here - makes me think of "organized crime!")

So regardless of whether religion is organized or not, what *does* it tell us? We all belong to or subscribe to some religion, or we may choose to be agnostic or atheist. It doesn't really matter because, first, if there is a God (and there is), wouldn't there only really be *one* God? And secondly, if God does exist, then do you think that it matters to God that you don't believe in Him or It?

Do you think that the "Alpha and the Omega," as Jim Carrey said he was, while he was "playing" God in the movie *Bruce Almighty*; the Creator of the Universe, would care if you did not believe in Him?

Some folks may think that it does not matter to Him, or simply that it *cannot* matter to Him because He is the Almighty Creator of all that is. I have really struggled with this question, but ultimately come up with an answer to it. You may or may not agree with me on this one, but in my opinion, the answer to that is, yes *and* no!

"Yes," because God or Spirit is *always* communicating with us, in His own way, and He is doing so because He wants us to make it a *dialogue* with Him, and not just let it remain a *monologue*, a one-way communiqué. As I have said in Chapter 6, God always remembers and acknowledges our existence because He created you and me. And not only that, He is always trying to remind us of our mission in life, and even helping us, if we ask for His help, achieve that mission.

Definitions

(What, do you think these are: Spontaneous new ideas, the inspiration to do something, intuition or a "gut feeling" about something? They are messages or communication *from* God!)

On the other hand, the answer is also "no," at least, it is a no in the religious sense. God does, obviously, care about all of us, *equally*. And that is exactly why He sends out His communication to all, as I mentioned above. But He could not or would not be diminished by one or more of us not believing in His existence because, after all, He is the Almighty! (He wouldn't be so if He were diminished by the non-belief of some people, or for that matter, of all people.) He does care for and about us, as His creations. However, it would not make sense that He would care about the fact that some of us do not believe in His existence. Or that He would be bothered by it or that it would matter to Him. At least, not in the way we would think that it would.

But does that also mean that He is totally and completely oblivious to our plight if we don't believe in Him? That He simply does not or would not care about the non-believers? Or is it that the complete opposite of that is true; the other extreme; i.e., the "micromanager" scenario that I have talked about before and do mention again in the definition of God, later on in this chapter?

(I do not accept the notion of a vengeful and punitive God that metes out sentences of pain and suffering on the one who does not believe in Him, and I also reject the notion of a fear-based belief and following of religion, for that same reason. In other words, true religion is love and freedom centered, and is non-dogmatic.)

Anybody who has seen the documentary, or read the book, *The Secret*, knows that there exists this Law of Attraction. And I am hoping that the viewers or the readers have realized that it is another name for *one* of the many *powers* of God. And therefore, one can surmise that God has given *us* the tools to create the life that we want for ourselves. It's not that He does not care, He just knows that it

God=mc²?

is not His job *to* care (i.e., to care so as to micro-manage and control every detail of our lives) simply because He has given *us* that responsibility, and along with that responsibility, also the power to create the life that we want. And ideally, even we are not supposed to try to micro-manage and control every detail of our own life; however, we have been given the power to create it the way we want it to be by other means.

(I discuss the Law of Attraction in much detail, and also mention sure-fire ways to get it to work for you in your life, in other chapters of this book. This way, we will learn how *not* to micro-manage our own life but still be able to create one of our dreams.)

Anyway, all religion has told us, cutting out the fat, if you will; that in order to bring good things to ourselves - on *any* level - physical, financial, mental, emotional, relational, or spiritual, we have to have faith in God, and *do* good deeds, and *think* good thoughts, and *be* good people. This is because God is good, and in being good, we are being god-like. And being god-like, and eventually merging with God; i.e., attaining God-Realization or Self-Realization, is our ultimate mission in life. And I understand that the meaning of "good"; as much as there are clear definitions of that word; can sometimes be subjective.

Murder is always bad; saving somebody's life is always good. Right? Or is it?

Imagine this scenario: A person cold-bloodedly and intentionally kills another person by shooting them! Is that murder and therefore "bad?" Well, the honest truth is that you don't know!

Well, you can only answer that question when you put things in the proper context. Now, I would say that the "cold-blooded person who intentionally shot the other person" is a United States Marine, who shot and killed an enemy combatant who was just about to throw a grenade at the former and his platoon, intending to kill them all. (Of course, this is in a setting of combat in a war, and you

Definitions

could always argue that war, itself, is bad, and I would agree with that, however, that is not the point of argument here.)

Or to use another scenario, the former; i.e., the "killer," is a father who, in the attempt to protect his teenaged daughter from being raped and murdered, and his whole family, which includes his son and his wife from being beaten up and left for dead, had found a baseball bat and beat the life out of the latter, an intruder - who was a serial rapist and killer.

So, yes, even though the act of intentionally killing another human being in these above examples was still, technically, murder, can it be defined as "bad?" These examples were, in fact, extreme ones, and I do hope and pray that one never has to make those kinds of decisions. One should never have to be in a situation where one has to even *think* about taking another person's life! The exception, if there would be any, is in the case of self-defense. (Or in the case of defense of another who may not be capable of defending oneself against the threat of imminent death.) Regardless, we all now know that the Karma of any action cannot be undone or mitigated. Well, at least, not under "normal" circumstances.

I understand that sometimes in life, *sometimes*, not most of the times, we may have to walk this fine line and it is not always easy to determine what the "right" or the "good" thing to do is. And that is where the Conscience comes into play.

If you do something that may be a crime or hurt somebody in any way, or be the cause for somebody's pain - whether or not you get caught - has no bearing on your conscience. It will always *know* that you did not do something right!

Consciousness and Conscience, well, those subjects are covered more thoroughly in another sub-chapter. I know that this may seem as a diversion and a digression, but in this case, it is not. These subjects of Religion, God, Spirituality, Consciousness, Conscience, Science, Faith, etc., are all so intertwined that it is impossible to define or clarify one without mentioning one or more of the others.

God=mc²?

Ultimately, I think we all, meaning all the people of Earth, and for that matter, all the religions and spiritual traditions on the planet, would agree that *doing* good and *being* good and having faith in God and treating everybody else as one would have themselves be treated, i.e., in accordance with the Golden Rule, is the crux of what *any* religion teaches its followers.

And it does so by asking us to realize who we really are - a piece of the Divine, a spirit - which is a small part of the Primary Spirit. So, if everybody else, and we, ourselves, are a piece of the Divine, how could we get ourselves to hurt anybody else? It also reminds us of the Law of Karma, the Law of Dharma, and also the Law of Attraction. Maybe these principles are defined using other words and terms in science or non-denominational spirituality, however, the basic instructions are the same as what religion teaches.

And why, exactly, should we follow these principles? To bring our own good to us; so that we can create and lead the life of our dreams, and ultimately, become blissful.

God Decoded

Who (or what) is God? Now, really, who or what is this entity, or thing or being that we call God? Is He a "Cosmic Bellboy?" as Dr. Wayne Dyer would ask us rhetorically? Although, we do treat Him as such, don't we? We pray and say that, "Please God, if you let me have this or that, I promise I will do this or refrain from doing that." We think God does respond to it, and that is simply not true.

We think that if we sacrifice something or promise to *not* do something; i.e., if we promise to refrain from an act which could be considered a "sin," we can gain "Divine Favor" and gain the good graces of God and actually receive the "good" things, status, or circumstances that we may want.

We think that God is like a corrupt government official whom we can bribe with the promises of good deeds, or ones to refrain from bad deeds, to get Him to do our bidding.

Definitions

(Government officials, especially the IRS officials, please note that I did *not* say "corrupt like a government official"; I said "like a corrupt government official" - suggesting that some - *very few* can be and, in fact, are corrupt, but not all of them are so.)

Also, we think of God as the micro-manager of the Universe - and hence, of every single human being and for that matter, every being and every*thing* in the Universe. Do we really think that is what God is? I mean, really? Do we think of Him as sitting in front of the computer and answering prayer email, one-by-one as they had shown in *Bruce Almighty*?

No, folks, we have all been wrong. Or more accurately, it has been the *people* - religious leaders and the folks who interpret the sacred texts for us - who have given us the wrong meaning of God. I do prefer to think that it was done mistakenly and not by intent.

God is simply the power that creates everything in existence. It is the power that creates *existence* itself! As it was said in *The Secret*, by several different scientists, doctors, authors, and teachers; in several different ways: Everything is energy! One of the featured experts from this hit film, James Arthur Ray, who has landed into a lot of trouble lately, had something very poignant to say about the relationship between God and energy. (I write about the event that got him in trouble and the lessons that I have learnt from it, at the end of this section as an epilogue to it.)

To paraphrase him, when one asks a Quantum Physicist what created life, he/she would say "Energy!" "It can never be created or destroyed, always was and always will be; it is always moving into form, through form, and out of form."

According to the Law of Conservation of Energy, energy is never "lost" or "created," it just changes form; i.e., it goes from one *form* of energy to another *form* of energy! Also, that the mass of a particular thing, meaning, the physical substance or "stuff" that makes up a physical thing, can be converted into energy, and vice versa. For

God=mc²?

example, Heat energy is converted into Kinetic energy - the energy used to create physical movement - when steam is used to power a locomotive. In that particular example, coal is burnt in order to heat water and create steam, and then the steam is used to power an engine. So, the mass of the coal is converted to Heat energy, and then the Heat energy is converted into Kinetic energy, which, in turn, moves the engine. By the way, the human body uses a similar, but a more complex and detailed process to convert food into energy. The body uses this energy to function properly and to be able to move around and to be able to do all the things that it is capable of doing. Then there is Potential energy - the kind that is stored in a body when the force of Gravity is acting upon it - for example, when you pick up a ball from the ground and hold it in your hands - it has Potential energy - that energy is what drops it to the ground if you let go of it.

James Ray further adds, "And when you ask a Theologian what created the Universe, he or she would say 'God; always was, and always will be, never can be created or destroyed, and is always moving into form, through form and out of form.'"

About four years ago, I had been watching the sleeper hit hybrid film *What the Bleep do we (k)now!?* and I saw the interview with Dr. John Hagelin, and he was talking about a "Field" that is ever present - the Unified Field. It is this Field out of which everything emanates. Per what he was saying, *it is everywhere*. There is nowhere that it is not, as I have mentioned before.

And I clearly remember saying to myself, "Hey, you are talking about God!" Here a Scientist, a Quantum Physicist, was saying that God exists! God has been described as the Omnipresent, the Omniscient, and the Omnipotent. The One that is present everywhere and at all times, and the all knowing, and the all powerful. As I had mentioned in Chapter 5, I had noticed this explanation and thought that it was very odd that *science* was talking about God's existence.

Well, if everything *does* emanate *from* energy, *is* energy, or can be converted *into* energy, and E - the mathematical representation of

Definitions

all the energy in the Universe - is equal to the product of the mass of all "things" in the Universe, times the speed of light, squared - that number is simply a number that is just too hard for any of us to even comprehend.

This, by the way, is the most famous and the most recognized equation of all time - $E=mc^2$!

Combined with the concepts above, I figured that it was only a natural conclusion to replace the "E" in Einstein's equation with "God." Also, that led me to come up with the title of this book - "$God=mc^2$?"

The question mark at the end of that equation simply suggests that I am not asserting that God replaces E; I am just posing a question. However, if God is truly *everything* - then the real equation would be $God = God \times God^{God}$ - God being everything there is in existence. God would replace everything in that equation, and for that matter, *all* equations in existence. It would also be right to put forth this *new* equation, God=Everyone+Everything! And on various levels of consciousness and existence, that equation *is* true!

Ainslie MacLeod, in his brilliant book, *The Instruction*, had said that it would take us a *billion* years while traveling at the speed of light to traverse the Universe (in other words, it would take a billion Light Years). And the speed of Light is approximately 6 *trillion miles* per year - 6,000,000,000,000 miles in a year, if I got the number of zeroes right. So, traveling at the speed of 6 TM/year, it would take us a *billion* years to get from one end of the Universe to the other.

(Well, practically, one could never traverse the Universe, and not even in a billion years, because the expansion of the Universe is the only thing that is occurring at a speed that is faster than Light-Speed. And since the Universe has been expanding for close to 14 billion years now, and since nothing else can travel faster than the speed of light, we would *never* be able to go from one end of the Universe to the other.)

God=mc²?

Anyway, if we *could* do that, do you know how many football-field lengths *that* distance would be? I will let *you* do the math on that!

What is the point of talking about all of this? I am glad you asked. The Universe is so vast and all the energy in it is such a huge amount, that it is *beyond* comprehension of the human *mind*. It simply cannot be fathomed by physical means, ever! It *can* be fathomed, however! Only by spiritual means. Just like God, Divine Energy or Supreme Consciousness - the entity, being or thing that is described by other synonyms such as Source, Spirit or Force - needs to be understood, fathomed and realized.

Epilogue to this item

Author, speaker, and featured expert from *The Secret*, James Arthur Ray, is being held criminally responsible for the deaths of three people who attended his "Spiritual Warrior" retreat near Sedona, Arizona late last year.

I did not want to comment extensively about these events in the section that defines God; however, these events were significant in the overall context of what we are discussing here, so I wanted to address them. Quite frankly, I *had* to address them.

The events in which three individuals lost their lives, and several others got sick or were otherwise injured, were tragic, and in fact, unnecessary. The final part of this "Spiritual Warrior" retreat involved the attendees to be enclosed in a makeshift hut; namely, the sweat lodge, and partake in this "purification ceremony." There was a hole in the ground inside this sweat lodge, and then there were hot rocks placed in this hole. Then, there was water poured onto these hot rocks to create steam. The resulting heat and steam was supposed to purify the spirits of the retreat attendees, from what I understand of this process.

Definitions

There were three important lessons that I learnt from this and thought that is was important that I share them with you. These three lessons are enumerated as follows:

1) Karma is inescapable – One may be able to escape the "Long Arm of the Law" but one cannot elude the Law of Karma and its effects.

Nobody ever gets away with anything. Ever!

Maybe James Ray is truly responsible for the deaths and injuries to his retreat attendees, as mentioned above. And maybe Ray is also truly responsible for saving tens or hundreds of lives of people who may have come to him at a time of dire need and he may have helped them, and maybe even prevented them from committing suicide. The fact is that he will have to pay for his bad deeds, and he will also get the reward for his good ones. A good deed does not directly mitigate an equally bad deed, as I have mentioned in the chapter on Karma.

While Civil and Criminal Law do their thing, justice, in the form of Karmic creation and the resulting debt, will be done. This judgment, if you can even call it that; more an evaluation, is carried out by one's own soul. In the meantime, as the laws of our society are implemented and applied, it is not the job of the rest of us to pass judgment. (I know that it can be very easy to say that but is very difficult to do. However, I can only implore you to do so, if possible.)

In my opinion, what we can and should do is this: Have the departed in our thoughts and prayers and wish well to the ones who were injured. And also do the same for Ray.

2) The message is important; not the messenger – The message that is being delivered, in most cases, is of more importance than the messenger; i.e., the conveyor or even the source of the message. (In *most* cases; sometimes you do want to consider the source also.) So, if a person is delivering a valid and true message, a Universal Truth, if you will, then the message is still valid and true, regardless of the true nature, intent, or reputation of the messenger.

God=mc²?

That is the reason why I did not remove James Arthur Ray's mention from my book because even though the reputation of the messenger may have become tainted, the message has not. (I had paraphrased what James Ray had said in *The Secret* a long time before the tragic events of the sweat lodge.) Another thing is that we live in a land where a person charged with a crime is considered innocent until *proven* guilty.

Regardless of whether James Ray is ultimately held guilty or innocent of these charges, his reputation may have been tainted beyond repair. However, it does *not* change the fact that he said something extremely poignant in the documentary.

3) The (non) significance of spiritual or religious rites, rituals, and ceremonies – In my humble opinion, these are only significant as far as the *metaphorical* transformation that they represent.

I do not recommend that one engage in any rite, ritual, or ceremony that may be even *perceived* to be *potentially* harmful to any aspect of the human being – physical, mental, emotional, spiritual, or otherwise. It is just not necessary. It is not necessary because life already throws at us events and circumstances that test our mettle in all areas of our life. All of our faculties are constantly challenged and tested throughout life!

You might have heard, "What does not kill you only makes you stronger." Right? Well, it *is* true, but that does not mean that we go *looking* for things that may kill us, quite literally, just so that we can triumph over them and thus, become stronger. And this is coming from a person who did go through three days of complete fasting himself (just as the attendees of the retreat had done *before* getting to the final Rite of Passage – the purification ceremony in the sweat lodge).

I write a lot more about religious rituals and ceremonies in Chapter 34; however, for now, I beg you to realize this: There is

Definitions

simply no need to *become* a "Spiritual Warrior" because you *are* one already! (Besides, the phrase *Spiritual Warrior* is an oxymoron; a contradiction in terms. *Spiritual Adventurer* is more accurate a description, as Mike Dooley, also a featured expert from *The Secret*, calls us all. Regardless, to reiterate, we don't need to become one because we are Spiritual Adventurers innately.)

Science Demystified

Science, from the Latin *scientia*, means "knowledge." It is humanity's collective and organized effort to understand or to understand *better*, how the physical world works.

Science always uses "empirical," meaning, first and foremost, physical, and then, experimentally and experientially observable data as a basis of that understanding of the physical world. This understanding can and does lead to the desired knowledge of how the physical world operates.

In other words, scientists look at existing physical phenomena or try to re-create those particular phenomena, under a controlled environment, and observe and record them as such. These phenomena could be things, events, reactions, or other such happenings. Regardless of what these phenomena may be, scientists want to see reproducible effects of any and all physical phenomena in a lab, or some other "controlled area." In other words, they conduct experiments on whatever phenomenon or process they want to learn more about. They may conduct exactly the same experiment several times in order to verify reproducibility of a particular effect. Then they study the experimental results of these phenomena until they come up with sufficient usable data. Then they come up with a conclusion and/or an agreement (with others, if others are involved) about the meaning of the collected data, and how it can be used to create something to make human life better.

And ever-present, in the discussions or definitions of "science," is the "Scientific Method."

God=mc²?

Scientific Method has already been defined, partially, in the previous paragraphs. It is that *process* or *method* of using reproductions of a particular natural (specifically, physical) phenomenon, to make predictions that may be useful for the advancement of humanity. In other words, scientists use this standard procedure, which is accepted by all scientists, to constantly invent new products, ideas or solutions to existing problems in not just scientific and technological fields, but life, in general.

After searching for the meaning of the word "Science," and the "Scientific Method," I have come to a conclusion that after considering all the things that we consider "Science," and thus consider them to be absolutely true, it is a fact, and yes, an absolute fact that Spirituality is *more* of a *true* science than anything else that could be considered "Science!"

Ironically, I would have to use the "Scientific Method" to prove that! And I will do so hereby:

Any and all fields of knowledge or of study that have the word "Science" attached to them - for example, Computer Science, or otherwise are considered Empirical Sciences - like Biology, Physics, Chemistry, etc. - all of these fields have had their core ideas changed dramatically or proven completely false. Similarly, a lot of the ideas first posited by the people in these fields as "truth," or "scientific evidence" have been proven to be theories that simply weren't either of those things!

However, the basic tenets of spirituality, or even religion, have remained the same. It is just that, now, they are being demystified and truly explained in the context that they were meant to be understood. For millennia, and not just for centuries, the message has remained the same! Now, we are truly "getting it." And the results of practicing spirituality or religion also have remained the same - enlightenment, and ultimately, bliss.

Definitions

I will discuss more of the existing empirical evidence of the benefits of practicing spirituality in a scientific manner in Section IV, the Action Section.

Faith Fathomed

The belief in something, anything at all, with complete trust can be defined as "faith." So, basically, you could even call it "trust." One does not, absolutely and always, require proof of something in order to believe that it exists or that it is true. Of course, the perfect example, and apropos to what we are talking about in this book, would be faith in God.

I do have to say that I am not a big fan of the phrase "*blind* faith," because like I just mentioned, faith, by its very nature, *is* blind. It could be considered "blind" because it does not ask for, or require proof, or even evidence, to trust in the existence of some phenomenon. So, in my opinion, it is redundant to add the *blind* in front of it.

You don't *need* proof to have faith! Please don't get me wrong, it would be very nice to have proof, but again, it is not required.

However, you do absolutely need proof to believe, if you are approaching whatever you want to believe in, *only* with empirical or scientific "eyes." (Or you could be using any or all of the five physical senses. The key being, you are relying on your physical senses, alone, and you are also trying to observe a *physical* phenomenon. The physical phenomenon being whatever it is that you want to believe in.)

Then there is "blind belief," and that is exactly what a lot of people *suffer* from – "blind" belief.

By the way, I think everybody has faith in *something*. Believers, obviously, have faith in God. Whereas Atheists have faith in the non-existence of God, while they may also have faith in science. Probably, the only ones who don't have faith in anything at all might be the Agnostics. And maybe even they have faith in something – in the fact

God=mc²?

that they are absolutely sure about *not being sure* about God's existence. (Okay, I only say that tongue-in-cheek.)

Conscience Comprehended

"You are like my conscience, except that I heed you." - Takizo Kanzei, *Heroes*, Season 2, Episode 3. Takizo Kanzei was a character in the super-hit show on NBC, *Heroes*; he was first a fast friend of the protagonist named Hiro, and then, his mortal enemy.

When I heard that line, I could not help committing it to memory because that is the only difference between a "sinner" and a "saint," isn't it? Whoever listens to and heeds his conscience is the saint. Obviously, the one who doesn't is the sinner.

So, where does this word *conscience* come from? And of course, more importantly, why do we care? Well, I am glad you asked.

Conscience is not the "science" of "conning" somebody (i.e., of playing the confidence game). *Con* means *with*, and *science* means *knowledge*. So, the word means, *with knowledge*. With knowledge of what?

Knowledge that we exist. The knowledge of consciousness itself. The knowledge or awareness of the "self." With this knowledge, haven't we conquered all? (Or at least that is our egoistic belief; I don't think we have even scratched the surface.) Well, the fact is that we *can* conquer all with this knowledge. That is important, i.e., to know that we can do this, and it is more important to know how we can do it. However, the *most* important is that we learn to "conquer" ourselves.

Anyway, I have digressed. So, the conscience is, in fact, a part of our soul, or an attribute of it. It is the highest part of who we are. It knows what the difference is between the right and the wrong. It is the voice of God within us.

If and when we try to do something that is not in accordance with the Golden Rule, our conscience lets us know of that. We simply

Definitions

"don't feel right" about it. Of course, we can surely override our conscience, if we choose to do so. However, the first time that we do just that, it does not feel right. It feels like we have stifled or muffled an inner voice. We do experience pain as if something inside of us just died. And in a way, that analogy is right. The innocence innate to us did die or does die when we don't listen to the voice of our conscience.

However, the good news is that this innocence does not actually die, ever. It is always ready to be resuscitated, and the voice of our conscience is never ever completely muted. It still does try to shout to us, but we have turned its volume down to the point where it only sounds like a whisper to us, and at the same time, we have turned up the volume of our desires of that which may not necessarily be congruent with the greater good, meaning, the good of not just ourselves, but also the rest of humanity, as a whole.

When this happens; i.e., when we only think of what *we* want, and as long as we do get what we want, and don't care about whether or not it comes at the expense of another, then we don't think twice about violating the only rule that we should not be violating. And not only that, but we actually start believing that we are doing the right thing. That is the beginning of what some would call the "evil" in us!

The voice of our conscience is still there, and will always be trying to have itself heard. Like everything else, it is a matter of choice! Do we choose to heed our conscience or do we choose to ignore it?

That is one of the major deciding factors in where we end up on our quest for higher consciousness because our conscience is the voice of God; the God within us; and how can we expect to advance on a path towards God by ignoring what God is saying to us?!

Chapter 13
Know Thyself!
(What does that even mean?)

"Know Thyself"
- The Matrix, circa 1998;
"Know Thyself"
- Hinduism, circa who knows when!

In the first part of the Trilogy that is *The Matrix* movies, when Neo goes to see the Oracle for the first time, she points to a wall-piece with the saying from the "original" Oracle of Delphi which says "Know Thyself," in Latin.

Hindu philosophy has said that from ever since it has existed, which, by the way, no researcher has truly been able to give an age to, so that's why I said "circa who knows when!"

What does that even mean, "Know yourself?" Well, to answer that we must ask the question that if we *do* already *know* ourselves, how is it that we would *define* ourselves? To be able to answer that question, we have to become introspective, to "look within."

Would we define ourselves as a "human being" first, or as a man or a woman; as an American or an Indian; as a Muslim or a Christian; as a Brahmin or a Vaishya; as a Businessman or a Sales Person; as a Billionaire or a Pauper? What do we define ourselves as?

God=mc²?

The fact is that all of those "definitions" are examples of what our *bodies* are, or what we *do*, or what *religion* we subscribe to. Or they may be our *professions*, or our *possessions*, or our *social* or *economic* status. However, that's not who we really *are*; we are not what we have or what our bodies are or what we do or our race or our religion. These are the things that our ego tells us we are!

A good example of the question we should be asking ourselves is what Dr. Wayne Dyer has asked, "If we are what we have or what we do, then when we don't have what we had or we no longer do what we used to do, are we *not*, then?"

Do we *stop* existing simply because we don't have a particular possession or a profession? The obvious answer to that is, of course, no. And quite frankly, we don't stop existing even after we die - that is, when our *physical* body dies.

(However, sadly, you might have heard of somebody who might have just retired from a job or profession and, within months or a few short years, died because they identified so much with what they did, in terms of their job or profession. Their means of earning a living was, in fact, also their purpose in life, and as soon as that was gone, they felt that they had no reason to remain alive anymore. I am not saying that they may have deliberately ended their lives. Just that they truly believed and felt, in their mind and their heart, that they had no reason to continue living, and their body agreed with that, and it, unwittingly, took on some disease and they died from it.)

Anyway, when we find out, or rather, remember, who we really are, we understand the How and the Why of Life.

In the movie *Bulletproof Monk*, Chow Yun Fat as "the monk with no name," says to Kar, the character played by Seann William Scott, that "The Wise know others; the Enlightened know themselves." And this whole process, this life, this book - *everything* - is to get us to be enlightened. To find out who we really are, and to really get to know ourselves like we have never done before. And to bask in

Know Thyself!

the glory and the almost-blinding brilliance of that knowledge; to experience bliss.

"Who am I?" This is one of the questions that, pretty much, every single one of the almost seven billion souls on this planet have. And it *has* to be an individual journey for each one of those seven billion people to find the answer to this, and other spiritual questions. I say it *has* to be because it necessarily cannot be otherwise.

Think about this for a while - nobody *else* can tell you who *you* are, right? You have to figure that out for yourself now, don't you? But that doesn't mean that we all should be Reinventing the Wheel, so to speak; we don't absolutely *need* to start at Square One, to mix metaphors.

An unshakably firm foundation has already been laid by the numerous religious and spiritual traditions of the world. There exist various Holy books that originated from these traditions such as the Bhagavad Gita, the Torah, the Qur'an, the Bible, and various other literary works on these subjects. All of those sacred texts are walls of that foundation. And, along with all of the other books on spirituality and/or religion, this book is a singular brick in one wall of that foundation.

And now, even science is helping in our quest for the True Self by shining the light on the similarities between science and spirituality. (Although I believe that this is an *unintended* consequence of the advances in science.)

What to do next is our individual responsibility. We can build further on that already existing foundation. We can start that Quest; i.e., the search for who we really are, and to *experientially* find our higher selves.

You know, to start the quest to truly get to know thyself.

Chapter 14
Are you a (*The*) *Secret* admirer?

It is February 14, 2009. Is it a co-incidence that I am writing about this on Valentine's Day? I think not.

Well, here's a question for you - are you a "secret admirer" of *The Secret*? Or are you an open and raving enthusiast and "in love" with it like I am? I do admire this work very much. It has brought the knowledge of the Law of Attraction to the masses, and it definitely deserves the credit for it.

Kudos!

(If you are not familiar with the Law of Attraction, please refer to the detailed and easy to understand definition of it provided at the end of Chapter 25 as the Epilogue to that chapter. There is also a detailed example of the Law of Attraction in action, along with the definition. However, you will read about various examples of it working, all throughout the book.)

God=mc²?

For me, however, *The Secret* was only a *validation* of something that I had found out about a year before the time I heard about *The Secret*.

Dr. Wayne Dyer's book, as I have mentioned before, *Being in Balance*, was the book that absolutely changed my life for the better, and forever. What I heard on the audio version of *The Secret* was something that I had heard before. Well, almost all of it; I should say that I had heard about 95% of it on the audio (live seminar) version of *Being in Balance*. So, it was nothing new to me.

Incidentally, I have neither actually seen the documentary, nor read the book version of *The Secret*. I have only heard the audio version, which I believe is the audio version of the book (as opposed to it being the audio version of the documentary). And the book/audio book does have more material than the original documentary did, as far as I know.

Regardless, I was trying to make a long story even longer (as my boss used to say, and I won't be like him and I won't do that) and more complicated than it needs to be. I will make it real short. The point was that I had known about the Law of Attraction before *The Secret*. The only difference had been that I had heard about this principle being called that; i.e., the Law of Attraction, very briefly. In *Being in Balance*, Dr. Wayne Dyer says, "You *get* what you *think* about, whether you *want it* or *not!*" He also mentions many other spiritual principles and practices that I have applied in my own life, and done so very successfully. Again, most of the things mentioned in *The Secret*, were written about in Dr. Dyer's book or talked about in his CDs.

Anyway, I absolutely loved his mantra, and here it is again, for emphasis, "You *get* what you *think* about, whether you *want it* or *not!*" I understood it the very first time I heard it, and knew it to be the absolute truth. It was so very profound for me because it validated what had happened in my life - good or bad. Please note that I

Are you a *(The) Secret* admirer?

examined what had *already* happened in my life to validate this principle, at least, initially. I found unequivocal *proof* in that validation!

This may be hard to believe (or maybe not) but I am a very scientific guy; a very "experimentally" and "empirically" oriented guy. Someone you would traditionally call a Scientist. I am not an actual scientist; it's just that I feel I have the same mentality as one. I am someone who has great respect for logic and the so-called Scientific Method, and one who believes, well, for the most part, that if it can be proven, it *has* to be real; and if it cannot be proven, it simply isn't or can't be real.

So, I had, and *still* have, the same mentality as a "Scientist."

You might recall that when I first immigrated to the United States, I wanted to be a Mechanical or an Automobile engineer, as I mentioned in Chapter 4.

Yes, I did resist, successfully, the temptation to feed the stereotype of becoming a Software Engineer or a Computer Scientist and considering my Indian background - I thought to myself - "Gee, I am an Indian who will end up being a Software Engineer or Computer Scientist - how novel, how unique." Despite that, I *still* went ahead and enrolled in the Computer Science undergraduate program at the UMass campus in Lowell, MA, after my stint at MBCC.

(If I had just listened to my instincts while I was attending MBCC, and just started to write professionally at that time, I would have been a published, and hopefully, a Best-Selling author a long, long time…..oh, sorry, I am writing out aloud again, aren't I?)

Anyhow, if my memory serves me well, I did attend exactly one semester in the Computer Science program there and promptly dropped out. (Thank God, and I most certainly *do* thank God for having done so – everyday.)

The point I am making is that, from ever since I can remember, I have been fascinated by the technological aspects of how things

God=mc²?

worked, and I still possess that same scientific mentality and curiosity that I possessed back then. It's just that, now, it is infused with spiritual curiosity also.

So, when I realized that what had happened in my life was simply the result of the *thoughts* that I had been thinking or of the long-term beliefs and related attitudes that I had held, I also realized that I absolutely needed to do something about it.

Of course, that "something" would be to change the way that I was thinking. And once I did that, my life started to change radically.

At first, as I mentioned before, I found the validation of this new-found principle by checking its validity against what had transpired in my life up until that moment. From that, I had a knowing that the events and the circumstances of my life had truly been the result of what I had been thinking about, whether I had wanted it or not; whatever "it" happened to be.

Then, I started to experiment with it to see if I could really manifest what I wanted. Although, I did not really *need* any more proof that this process - this Law of Attraction - really worked. I guess I wanted to be doubly-sure.

The following is a story that will demonstrate the kinds of things that started to happen to me:

It was July 31, 2007 when I was going to stop by my parents' place for lunch or just to see them; I don't remember exactly. As I got out of my car, I just happened to notice the "Open" sign on the door of Cobb's Lock & Key Service, the locksmith store located diagonally across the street from the building in which my parents lived. I thought to myself, "Perfect! Dad needs a new car key, and I can get it made today."

My dad had a set of keys to my car and home, just in case we would ever need them if we lost ours, and also because of the fact that he would often borrow my car to run his errands. My dad had

Are you a (*The*) **Secret** admirer?

lost his car key a few months back (about five months before that day) and I had been meaning to have a copy made for him since then. I knew that I had been procrastinating long enough.

So, that day, I walked into the store and waited for the gentleman who was minding the counter to be free. (By the way, this reminds me of the hilariously funny British sitcom about a bunch of salespeople working at Grace Brothers, a department store in London. You guessed it, *Are you being served?* I can almost hear Mrs. Slocombe ask, "Are you free, Captain Peacock?" And then Captain Peacock looks around, and says, "At the moment." Incidentally, growing up in India, this was one of the first TV shows that I had a chance to watch. The very first, though, was *The Lucy Show*.)

Anyway, once the person at the counter was available, I handed him the key and started making small-talk with him.

I said, "My parents live right across from your store." Pointing to the apartment building in which they lived, I said, "Right there." I continued, "My dad borrows my car often, and he had lost his key to my car a while ago and today, it seems, was the day that I could have a new key made for him." I was almost embarrassed to admit that I hadn't gotten it done yet, not that he even needed to know any of this.

Regardless, it had been such a small chore, and still I had either procrastinated getting it done, or simply forgotten about it, from time to time. Sometimes I would remember that I needed to get a new key made when I visited them due to the locksmith being right across the street, but I would find the store closed at that time. However, on that day, the "stars must have been perfectly aligned," and I was there at just the right time.

Anyway, near the end of the transaction, he reached behind the counter and pulled out a fake million dollar bill and handed it to me. You could not have imagined the joy I felt at that time. I felt as if I had actually gotten a million bucks! In *real* U.S. legal tender!

God=mc²?

So, why was I *so* excited about having received a *fake* million dollar bill? Because at that moment, I wanted nothing more than a fake million dollar bill! Well, other than actually getting my grubby little hands on the *real* currency, and of course, having a new car key made. But then again, if I had the actual "dough," I would just have a new *car* made for my dad. Or at the very least, I could *buy* him a new one that was *already* made. I will take this literal example and make it a metaphoric one by saying that I had been taking a ride and somehow gotten off on a detour, and now I need to get back to the main road.

So, this event was taking place exactly around the time that I had been thinking that it would be really nice to have a fake million dollar bill to use as a visualization tool. I had been thinking about getting it so that I could look at it and imagine having a millionaire's lifestyle just as Jack Canfield had said he had done to create *his* dream lifestyle in *The Secret*. I had been thinking about it for several days and that I should just try to find one somewhere. I thought that maybe a specialty gift store or some similar place would sell something like that, but I had just not gotten around to looking for it. (You might have noticed a little bit of a pattern developing here, as far as procrastination is concerned.) Anyhow, I really did want one so that I could use it just like Jack Canfield had done. Well, in his story, he had said that he used a fake $100,000 bill, but you get the point.

After that simple yet profoundly life-changing transaction at the locksmith's store, I was grinning ear to ear while I was walking back to my car to make sure that the newly-made key did work properly. And then for days, and weeks, and months since then, every time I thought about this episode, I would smile. I even shared that story with many people; some of them had been folks with whom I had also shared *The Secret*, so they had known the significance and context of the million dollar bill.

(Incidentally, I have saved the receipt of that transaction from that day and that's why I know the exact date of when it happened. And you may be able to see why, exactly, I saved it.)

Are you a (*The*) *Secret* admirer?

I knew; I just knew - for a fact and without a doubt - that Divine Energy, Source, Spirit, or God had brought that million dollar bill to me. And It had done so simply because I had wanted it, and there had been no conflicts within myself about wanting it.

It was simple as that. That did it for me. I was a "believer" of the Law of Attraction.

This is how I became an open and raving enthusiast of *The Secret* as opposed to a "secret admirer" of it.

So, which one are you?

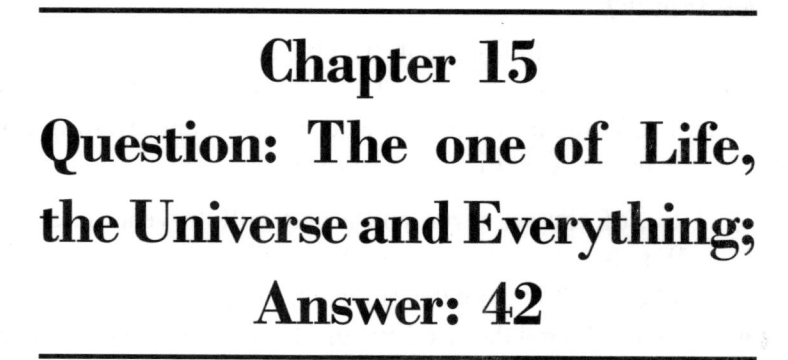

Chapter 15
Question: The one of Life, the Universe and Everything; Answer: 42

You might recognize that line as one from the movie *The Hitchhiker's Guide to the Galaxy*. If you don't recognize it, or have not seen this movie, I do recommend it highly. In my opinion, it is in a whole new genre by itself. It is in the Sci-Spi-Fi category. It is a Science Fiction movie, with overtones of Spirituality. The movie is actually based on a series of books by English humorist and science-fiction novelist, Douglas Adams.

Here are a few lines from the movie to give you proper context of what this is all about: "Many millions of years ago, a race of hyper-intelligent, pan-dimensional beings got so fed up with the constant bickering about the meaning of life that they commissioned two of their brightest and best to design and build a stupendous super-computer to calculate the answer to Life, the Universe, and Everything."

In the movie, they show these two little girls who are the "best and the brightest" on a planet called Magrathea, who design this

God=mc²?

super-computer and name it "Deep Thought." Then, they ask it do what it was designed to do. The computer, which is voice-enabled and all, asks them to return in exactly seven and a half million years "to get the answer to *the* question."

So, of course, seven and a half million years later, there is a huge Woodstock-style crowd gathered around the super-computer on Magrathea in order to celebrate receiving the answer to the greatest question of all, and the two little girls that created the computer come up to it and ask for the answer.

And Deep Thought's answer was......simply, the number 42! (That is after 7.5 *million* years of computing!!!!)

Ha! Of course, that was fiction, and this is not. But I thought that it was poignantly funny that even after seven and half million years of computing, it came up with an unexpected answer such as that. I think the moral of it is that one has to try to find the answer to that question on one's own. Like I have said before; however, that doesn't mean one has to start from scratch.

By the way, I would like to reiterate the suggestion that you watch the movie, if you already haven't done so. And if you have already watched it, it is my humble suggestion that you watch it again, if possible. You can, of course, also read Douglas Adams' books.

And that is a perfect segue back to the movie. Since Deep Thought had come up with such a non-profound answer to *the* question, everybody, including the creators of the computer, was very, very disappointed. So, instead of asking the computer to churn out the ultimate *answer*, they ask the computer to now calculate the ultimate *question*.

So, in response, Deep Thought says that it won't be able to compute the Ultimate Question; however, it did know that it would have to be *another* computer that would be able to do that.

Question: The one of Life, the Universe, and....

Deep Thought says, "A computer that will calculate the Ultimate Question! A computer of such infinite complexity that life itself will form part of its operational matrix! And you, yourselves, shall take on new, more primitive forms and go down into the computer to navigate its 10 million year program!

I shall design this computer for you, and it shall be called......Earth!"

The "experiment" or the "computer" that could churn out the ultimate question of Life, the Universe, and Everything was supposed to be the Earth. Not *on* Earth, but the Earth itself. With all its life and complexity.

In my opinion, this makes perfect sense! Only by actually living life, can we know what life is all about, right? By doing so, not only can we come up with the right questions we should be asking, we can also come up with the right answers to those questions. As I mentioned in Chapter 6, we have a mission in life, and it can only be accomplished *by* living life, and in the process, achieving the objectives we have planned to achieve, and thereby achieving the overall and ultimate goal of life, bliss.

So, what are all the big questions? *The* questions? The ones that we all ponder? What or who are we? Why are we here? Why was the Universe created? Who or what is God? *Is* there a God? What is a Soul? Is there a heaven and a hell? Et cetera, et cetera.

Just like the question of the meaning of life itself, there are these other questions, like the ones mentioned above. We can arrive at answers to some of them only by experiencing, first-hand, some of those things. Whereas with some other ones, we can look at the clues left by the evidence surrounding some "odd" phenomena.

Like the ones that we will be discussing in the next section.

SECTION III: Phenomena - Spiritual Phenomena On The Verge Of And Now Explicable By Science; And Vice Versa!

This is what I am calling the Phenomena Section of the book. Here, I hone in on phenomena which, up until very recently, scientists were simply not willing to do research on. And even still, unfortunately, the members of the modern scientific community who are willing to put their reputation on the line, and face ridicule by taking up research in the field of supernatural, paranormal or metaphysical phenomena are few and far between.

Some of the examples of "spooky" or "mysterious" phenomena are ghosts or earth-bound spirits; psychic phenomena such as telepathy, clairvoyance, precognition, remote viewing; Near-Death and Out-of-Body-Experiences; death and the Afterlife; reincarnation, déjà vu, etc. These, I consider as spiritual phenomena now on the verge of science. I have covered a few of the above since I would not have been able to cover them all within the scope of this book.

The scientific phenomena, on the other hand, which could be considered as being on the verge of spirituality, are Time Travel, Teleportation, Bilocation, Quantum Mechanics, UFOs and Extra Terrestrials, etc.

There can be individual books written about each one of these phenomena, and, in fact, there have been many already written about few or all of them. Despite each one of these phenomena being a huge topic of discussion and possible research, the reason I decided to mention them in this book is because each one of these phenomena is an extremely important piece of the puzzle of our existence.

God=mc²?

Careful examination of scientific evidence pertaining to any of these phenomena; if available, and it *is* available in certain cases; will lead to us coming up with some solid conclusions regarding the existence of God. At the very least, each piece of evidence from each of these phenomena, when put together with every other piece, will provide convincing proof of the existence of Divine Energy or Supreme Consciousness. In other words, of God.

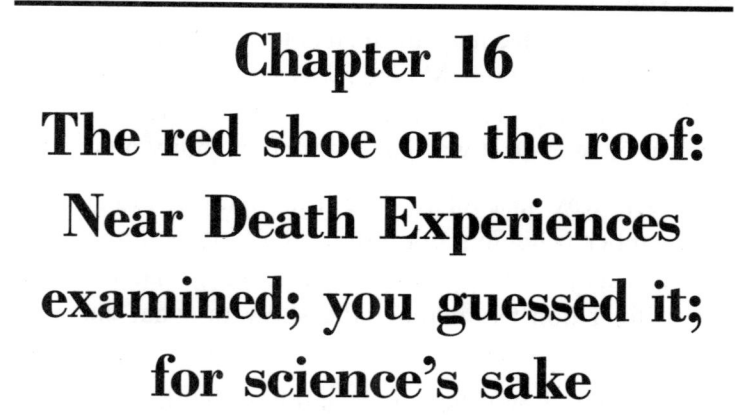

Chapter 16
The red shoe on the roof: Near Death Experiences examined; you guessed it; for science's sake

Near Death Experiences or NDEs, as they are called in the "business," are phenomena that are relatively new because of usage of defibrillators and adrenaline and other such life-resuscitating technologies in Medicine. Well, they are also "relatively new" in terms of the *official* reports of NDE occurrences.

So, they are now more common phenomena then ever before because we hear about them a lot more, and also because of the medical reason that I mentioned above. However, I had first come across NDEs via the 1990 movie, *Flatliners*, which I had seen when I was still living in India. In this movie, which I consider groundbreaking, five medical students experiment with their own life and death by having each one's heart stopped, and then revived, so that they can experience and learn about what lies beyond death.

And then, I was re-introduced to this phenomenon via another movie, *Hideaway*, released in 1995. After watching this movie, I had been scared witless! So I cannot tell you what the insane reason was for

God=mc²?

my having watched it again and that too within a matter of a few weeks from the first viewing. Maybe I was a glutton for the morbid curiosity of the possibility of having my own heart stopped via the experience of a terror or two. Or it was just plain ol' stupidity on my part.

Anyway, fast-forwarding from that time, to around a time that I remember watching a program on TV about three years or so ago, and the subject was NDEs or something related to death and the Afterlife. I don't remember the show or what channel it was on; however, the impact of what I watched was irreversible.

In the show, they were talking about a lady that had been brought to the hospital in a critical condition. And then she "died" for a few minutes, and what she experienced, while she was dead, was documented in the program. She had been resuscitated by the doctors there, but while she had been "dead," she claimed to have had a feeling of rising from her body and then rising to the ceiling and then going through it and coming up through the floor above and so on and so forth. Then, as she had claimed, she had reached the roof, and had been hovering there and had happened to see an object on the roof there. She claimed that it had been a red shoe.

As she told this story to the doctors, they sent a person upstairs to see what they would find, and the person came downstairs holding a red shoe! Now, one can say that she had known that before she got to the hospital and this whole thing was a hoax, but then how do you explain her being able to "die" at will, and then come back to life? The answer is that you *cannot*!

There have been numerous stories of people dying and coming back to life after several minutes, or even hours, and in rare cases, even after days, and describing and explaining what happened to them while they were "dead."

Some or most of these stories have very subjective elements to them, and one cannot verify that what a "dead" person experienced while he/she was dead did actually happen to them. However, there have also been several stories reported by P. M. H. Atwater, the

The red shoe on the roof: Near Death Experiences....

foremost researcher of NDEs, in her book, *The Big Book of Near-Death Experiences*, that defy logic and scientific explanation.

I highly recommend this book to anybody who may be interested in the particular subject of NDEs, and also to somebody like yourself, who may be interested in metaphysics.

In her book, Ms. Atwater does, in fact, mention the episodes of several people who, when they were clinically "dead" and supposedly out of their bodies, saw and perceived things that they possibly could not have. Things just like the lady on the roof had claimed to have experienced.

By the way, a very similar story to that was reported by Ms. Atwater in her book. However, in that story, the "dead" lady was hovering in mid-air right outside the window of the hospital room that she had been in, and happened to catch a glimpse of a blue tennis shoe, on a window ledge somewhere on the side of the building. Upon investigation, it was found that, in fact, there had been a blue sneaker stuck on a ledge; however, it was not visible from anywhere at all - either from the ground or from any windows of the hospital. Or if it were visible, the scuff mark that she claimed she saw, and also the fact that the laces were tucked underneath the sole, would have been facts that she could not have been able to know, unless she had been "hovering" right in front of the shoe.

(Maybe this story that I saw on TV was about the same person, and the details may have been changed, for privacy reasons or whatever.)

Another truly incredible episode mentioned in Ms. Atwater's book had been one of George Rodonaia, who was a Russian doctorate student of research psychology and an open dissenter of the Soviet Union during the Cold War. He had "passed away," and then had come alive, on his own, three days later, while his body was on the autopsy table, with his chest cut wide open. He had been murdered, supposedly by the KGB, via the process of being run over twice by the same car.

God=mc²?

While he had been dead, his consciousness had floated out of his body, and had roamed the world. Not only that, it had roamed different *times* of the world. Right before he got back to his body, he had heard a child crying incessantly in the Nursery of a Maternity ward in a nearby hospital where a friend's wife had just given birth. He (his out-of-body spirit, that is) floated into the Nursery to check on the crying infant. It was a new-born baby girl, and she had been crying uncontrollably. As soon as he approached her, the baby was startled, as if she could see him.

This man said that he felt like he had X-ray vision, just like Superman, and he scanned the baby's body to see what was causing her pain, and he could see that the baby had a broken hip.

So, after being sucked back into his body, as soon as he was "alive" and able to speak again, he mentioned the baby girl in the Nursery, and the fact that she was crying so much was because she had a broken bone in her body.

So, the doctors took an X-ray of the child and found that, in fact, she had a broken hip-bone! Later on, after some questioning by the doctors, a nurse there fessed-up to having dropped the baby.

If we were to accept the phenomenon of NDEs as real, and scientifically verifiable via these corroborating pieces of evidence presented by the experiencers or NDEers, as they are called, then we can very easily come to a conclusion that our consciousness, or soul or spirit does survive the physical death of our body. And that consciousness is not limited to a location within our bodies, i.e., our brains. That it is "Non-Local." That it can be located anywhere, and that it really is pervasive of all of space. That it is, in fact, everywhere.

Gee, that reminds me of a particular word, and it is right on the tip of my tongue........what is it....oh, yes, *omnipresent*!

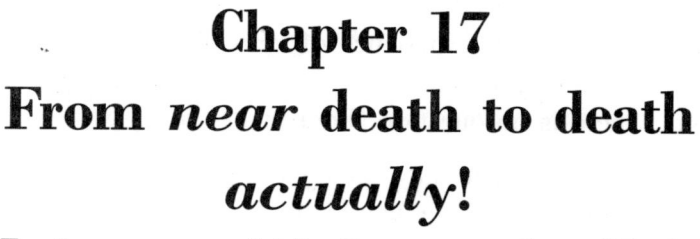

Chapter 17
From *near* death to death *actually*!
Is it so morbid that we shouldn't talk about it? Naaaah!

Death!

It is such a "scary" and "sad" word, isn't it? I put the quotes on those words because we have *made* it scary and sad. I am not saying that death is not scary or sad, currently. It surely is. It's just that it *is* so scary and sad because we have *made* it so.

I just think that it was never meant to be scary, sad, or morbid. We have made it that way because we are so focused on the physical world and so we assume that the physical death of any person is the ultimate end to their existence.

When somebody dies, our assumption and even our experience is that they are gone. Forever! We will never experience all the good things about them because if there were bad things about them, we would not miss them anyway. If *some* aspects of the departed were undesirable, we would not miss those aspects, and so we mourn the

God=mc²?

loss of the good traits and good attributes that they possessed. We loved them for those qualities. And therefore, we mourn the loss and absence of the person who had them.

There is an experience of very real pain and suffering, and genuine feelings of loss and grief associated with the death of a loved one. There is no question about that.

However, you may agree with the fact that *we* miss them. So, on some level, this pain that we feel is somewhat of a selfish nature, isn't it? *We* are the ones feeling the pain of missing the company of the departed. And if they missed us also, they would stick around, and not actually go – if they had the power, spiritually speaking – to stay. (And sometimes, they *do* stick around in this physical realm of existence, as you will read about it in the chapter about ghosts or earth-bound spirits. However, in most cases, they do not stick around.)

I am not saying that we should not mourn our loss just because it is *our* loss that we are really feeling the grief from. It is perfectly natural and normal to do so. In fact, it would be abnormal *not* to feel the pain and the grief of this loss because it is out of our love for the one who has passed away that we feel those emotions. Not only that, the grieving process is the way to fully experience that loss, and not to deny it. But then, we have to let go. It is the way to be able to move on.

And *why* would we want to move on? So that we can start to focus on the purpose of our own life again, which is still existent. Of course, we could always use the grief in a positive way to make life better for others in a very meaningful way. And you might have heard numerous stories of people doing exactly that after experiencing a tremendous loss of this nature, and therefore, having done something selfless with it.

The exception to this mourning being somewhat of a selfish nature is when one mourns the fact that the person who has died will

From *near* death to death *actually*!

not be able to enjoy all the things that life had to offer them. When the grief felt is *more* for the loss of the person who has died, and not for the loss felt by the ones left behind.

However, in that situation, it is our assumption that what the Afterlife has to offer is nothing at all because there is no such thing as an Afterlife, and the person is just not existent anymore - in any realm - physical or spiritual. Or, one of the other assumptions is that the person's soul is in a realm which is lesser than the one they were in while they were alive. One may also make the assumption - if one believes in reincarnation - that the soul of the dead has reincarnated into what could be a better or a worse life than the one they just left, as another possibility of where the loved one has gone.

Of course, one could always assume the worst possible scenario and that is that the dead are in hell. That would surely be mournful and even dreadful if that were the case.

However, consider the other scenario - the best possible one - the one of them having ended up in heaven. Well, in that case, one should rejoice. And most people *do* think, or would *like* to think, that their loved one is in heaven. Well, in that case, the dearly departed are experiencing the bliss that we all want to experience. We should really celebrate the fact that they are in heaven and one with God now.

Well, maybe that can lead to the thought that *we* are not *with* them, in heaven, and therefore, the resulting mourning.

In spite of considering the fact that every person or living being that has been physically born, will also physically die, and that it has been happening ever since the beginning of life, we know so very little about death, don't we?

So, death, in and of itself, is a very mysterious phenomenon. Although it is a very natural and a normal one, it surely has spiritual and metaphysical implications, doesn't it?

We may say that dead people don't come back to tell us what is going on with them after they have died. Or dead men tell no tales.

God=mc²?

Well, they *do* come back, as experiencers of Near-Death states! And they *do* tell us tales, as ghosts or earth-bound spirits! (As I had heard a spirit Medium say once.)

A person's physical death being the ultimate end to them or their existence, as we have discussed, simply isn't so.

I love how metaphysical teachers Esther and Jerry Hicks call death "your croakin' experience." They call it that because they say that there is really no such thing as "death."

(Well, Esther Hicks claims that these ideas and spiritual concepts that she talks about come from the non-physical entities that the Hicks' call "Abraham." Esther channels the collective teachings of Abraham via her consciousness. By the way, Esther and Jerry Hicks are, in my opinion, and probably in fact, one of the pioneers of the teachings and principles of what is now known as the Law of Attraction. Well, at least, as far as our times are concerned. And so I was unpleasantly surprised that they were neither featured as one of the many teachers in *The Secret*, nor were they even mentioned in it. Maybe there was some reason for that. Maybe the fact that they claim to channel knowledge conveyed by spiritual or non-physical entities would have been just too "out there" for some people. Quite frankly, Channeling used to be a little out there for me, too. However, I have come to realize that the message, itself, is important, and not how, necessarily, the message is being delivered.)

Anyway, they refer to death with such disrespect that they even want to make fun of it, and in fact, they are doing just that. They are doing so, in my opinion, because they know that in the physical death of the body, the soul rejoins the "stream of consciousness" which experiences only pure positive bliss. And that, truly, it becomes one with its Source.

Abraham, the spiritual entities (yes, the name suggests a singular entity, however, there are more than one) say, via Esther, that everyone will experience that Oneness when we "croak," however, it is *not* necessary for us to "croak" to experience it.

From *near* death to death *actually*!

Dr. Dyer calls it "dying while you are alive." Spiritual Enlightenment or having an experience of Unity Consciousness, that is, the experience of actually being one with the Universe, is the experience we would have when we die. However, again, we don't *have* to die to experience it. (I have tried to describe the state of Unity Consciousness in Chapters 6 and 7, and how we may be able to experience it while being alive.)

We can choose to either see a trailer of the Coming Attraction, or we can choose to see the whole movie.

Meaning, by our moving towards achieving higher consciousness, we can have a one-time spiritual experience of the magnitude of what would be considered Unitive (or Unity) Consciousness, and therefore *know* what to expect when we die, and consequently *lose* the fear of death, and also experience other spiritual "side effects" of a positive nature. Or we can choose to continue our "inner" work after having that one-time experience so that we can have multiple such experiences, and then, eventually, we can become spiritually capable of living in those states all the time.

At that point, in my opinion, not only would we *not* be afraid to die, we actually won't even *need* to die. We would be able to *choose* the time, place and the way we leave our body, once and for all.

I do want to clarify that this is not dying or anything like dying. It is by will, and by choice. We could, very easily, continue living in physical form, if we were to choose to do so. However, at that point we may find that we have no need for the body and for human life, as it may be, because the purpose of life - full and complete spiritual bliss - would have been achieved.

Or after leaving this body at will, we may *choose* to return to this physical realm by taking birth into a life where we dedicate our life to serving humanity; for example, and these are only a *few* of several examples, as a person like Mother Teresa, Nelson Mandela,

God=mc²?

Mahatma Gandhi, Saint Jalaram, Warren Buffet, or Bill Gates. The former four on this list may be clear examples of actual Saints or Saintly beings who have made non-monetary or even significant other material contributions that changed the whole world for the better. However, the latter two may not seem to be such obvious choices, but since they have contributed tens of billions of dollars to charitable causes and thereby served humanity in ways that others could not have, one could choose to return in such a role also, and of course, one would be granted such a choice. (Of course, only if one has reached that level of spiritual advancement.)

This pertains to another very controversial topic which provides scientific evidence of the existence of our spirit, and that it is of an eternal and infinite nature: Reincarnation. Even though we will discuss it only briefly, this topic happens to be a natural segue into the next chapter.

Chapter 18
Are you a Sinner or a Saint?

Even if we know that we *are* a sinner or *might* be a sinner, we don't like to admit the same, do we? The reason being that once we do admit that, we know where we are going, after we die. That would be a very unpleasant place called Hell.

On the other hand, when we are told we are saints, we do tend to vehemently resist *that* also. Eknath Easwaran, an Indian author of spiritual books, said in his book, *The Bhagvad Gita for Daily Living*, that "If somebody tells us that we are a saint, and they keep insisting upon it being the truth, no matter how much we may disagree with that, we do eventually give in, and become one."

I like that approach. No, I *love* that approach because that is the approach of God! Nobody, really *nobody*, likes to hear that they are no good. Even if they know, deep down and for sure, that they are no good. Everybody, really *everybody*, likes to hear that they are good and that they are great. Even if they know, deep down and for

God=mc²?

sure, that they are not. They may resist it or disagree with it, but they still like hearing it. They might feign modesty or even express genuine humility, but they will still like hearing the words of their praise.

It all depends on what you really want out of somebody when you call them "good" or "bad." Are you passing judgment on somebody when you are doing that? Or do you want to acknowledge good behavior or their genuine "goodness," or are you trying to mete out negative reinforcement to change their behavior for the better; i.e., the kind that you want from them?

I love Eknath Easwaran's approach because regardless of how somebody really is - good or bad; saint or a sinner - once you start saying and insisting that they are a saint, they will become saintly.

Do you know why this approach works? It works because the soul, the spiritual core of ours, is not only saintly, it is godly! And when there is an unwavering insistence for it to show its real self, it does. Do you understand the power of this insistence to transform any "wrong-doer," "criminal," or "sinner" into a person who possesses all the opposite characteristics? This insistence can come from within, meaning, the self, or it can come from without, meaning, somebody else.

Of course, this talk about "sinners" and "saints" also bring up the other-worldly realms of heaven and hell.

Since I was born into a Hindu family, reincarnation is something that I have always believed to be a fact of life and even of death, so to speak. Although I am neither a deeply religious person, in terms of all the tenets of Hinduism, nor am I a follower of rituals, I do believe that ultimately, we all end up being one with God.

That sooner or later, all souls will merge back into the Supreme. All "Atmans" will reunite with the "Param Atman." That is our destiny because, ultimately, we *are* God, or at the very least, *a part of* God.

Are you a Sinner or a Saint?

I do believe that if there is a hell or a heaven, it is right here, on earth. And we experience either of those states at any given time, in our lives here. In my opinion, living in conditions that you don't want to live in, is hell. Conditions that are ideal and pleasant are akin to heaven. These two states of being are what we think or imagine them to be, because they are really mental states. Simple as that. I also believe that we have the Free Will to choose what we *want* to experience. We may not *always* have a Free Will to choose the exact events or circumstances of our life; however, we always have a Free Will to choose our thoughts and our reactions to those positive or negative events or circumstances. In other words, to choose to experience "hellish" or "heavenly" states regardless of the nature of the underlying event to which we are reacting.

Just like in life, we have this Free Will to choose, we have the Free Will to choose, even in death. We can choose to come back, and we can even choose to come back in another physical form, as an animal or a bird or an insect.

Since life is about *evolving* to a higher level of consciousness, we would generally choose to come back as a higher form of consciousness, the next time around. Or we may choose to reincarnate into conditions that are more conducive to our spiritual advancement. So, for example, a person who might have led a very tough life, and had found it difficult to start on a path to higher consciousness during this lifetime, might choose to take birth into a household where spirituality is already a way of life. This would ensure the ascension of the soul of this person.

Sometimes, we might make a move that may seem like spiritual retreat, or de-evolution, if we simply need to experience some other form of life, in order to eventually move towards a higher level of consciousness, or to burn off some Karmic debt that we may owe. By the way, do you see the reason to not have *any* Karmic debt whatsoever, either good or bad, built up in our Karmic Account? If we do, we will be *forced* to take birth to enjoy it or to pay for it. We would not have any choice in *that* matter.

God=mc²?

However, still, the Free Will to choose will always reign supreme. So, there is always a possibility of stagnating at the same level and of going from one birth to another, without making any real progress. Conversely, there also exists the possibility of making spiritual advancement by leaps and bounds by making Self-Realization a goal to be achieved within the span of a particular lifetime, and moving in that direction.

So, having come full-circle, because of the fact that we do have Free Will, an act of "sin" would be to move *away* from God by denying our own primary nature, which is spiritual, and by not heeding our conscience.

And anything we do to move *towards* God is "saintly." There are no *specific* acts, in my opinion, that are deemed as either sins or saintly in nature.

Chapter 19
You got ghosts?
Whoyagonna call?

What are they? And why do they matter? One can say that the existence of ghosts, or as Mary Ann Winkowski, the author of *When Ghosts Speak*, and consultant for the hit show on CBS, *Ghost Whisperer*, calls them - "earthbound spirits," proves, without a shadow of a doubt, that human beings are spiritual beings because that is exactly what is left behind of them when they die - their spirits.

Incidentally, the Show is based on Mary Ann's life, and the character played by the gorgeous Jennifer Love Hewitt is supposed to be the on-screen version of her. (Incidentally, I used to have a huge crush on the lovely Ms. Hewitt during her *Party of Five* days.)

Of course, one has to *actually believe* that what Mary Ann has the capability to do is, in fact, real. And that is, to be able to communicate with these earthbound spirits. There has been many a proof of her "taking care" of the "problem" and then things returning

God=mc²?

to normal at the residence of, say, a happy couple that had been inexplicably fighting a lot ever since they moved into their new house.

Unbeknownst to them, there had been an earthbound spirit residing there already and did not like the new company arriving, for whatever reason. Let it be known that per what Mary Ann says, these earthbound spirits do, in fact, *need* humans to be around to provide them with the energy they need to "survive" and to be active.

They, basically, "feed" off of this energy created by couples fighting with one another, or people being frustrated about, say, not finding the remote control of their TV or not being able to find their car keys and other such anger or frustration-inducing situations. Logically, I would think that these earthbounds could feed off of positive, loving energy and thoughts also; however, the "bursts" of negative energy might be more intense due to their having more emotion packed into a very short period of time, and thus, they might *prefer* the negative to the positive kinds of energy. However, that is just speculation on my part. I am sure that Mary Ann can shed a whole lot more light on that subject than I can.

So, it could very well be the case that a "resident" spirit may not be very thrilled if a really happy couple moves in and is not fighting at all (or not fighting enough) for the earthbound spirit to get its energy "fix." So, the earthbound spirit "causes" the couple to fight often or tries to get them to move out of the place so that a more "fruitful" couple - one that is a lot more unstable and highly volatile - can replace them. So, that's the scenario that Mary Ann Winkowski would mention.

Then there are these guys, the *Ghost Hunters*, the members of the team by the same name, and also a TV show on the Sci-Fi channel (now called SyFy), who use sophisticated electrical and electronic devices to measure ghostly activity in a particular "haunted" place. They use EMF, Electro-Magnetic Field, detectors to find out if there are higher levels of readings present somewhere to indicate a presence

You got ghosts? Whoyagonna call?

of a ghost in that location or vicinity. Using other sophisticated equipment, these Ghost Hunters also record EVP, Electronic Voice Phenomena, which they claim are the voices of ghosts talking. (Of course, the "original" on-screen ghost hunter-gatherers were known as the *Ghostbusters*, as in the movie and subsequent sequel.)

By the way, now, there are two other similar shows, that I know of, on TV – one of them is called *Ghost Adventures* and it is shown on the Travel Channel, and the other one is a very scientific-sounding *Ghost Lab* on the Discovery Channel.

(Please don't get me wrong. I am not saying that this is proof-positive of the existence of ghosts, just that it is *adding* to the evidence that is out there already.)

So, even traditional science, as opposed to Quantum Mechanics, is surely moving in the direction of proving the phenomenon of "Non-Local" consciousness, or existence of disembodied spirits. Meaning, consciousness existing outside of the human body – as we talked about in the chapter on Near-Death Experiences, and as we are talking about now – in the case of ghosts or earthbound spirits.

And if these spirits do exist, then think about what their source could be. Well, *other* than the *body* that they came from because even though the body was holding the spirit, it was not the source of the spirit, it was simply a vessel for it. This contemplation, deduction, and the resulting conclusion is going to be a very positive and uplifting one. (I just thought that I should mention that.)

If a physical human being exists, so do its parents, right? Do you need to do scientific research to find out whether or not a child's parents were really alive or not? No, you simply know, with 100% certainty, that the source and the creator of a particular child exists or existed. The parents *had* to have existed; otherwise their child would not exist. (I am not talking about Immaculate Conception here, although, even in that case, a parent - singular - still had to exist, right?)

God=mc²?

So, if a soul or a spirit of a human being lingers on, in this physical plane, and there is scientific evidence of its existence, then one must, necessarily, come up with the conclusion that the source of the spirit must also exist. Meaning, that there *must* exist a place or space from which this spirit emanated. And as all religious and spiritual traditions have told us, Primary Spirit, or Source, or God *is* the source of that individuated spirit.

If a child exists, so must its parent(s). Ghosts prove that God exists! And in fact, that was exactly the rationale that I used to rely on to get rid of my fear of ghosts. (And yes, I did have a fear of ghosts, and one that would often induce a state of temporary paralysis.) I used the following logic: If ghosts exist, then so does God, and if God exists, then what do I have to fear?

And this is only *one* of the *several* pieces of evidence that proves God's existence.

Chapter 20
Conversations with a *real* psychic: My 11-year old niece!

It had been a Friday evening, about two and a half years ago, now. My niece, my sister's daughter, Radhika, had come over to stay overnight as she often does. Radhika loves to stay at our place because my wife happens to be her favorite aunt because she "spoils" her, and she has a lot more freedom - freedom to do what she wants; i.e., stay up late, watch TV, talk on the phone with her friends for hours, etc. - in our house than she does at her own place.

Anyway, she was an 11-year old, at that time, who often predicted little occurrences. And I should say she did it accurately. So, that Friday evening, we had started to talk about her abilities and the fact that I was writing a book on spirituality and how it compared to modern science (i.e., this book), and that her psychic abilities were something that I wanted to mention in the book. She was very excited to hear that she and her "powers" would be featured in the book, and so we talked a lot more about spirituality and psychic phenomena and

God=mc²?

other such topics of a metaphysical nature. I think we were up until 3:00 o'clock that morning.

She had accurately predicted that my wife was pregnant (*before* we had probably even known, or it may have been the exact day that we had found out, but had yet to tell anyone), and that we were going to have a baby *boy* and that he was going to be born on September 7, 2007.

My wife gave birth to Krish, our son, at 11:54 PM. Only six minutes *short* of the date on the calendar changing to September 8, 2007, which would have been a date that would have proven my niece wrong.

So, not only did she know that we were expecting a child, and maybe even before *we* knew about the pregnancy, she also accurately predicted the gender of the baby, and his date of birth. To be 100% positive about any one of these things would be impressive, in and of itself. Well, the probability of accurately guessing the gender of a child to be born is 50-50, so guessing that is not very impressive, but to be 100% adamant that it is a baby boy, *and* to predict his date of birth was something else.

She is a very spiritual person. Or it would be more accurate to say that she *was* a spiritual person because, now, she seems to have lost all, or some of those "powers" as she has grown older and lost some of that innocence that is innate to a child, and has grown to be more physically oriented. (By the way, this is exactly what happens to all children as they grow older – they become less spiritually oriented, and more physically focused because they are taught to do so by the physically-oriented world.)

Anyway, on that evening when we had stayed up and talked for hours, we had talked a lot about the general topic of spirituality and what that entails. She had told me some very amazing things. Things that would be considered amazing even for an adult, let alone an 11-year old child.

Conversations with a *real* psychic....

Unfortunately, I don't remember all of what she said and she doesn't either. However, I do remember one thing very clearly. She had said, very cooly and calmly, "Prasann uncle, everything in the Universe - even if it is *not* a living being - *has* life, or at least, *wants* to experience life." And that "everything wants to be more." After hearing her statement, I must have had the oddest combination of an expression on my face. One aspect would have indicated a "Huh?" whereas another component of my face would have been expressing pride at hearing such a profound statement from my niece.

Since she saw the apparent confusion on my face after hearing her nonchalant, but very profound statement, she decided to give me an example so I would better understand what she was trying to tell me. She said, "For example, this couch," as she pressed down with both of her hands, on the soft leather surface of the black couch that we had been perched on. Then she continued, "this couch that we are sitting on is 'alive,' and not only that, it wants to be 'more' alive."

She was saying, not in those words exactly, that everything wants to, and is, evolving towards God. In other words still, every living and non-living thing in the Universe *is* God, just at different levels of awareness about the fact that it is God, or at least, a part of God. God is Divine Energy, as we have defined before, and if everything has energy and is vibrating at a particular unique frequency, everything can be defined as "alive" *with* that vibration.

Among the other things I do remember her saying is that she used to get this feeling of wanting to help others with their issues, and that when she approached a question somebody might be posing to her with that attitude - one of providing selfless assistance - she was able to give a genuinely accurate and helpful answer to them. And she also said that whenever she approached the question with selfish reasons, she was not able to accurately predict or divine an answer.

It is very easy to forget that these words were coming from the mouth of an 11-year old girl. Not just that, but an 11-year old who

God=mc²?

has never read or come across spiritual books or material of such sort. Anyway, when I heard these things, it was the first time that I made the connection between psychics and spiritual people. It was an "a-ha" moment for me. After that connection, it just made sense to me that psychic abilities were, in fact, spiritual abilities. I realized that, here in my living room, talking to me at 3:00 AM, was a *Spiritual Master*, of sorts!

So, getting back to her powers, she had once told me that I was going to be very, very close to winning a $20 Million dollar lottery ticket, but my numbers were going to be off by two digits. I did, in fact, end up coming very close to winning, not the jackpot, but a $200,000 prize in that same drawing. It was part of a Sweepstakes by the Massachusetts State Lottery in July of 2007, where they were going to announce the winning numbers on Independence Day.

The lottery/sweepstakes ticket was a $20 ticket which had a seven digit number which, obviously, if matched the drawn winning numbers for the jackpot, would have resulted in that ticket being the winning one of the $20 Million prize. I did not come close to that or even the $1 Million dollar prize, which was the next prize in the drawing. I had the same numbers - the first four digits matched exactly - even the order, but with the last three, although the numbers matched the winning numbers, the order was off. If the order had been right, I would have won the $200,000 prize!

Anyhow, the point here is that we all - my sister's family, and my family - had come to an agreement, based on the evidence, that my niece did possess *some* genuine psychic abilities.

Psychic phenomena or abilities are not only the ones represented by your neighborhood Tarot Card reader. Although that is surely one of them. Precognition, the ability to see or predict the future; Clairvoyance, the ability to see clearly what others are not able to; Telepathy, the ability to read the thoughts of another; Remote

Conversations with a *real* psychic....

Viewing, the ability to "see" physical objects, or people located miles away without physically going there; Telekinesis, the ability to move objects simply by using the mind - these are all examples of psychic abilities.

(By the way, not all Tarot Card readers are genuine; however, a good friend and ex-coworker of mine, Christy Sherman, does provide some very accurate Tarot Card readings - and she does not do it for money. So, she has no ulterior motives - not that doing it to earn a living would mean that she did have ulterior motives - and she only does it for friends and family, too. I know, I know, the evidence provided is only anecdotal, but in my opinion, she is the real thing.)

Incidentally, Edgar Cayce, a gentleman whose name you may have heard, was a very well known "real" psychic and intuitive healer who would go into a self-induced trance and was able to cure thousands of people of their ailments. While he would be in a trance, his wife or another assistant would describe a particular medical condition or problem a person may have been suffering from. While he was still in his trance, he would "prescribe" a sure-fire cure for whatever the problem was, and in most cases, it would be a medical condition for which doctors had not been able to do anything about. In other words, it would have been a condition that had no cure or treatment. Oh, and by the way, he was *not* a doctor. He was also known to be able to predict the future accurately. Edgar Cayce has provided around 14,000 *documented* cases of accurate readings and/or "miraculous" cures.

Science: Please explain that, and I will give up all of this talk of the paranormal, supernatural and the metaphysical!

Non-scientific claims about Edgar Cayce's abilities are that he used to be able to access what are called the "Akashic Records." These are records that are available to *anybody* who can train themselves to access the spiritual plane where they are located.

God=mc²?

Claims are that these "Akashic Records" hold all the information about all the events that have ever occurred and will ever occur.

The existence of these abilities, among other phenomena such as NDEs, Ghosts, etc., proves that consciousness is not confined to the human *brain*, or even to the human *body*. It is not confined by space, and the fact that some people are able to "see" and accurately foretell the future also proves that consciousness is not limited by time, either. In other words, consciousness is Non-Local.

As I have mentioned in the introduction to this section about Phenomena, there are several books written on each of these subjects and I do recommend a few of them. Please see the Recommendations and Sources section located near the end of the book for those.

Anyhow, *mainstream* science has been unofficially banned from doing research in these fields, and I can only offer speculation as to why. Well, *one* of the most important reasons, or even *the* most important reason, for this "taboo" could be that scientists would discover further proof of God's existence, and therefore turn all of Science on its head. However, I just cannot be absolutely sure about the *why*.

I would recommend that you watch the sequel to the original *What the Bleep do we (k)now?!* movie, *What the Bleep: Down the Rabbit Hole*. As featured in the movie, Dr. Dean Radin, PhD, a chief scientist at the Institute of Noetic Sciences, mentions this taboo, and says that there is even a taboo on even *mentioning* this taboo.

One must wonder *why*, as I asked before. What is *so* threatening to scientists or to the entire world, if not to scientists, that they are being prevented from doing this research? It is not that they are being physically prevented from doing it; it's just that they know that they will be branded as "loons," and that they will end up losing all credibility in mainstream science if they endeavor to undertake this sort of a research. For all intents and purposes, their career would be over before it even takes off.

Conversations with a *real* psychic....

Regardless, I can tell you that even I possess some of these psychic abilities; however, they may show themselves as very trivial manifestations. (Although, something is only trivial when compared to something else that is much bigger. In my opinion, there is *nothing* that is really trivial.)

I can recall several times, when I had been listening to the radio and been thinking about a particular song that I had not heard in years, and then the next song on that particular station starts playing and it was the one that I had been thinking about. Or I had been thinking about a specific word, for whatever reason, and I see that word on a billboard or in a magazine or a newspaper, almost instantly.

Here's an example of something that happened to me recently, and you be the judge of whether this was coincidental or a psychic-type phenomenon. This incident is more significant than the "trivial" examples mentioned above.

About a year ago, I had been watching CNBC, my favorite channel, and a segment called *Squawk on the Street*, with anchors Mark Haines and Erin Burnett, had been on. (Or it might have been another segment known as *Street Signs*; I don't remember exactly.) I had been walking past the TV screen, and just as I was noticing that there was a tiny spider hanging from the ceiling, right at eye-level, and that it was visible in the background of the wall behind the TV, I heard Erin say that an insect or something had just bit her or that some insect had been hanging from the ceiling and had landed on her head, or something to that effect. And then she had realized that it had been a small spider. My noticing the spider in my own home, and Erin noticing the one hanging near her head - these two events happened almost at the same time - maybe one second apart, if that. And this was live television!

I have now come to a point in my life that when these things happen; things most of us would consider highly improbable coincidences, however, coincidences still; I try to figure out what that event is trying to tell me.

God=mc²?

Quickly, I ran up the stairs to my third-floor bedroom where the bigger one of my bookshelves was located and hurriedly found a book entitled *Messages from Spirit* by Colette Baron-Reid, who is an author and a popular spiritual intuitive. I wanted to find out what she had to say about a spider as a "sacred sign-bearer."

And there it was, on page 220 of her book, on the sixth line down from the top: "Spider: creativity, writing, sewing."

Well, I am not sure what "sewing" had to do with me, but I surely got the message that was being delivered to me - to continue to write, and to be creative.

This had been a very important decision making time for me because after I had gotten laid-off from my job at the Phone Company, I had attempted to make a living as a health insurance salesman. And around the time "spidey" was landing on Erin's head and dangling from my ceiling, I had been getting doubtful about whether or not this book was going to come to fruition. It was not a doubt about whether or not I would finish writing the book, it was more of a doubt about what would I do *until* the book was done, meaning, how would I pay the bills until then.

(The actual date of the "spider event" may have been May 12 or 13, 2009, and I know this because on May 15, I had sent an email to an old friend of mine from India, Anuj Hora, who now happens to be living in Australia; which, by the way, is where the author of *The Secret*, Rhonda Byrne, is from. And in that email to Anuj, I had mentioned this incident to him.)

Anyway, I had not really focused on selling health insurance because my heart was not really in it. It was really in the book. My manager at the health insurance company, Chris Smith, and that *is* his real name, had not been very pleased with my performance up until that time because I had only sold *one* policy by that time. And this was *months* into this new career. By the way, I think it is important to mention that he "happens" to be an Australian, who became a

Conversations with a *real* psychic....

Naturalized U.S. Citizen only very recently. Coincidence? I think not. Anyhow, he had given me an ultimatum to really "get going," or to get "going!" Don't get me wrong, he was genuinely nice about it and had given me all kinds of concessions in terms of the time I had needed to get started in this new career. So, at that point, I felt that I had not left him any choice.

So, this event, which I consider a spiritual and also a psychic one, allowed me to see that if I just stuck with what I *wanted* to do, things would take care of themselves. That, somehow, the money that I needed to pay the bills and to stay "afloat" would show up.

And it surely did. Almost exactly two weeks from the date of that incidence, I had a check for $16,358.93 in my hands. The detailed account of how that ended up coming about is in the first section of Chapter 26, the section on Wealth/Money/Abundance.

So, I did give my opinion of what I thought this was. Of course, you can make up your own mind about it because it was a very specific and individual event.

By the way, an interesting - and related thing - happened on June 19, 2009. I had gone to the CNBC studios in Englewood Cliffs, NJ, because I had gotten tickets to attend an in-studio taping of my favorite show, *Mad Money w/Jim Cramer*. It is a very "family friendly" show, and the proof of that is in the fact that this particular in-studio show was entitled "It's a Family Affair."

Anyway, since I had been traveling from my city in Massachusetts, and due to improper planning on my part, I did not end up getting there on time. And so I had been hanging out near the entrance to the *Mad Money* studios, within the main building, waiting for the Show to end so that I could, at least, say "hello" to Jim and maybe get to talk to my favorite TV personality and Stock Market guru.

The entrance to the Mad Money studio happened to be right near one of the points of egress to that building. So, I had been standing there when I noticed a person with a very familiar face

God=mc²?

walking in my direction. It was Erin Burnett! I actually did end up briefly meeting and talking to Erin. I do have to say that she is really sweet and nice, and she is even more beautiful in person, and is truly "wonderful and fabulous," as Jim Cramer always says she is. I was almost tongue-tied but somehow managed to get the words out that I was a big fan of hers and that CNBC is the only channel that is on, pretty much, all day at my home. She was on her way out and it did not strike me to mention this story to her, so now I am doing so, via the mention of it here.

I am not sure whether my running into Erin the way that I did, a little over a month later, had any other significance than just the reiteration of the first message - which was - to stay on the path that I was on. However, you can see the synchronicity or serendipity in these events, can't you?

Regardless of whether you can or cannot see it, here is an example of a very common psychic event, as opposed to the very specific and individual one that I just mentioned. You might have been thinking about a friend or a family member and about the fact that you had not communicated with them in a long time, and then the phone rings and it is that person on the other end of the line. Or you open your email account and there pops up an email from them.

These things happen to me *all* the time, but like I said, I consider them to be *small* examples of psychic abilities; however, it is a fact that they are such. And it is also a fact that we all possess them, just in varying degrees of manifestation. We can all learn to be experts at using these "powers" if we choose to build up their strength. I would recommend a book entitled *You Are Psychic* by Debra Lynn Katz, if you are interested in developing your psychic potential.

However, increasing the strength of these spiritual powers is, in fact, a very natural by-product or a positive "side-effect" of your progress on the path to higher consciousness. In other words, you

Conversations with a *real* psychic....

don't have to specifically work on developing these super powers if you are already working on achieving Self-Realization because that will happen automatically.

Anyhow, this goes back to the phenomenon of Entanglement from Quantum Physics. It says that before the Big Bang, everything that is now existent in the Universe, and in fact, the Universe itself, was a microscopic *dot* - the Primordial Atom – as it is called, and that all the elements that make up everything and every living being in the Universe were all physically together in that dot. Everything was "entangled" with everything else in that infinitely small space. In other words, everything *was* one. There was no separateness. And as far as instantaneous communication goes, we are all *still* one, and that's why we can communicate in that manner; i.e., instantaneously.

In other words still, there is only *one* consciousness and it is everywhere, all at once, as I have mentioned in Chapters 6 and 7. So, Entanglement explains psychic phenomena. It also explains how it is possible to experience the Unity Consciousness state of Enlightenment.

Chapter 21
E.T.'s and UFO's -
Science "fiction" or science "fact?"

Just what were the mathematical probabilities of our home, the Earth, ever coming into existence, and then on top of that, the "almost impossible" occurrence of all conditions coming together so perfectly so as to create life as we know it, of course, through the process of evolution?

Scientists might put it up there - maybe one in a billion or even one in 10 billion. (This is an arbitrary number from me; I actually don't know what the probability is. And neither can scientists know that because we can never really know, for sure, how big the Universe *really* is, and also because, for all we know, new galaxies may be popping into existence as you read these words. Also, it is a scientific fact that the Universe is expanding.)

Well, if that is the case then there are in existence *at least* one *trillion* other planets exactly like ours in the Universe - extrapolating that probability that I have come up with, on behalf of scientists.

God=mc²?

Astronomers say that there are *over* a 100 billion stars in our galaxy, the Milky Way, alone. That would mean that there are 10 "Earth-like" planets in our galaxy. That is, if you were to take into consideration the number of stars as a measure of the number of "possibilities" for Earth-like planets to come into existence as part of their solar (or stellar) systems. *Again, this is only in our galaxy!*

Astronomers also say that there are, at least, 100 billion galaxies in the Universe, "at last count." So, that would put the number of Earth-like planets at 10 times 100 billion; i.e., one *trillion* Earth-like planets!

This is actually an extremely *conservative* estimate because the number of stars in our own galaxy may be much higher than that, in reality. Also, the same case may be true for the number of galaxies.

However, still, let's go the other way; the way of being even more conservative, and not less. Let's say that there is only one Earth-like planet possible in each galaxy. And we have no choice but to assign, at least, that probability of one in a 100 billion because if it weren't so, the Earth, itself, would not have existed. And since it *does* exist, just in case you might not have noticed, and since it *is* a part of the solar system of *one* of the *100 billion* stars in the Milky Way galaxy, we are going to go with that probability. In terms of a percentage, in case you might be wondering, it is 0.000000001% chance.

Well, even using that very extremely conservative estimate, there would be, at least, 100 billion inhabitable planets which may be suitable for life, in the Universe.

Think about this - we know that the lotteries such as the Mega Millions or the Power Ball have incredible odds against the player - odds as *huge* as 1:175,000,000 - that is a chance of 1 in 175 million.

But people win these lottery jackpots "all" the time! Don't they? Okay, they don't win it everyday, but they almost certainly win it once every few days or even few weeks.

E.T.'s and UFO's - Science "fiction" or science "fact?"

Now, you could tell the person who has already won the lottery that they wasted their money by buying the ticket. That they had practically *no chance* of winning, and that they would have been better off leaving that dollar in the bank or better yet, buying gasoline with it, whatever fraction of a gallon that would buy at this moment. You could tell them that, and in theory, you would be absolutely right!

Of course, they would laugh at you harder than they have ever laughed at anybody, as they made their way to the bank to deposit their multi-million dollar check. Wouldn't they?

This reminds me of when the character played by Jim Carrey asks the one played by Lauren Holly; his romantic interest; in the stomach-achingly hilarious movie *Dumb & Dumber*, "What are the chances of a girl [sic] like me ending up with a guy [sic] like you?" Carrey misspeaking and referring to himself as a "girl," may have been part of the intended humor, but the even funnier part was that when Holly replies, "One in a million," we might expect Carrey's character to be heartbroken and disappointed beyond all belief, but instead he is ecstatically happy knowing that there *was* still a chance. (If we all could learn to see the "bright side" of things like he did, our lives would be totally transformed.)

All kidding aside, the point here is that regardless of how insurmountable the odds are, based on them there has to be, at least, 100 billion other planets exactly like ours in existence. So, not only 10, 50, or even 1000, but 100 *billion* or more "Earth-like" planets are in existence and that is if we have the number of stars and the number of galaxies accurately numbered. If those numbers are higher, then the number of planets also increase in proportion. Again, I do have to cede that there is no way of *really* knowing this. There could actually be 100 trillion planets like ours or "just" one million.

Also, we are assuming that only the conditions that exist on Earth are the ones that are absolutely required for life to exist elsewhere, and the fact is that there could be various other, what we might call

God=mc²?

"extreme," conditions in which life of different forms could not only survive, but thrive. This happens right here on Earth, doesn't it?

All kinds of creatures live in all kinds of extreme conditions - conditions that would be considered extreme for human beings - in the depths of oceanic trenches where the water pressure is extremely high, in the hottest of hot deserts, in the coldest Arctic or Antarctic regions of the world. There are even organisms that are capable of thriving in highly acidic environments, and then there are ones which can resist high levels of ultraviolet and even nuclear radiation.

There is even an appropriate name for these creatures and micro-organisms, "Extremophiles." If Extremophiles can exist right here, on Earth, based on that empirical evidence, we can conclude that evolved beings of all kinds could inhabit the rest of the Universe.

Then there is more evidence in the analysis of the statistical data regarding the conditions necessary for life, and the probabilities of such conditions existing elsewhere in the Universe. Based on those data and the number for the probability - however limited the data, and however small the number may be - it is an *impossibility* that intelligent life does not exist elsewhere!

To prove or disprove that possibility (or impossibility) there is now a new science called Astrobiology. Why do you think this new field of study has come into existence? I would think that because scientists are seeing the validity of this statistical argument.

If there is evidence presented that beings at different levels of evolution and advancement do inhabit the rest of the Universe, then we can also conclude that, most certainly, they would have reached points in their technological progress to have created spacecraft which can traverse the Universe in a short amount of time.

I read somewhere; I cannot remember where, "How arrogant is it for us to think that we (the Earth) are the only ones to have intelligent life!" Also, a joke that I had read somewhere was that the positive proof we have of the existence of *intelligent* life elsewhere in the Universe is that they haven't tried to contact us. Ha!

E.T.'s and UFO's - Science "fiction" or science "fact?"

In all seriousness, if you do believe the validity of the existence of extra terrestrial life and therefore of their vehicles or spacecraft, then they truly must have contacted us also. Of course, we have had numerous cases of sightings and reports of various encounters of "the third kind" and for that matter, encounters of all kinds.

We now have the show *UFO Hunters* on the History Channel and from the evidence that they provide, these ideas do not seem to be so far fetched now, do they? (I am not saying that we should rely on just the TV show for evidence regarding extra terrestrial life. I am suggesting that we should think about it for ourselves, and to weigh the logical and statistical data about probabilities; consider the *infinite* vastness of the Universe; the establishment of the new science of Astrobiology; other advancements in the study of consciousness; and progress in the overall field of Science and Quantum Mechanics.)

Anyhow, you might have been wondering, "What do E.T.'s and UFOs have to do with *spirituality*?"

Science is starting to agree that consciousness *must* pervade the entire Universe. Based on that, it would be very logical for us to conclude that it must be a fairly *common* phenomenon to have *conscious* beings in existence, living on habitable planets scattered throughout the Universe. (Because, naturally, they would have access to that Universal Consciousness that exists everywhere.)

As I said before, it is a *mathematical* and *scientific* impossibility that they don't. Also, "It would be an awful waste of Space," if we were all alone in the entire Universe, as Carl Sagan has said so famously.

Therefore, E.T.'s and UFO's must not only be scientific realities, they have to be spiritual realities, also.

Chapter 22
Time would be on your side in your travels if you could Teleport or Bilocate

I have always thought about the concept of time as really being our consciousness progressing through fixed events. Meaning, the past, the present and the future are happening all in the same "instance."

The best way to describe it is that I felt or imagined the passage of time as the frames on a reel of film going by very rapidly - as in a movie reel - 24 frames per second. Imagine your whole life as being shown on film. Well, it would have single frames frozen in time, if you will, on that film reel. Your consciousness experiences one frame at a time as you live your life, and thus, it experiences the passage of time.

However, scientists say that time only moves in one direction and that the "Arrow of Time" is pointed in the direction of the future, from the past and the present. However, again, this Arrow of Time seems to be applicable only to Newtonian Physics; i.e., the physics

God=mc²?

governing day-to-day objects like bowling balls, cars, buildings and such. From the perspective of Quantum Physics, the physics pertaining to atomic and sub-atomic particles, time does not even exist or if it does exist, it does not have an arrow, and it is non-linear.

I don't know if we will ever be able to travel up or down this timeline; however, I do know that when one is not in the physical body, one is not only *not* limited by space, one is also not limited by time. An out-of-body spirit can travel to any place on earth and probably anywhere else in the whole Universe, and to any time period in the past or the future by simply thinking about the place or time.

Imagine the possible applications of time travel if it were a scientific reality. However, time travel is the stuff of science fiction. Well, at least, for now. So is Teleportation; which is simply being in one physical place at one moment in time, then disappearing from that place and then re-appearing at another place the next moment in time. You know, the classic "Beam me up, Scotty!" way of transportation from *Star Trek*, which, by the way, would be the most efficient and "Green" way to travel. Bilocating, which is, quite literally, being in two or more places at one time, is also not in the realm of science fact, at this moment. But if it were, wouldn't your life be so much easier? It would give "multi-tasking" a whole new meaning.

However, Quantum Mechanics shows that microscopic particles *do* exhibit exactly these types of mysterious activity and phenomena which could be considered the stuff of miracles. Various Saints in history have been known to have the ability to travel through time, and also Teleport and Bilocate.

Einstein has been so famously and *repeatedly* quoted as calling some of these Quantum phenomena "spooky action at a distance." He could not explain how these things were possible.

So, these phenomena of being in two places at one time; or quantum particles being able to travel back in time or *seeming* to have the ability to travel back in time; "Entanglement," meaning

Time would be on your side in your travels if you....

instantaneous communication between two particles *regardless* of the distance between them; and other such scientifically observable or experimentally reproducible effects (at the quantum level, that is) are not explicable by traditional science.

(Entanglement would be impossible according to Einstein's theories because even if particles communicated with each other over hundreds of thousands of miles, there would be a slight "lag" from the time information was sent out by the first particle to the time it was received by the other particle. This is because the information could not possibly be traveling at a speed greater than the speed of light because nothing in the Universe can travel faster than that. So, even if the information was traveling *at* the speed of light, which is, approximately, 186,000 miles per second, then there would still be a lag of a second, or a proportional fraction thereof, to account for that journey through space. Instantaneous communication would be impossible, and therefore, Entanglement would also be impossible.)

As I mentioned earlier in this chapter that all of this seems to be the "stuff of miracles," and I would say that, in fact, it *is* the stuff of miracles that if we could master, we would be god-like in our abilities, just like the Saints of old were.

I do genuinely believe that we will come to a point, scientifically and technologically, when we will be able to Teleport and Bilocate, and maybe even travel through time, *without* employing spiritual methods. In the future, scientists could design a machine, or machines, that could allow us to do those things.

And no, we don't have to "be afraid, be very afraid," as quoted from the mid-80's movie, *The Fly*. It featured a brilliant scientist, played by Jeff Goldblum, who had invented these "Telepods" to transport matter from one place to another, via, you guessed it, Teleportation. I am sure that future scientists are going to be more careful than Seth Brundle, the character played by Goldblum, was.

God=mc²?

I reckon they will be careful, much more careful!

Regardless, this is just conjecture on my part, for now. I just don't know when any of these inventions might become reality - it could be 50 years from now, or it could be as far as 500 years from now. And technically, if time travel, among these other sci-fi possibilities, is actually possible, it would already be so, wouldn't it? And maybe it *is*.

However, spiritually, all of these things *are*, in fact, already possible.

Chapter 23
Quantum Possibilities!
A very "real" possibility of a "new" you?!

There is another quirky phenomenon in Quantum Mechanics known as the "Observer Effect." You may or may not have heard about this. Basically, what scientists say is that there is a finite, measurable effect an observer has on whatever is being observed. So, in case of a scientific experiment, let's say, whoever is physically watching a particular experiment take place is the "Observer." And this Observer, whether he/she wants to or not, is affecting the outcome of the experiment by the very act of observing it.

Then the argument could be made, "Why not have the experiment take place without any physical observation?" And let the chips fall where they may, so to speak. So, in this case, there would have to be some device to measure the result of the experiment, and we could also record the whole experiment, electronically, on audio-visual equipment - via a camera - or whatever sophisticated equipment that might be necessary to record the experiment for observation later on.

God=mc²?

The suggestion was that since there is nobody actually observing the experiment taking place, they cannot interfere with the results. However, what physicists found was that the very act of taking measurements via an appropriate device that would hold the measured data for viewing and analysis later on, and/or having the recording of the experiment - those things, in and of themselves - were "observations," and affected the results. Also, the fact that somebody had to, eventually, look at the results. So, consciousness would have to be involved at some stage of this process, and whenever it did get involved, the "observation" took place, and affected the results.

Yes, that means that the effects of the observation would have to travel back in time to affect whatever was going on when the actual experiment was taking place.

There is a very famous experiment which is called the Double-Slit experiment and this was shown very nicely in the hit hybrid film, *What the Bleep do we (k)now!?* This experiment showed the undeniable effects of the Observer. It showed how a particle, say an electron, would behave a certain way when it was *not* being observed, and that it would behave in another way when it *was* being observed.

Imagine this scenario: You are waiting for something or someone, for example, to get on a bus, and have been just "hanging around" the bus stop where there is nobody else waiting, and nobody else in sight. While you are waiting for your bus to come along, you are in your own world, maybe singing a song or kicking a can, or whatever. Then, suddenly, you get the feeling that you are being watched! You know, the psychic "I-feel-like-I-am-being-watched" feeling. And you are, in fact, being watched. There is a strange-looking figure watching you from the second floor window of a nearby house, observing and possibly judging your behavior. As soon as you know this, you start behaving in a different manner. You are just not so care-free in your demeanor anymore, and a lot more conscious of what you are doing. Hence, your behavior was one particular way when you knew that you were not being watched, and

Quantum Possibilities!

since finding out that you were being observed, your behavior became different. That would be an everyday example of the Observer Effect.

Scientists have come up with ways to minimize the effect of the Observer; however, they say that there is a finite limit that this "minimization" has reached. That no matter what you do, there will *always* be *some* effect of the Observer on whatever is being observed, however minute that effect may be. So, there is some effect of the Observer even when there is an effort made to *minimize* the effect; imagine what would happen if we were to try to *maximize* it!

The overall point in bringing this up was the following: The effect is brought about by a *conscious* observer. In other words, consciousness *itself* is the Observer.

In the world of Quantum Physics, there are no particles that exist, by themselves. There is only a potential for those particles to exist. In *What the Bleep: Down the Rabbit Hole*, Dr. Hagelin says, "It's not a world of electrons; it is a world of *potential* electrons." And guess what, based on the Double-Slit experiment, one can surmise that not only does consciousness create the Observer Effect; it actually creates the physical reality of a particle coming into existence *as* a particle. Before consciousness observed these potential particles - they existed only as possibilities - as "waves of probability," but not as "dots of actuality." In other words, consciousness creates *actual reality* from all the possibilities of *potential reality*.

You could even get biblical and say that consciousness, by virtue of it being self-aware, has the Free Will to choose a particular reality.

When you add deliberate intent to *maximize* the Observer Effect, instead of just having an "effect" on the reality that was going to come into existence anyway, you are actually creating the reality that is *wanted*.

(There is a conundrum in Quantum Physics, called Tangled Hierarchy, as I had mentioned in Chapter 8, and it states that, in fact,

God=mc²?

if there exists no Observer, there actually would be *no* reality, of *any* kind - wanted or unwanted - that would come into existence by its own. However, in my own thinking and based on the study of this as written by Dr. Amit Goswami, I resolve this by saying that the Universal Consciousness is the *pre-existing* Observer that created the reality that our consciousness exists in. Therefore, our observation, via our consciousness, is not creating a brand-new reality; it is just creating a new reality that is wanted by us.)

The whole Universe existed as a *potential* Universe before it came into actual existence. The same goes for all galaxies, stars, planets and other celestial bodies, and ultimately the same with human beings. Before our galaxy, the Milky Way, came into existence, it only existed as a *potential* galaxy - one among infinite possibilities of galaxies - i.e., it was, quite literally, *one* of the *infinite potential galaxies* that could ever come into existence. And as we all may know, infinite means countless, doesn't it? If we wanted to count the number of potential galaxies, we could start counting, and we would have to keep counting eternally, forever.

Well, then the natural question you might have is who created the Universe? The answer would be that Supreme, Self-Aware Consciousness; i.e., God, exercised Its Free Will to choose one of the infinite possible Universes, in order to actually bring it into existence!

You can apply the same paradigm to all the other things I mentioned above, and when you come to human beings, stop, and think. Please think and carefully consider what I am about to tell you.

I have heard a reference made by some older folks, mostly men, when they are talking to an adult child or adult children of their friends. This reference is something to the effect of "I knew your father when you were only a mere thought in his head." Another equivalent would be "Your father and I were pals when you were only a twinkle in his eye!"

Quantum Possibilities!

The phrase that I am talking about is a slightly different version of the ones mentioned above, but they all mean the same thing, ultimately. (It is a bit crude, at least in my opinion, so I won't mention it. It had something to do with an "itch" somewhere or something like that.) Why I mentioned that phrase will be clear after you read the next few paragraphs.

A fully-grown (*physically* fully-grown only, because we are not "fully-grown" spiritually until we attain God-consciousness or Self-Realization) human being was a young adult before the current state it is in, and before that, was a teen-ager, and before that, a pre-teen, and a toddler, and if you go further back, it was a new-born infant child. But as we all know, the child's existence did not start then, right?

(I do have to be very, very careful here, and not stir up the debate about when, exactly, does "life" start, in the context of a human being. This explanation of Quantum Possibilities is not provided to sway the Abortion Debate one way or another because that is not what this book is about at all. However, I do have to be very honest and say that, personally, my beliefs have changed about this topic after uncovering what I have uncovered while I researched this book. Regardless of my opinion on this Debate, the reason I put the quotes around the word *life* is exactly because of that. It is meant to be a reference to *physical* life; i.e., the life one experiences in a physical body only. In the spiritual context, life never started and it will never end. In my mind, there is no conflict or controversy over that, and that discussion is moot, as far as I am concerned. And quite frankly, you will read just a little bit later on that there is no conflict or controversy in my mind over when life starts physically also.)

In my humble opinion, and this is only an opinion, *physical* life starts at *any* moment of time *between* the process of conception; meaning the sperm cell fertilizing the ovum; and the time when the organs in a fetus are fully developed, and the heart has started to beat. I only draw this conclusion because physical life also *stops* at various states of the physical body.

God=mc²?

People survive illnesses and accidents in which they have suffered temporary total loss, permanent partial loss, and in certain cases, even permanent total loss of certain vital organs. So, having a perfectly formed body with all the proper functioning organs does not necessarily mean that a fetus is now ready for ensoulment. The soul could be ready for the body way *before* that time. Or conversely, way *after* that.

The exact moment of that is something that we will never know for sure, because quite frankly, I think it is different with each human being that comes into existence. I will let the OB/Gyn's offer their expert opinion on when they think life begins.

(This reminds me of what President George W. Bush once had said, "The OG/Byn's [sic] should be allowed to practice their love with their patients without any hindrance from the Government." Or something to that effect. However, here, I am only talking about the OB/Gyn's expressing their expert opinion based on the science behind their practices.)

All I will say is that there is definitely one thing we can all agree upon regardless of where we stand on this very important issue, and that is that *physical* life cannot start *before* the process of conception. (Pro-Life *and* Pro-Choice people can both agree on this, and won't find the need to go into any debate over it, as I had mentioned before.)

At the same time, I think we all can also agree that the physical attraction that a man feels for a woman or vice versa or both at the same time, and the resulting sexual union is the very reason why a human embryo comes into existence. (News flash: I bet you did not know that!)

As I said before, think about it. So, I am assuming that you are thinking about it. That physical attraction, itself, is a non-physical thing. It is a thought! Or at the very least, an indescribable *feeling* of attraction; an impulse. And it is "simply irresistible," as Robert Palmer sang in the late 80's. Isn't it?

Quantum Possibilities!

Whether or not this non-physical attraction generates a physical response; maybe aided by Viagara, Levitra or Cialis; is not the primary matter of discussion here. (Although, it is surely a part of the attraction process.) Sure, it is a non-physical feeling of attraction towards a physical being, and towards wanting to engage in a physical act, but ultimately, it is still a non-physical *feeling* that emanates from a non-physical *source*.

However, as I mentioned in Chapter 8, these things - this attraction - can be "explained away" as being chemical, and therefore, physical in nature. However, again, Quantum Physics is saying that when you keep reducing physical particles, you ultimately arrive at non-physical vibrating energy, thoughts, pure consciousness, or awareness - as the basic building blocks of any particle.

Well then, what happens in the process of the creation of a human being is very clear to us. A physical human being, with anywhere from 50 to a 100 *trillion* cells, is "only" a *thought* or a *feeling* first.

What I would say, after *just* having had a major epiphany and it truly was an epiphany - in the truest sense of the word - is this: Nothing that is physical is purely physical; it is *always* both, physical *and* spiritual. Only the spiritual is *purely* spiritual.

This reminds me of something that my friend and mentor, Dr. Vipul Chitalia, says often. He says, "Everything is in everything!" We could compare a human body with its 100 trillion cells to the Universe with all of its stars. Nobody really knows, for sure, how many stars there are in the Universe, and maybe a 100 trillion might be too few, you might argue. Okay, so at the very least, we could compare the body to a collection of galaxies.

If we, humans, can create another human being from thought, why can't God create a Universe from His thought?

The above was a rhetorical question. The point is that our physical existence *begins* in the spiritual realm. There is not an iota

God=mc²?

of a doubt about that in my mind. After the just-provided evidence, can there be any doubt in yours?

And so any particular human being is only *one* out of the *infinite possible human beings* it could have been. In the same way, I am also one of the infinite number of human beings that could have possibly ever come into existence. And so are you.

You, I, and all the human beings alive today, and those that ever lived, and those that will ever live were, and will be a result of choice. This choice was either conscious or sub-conscious, but it was still a choice. (In the context of human consciousness versus Universal Consciousness, that is.)

Coming full circle, I would say that whatever state our lives are in right now - whatever we are doing, whatever we may have accomplished, whomever we may be married to or in a relationship with, whatever our career may or may not be, whether we are homeless or living in a multi-million dollar mansion - all of these and more are simply results of our choices. It is as simple as that.

In fact, for every single variable that we may have come across in our life, we *must* have made a choice about which one we prefer. Since there really have been *infinite variables*, and therefore *infinite choices* related to those infinite variables; we must have made those infinite number of choices. That is the only way we would have gotten here. We *had* to have *chosen* from among those variables; those infinite possibilities.

We don't have a choice, but to choose! Yes, ironic, isn't it? Like so many principles in spirituality. Think about all the variables and possibilities that you have come across all your life. Whether to turn left or right? To wear this or that? Should I go to that party or not? Should I say "yes" or should I say "no?" Paper or Plastic? Should I stay or should I go? This list can truly go on forever because these are not just one-time choices; you may have come up against them over and over again, and you will continue to come across them all your life.

Quantum Possibilities!

So, ultimately, this world and your life are created by choices: Yours! Whether you believe it or not; like it or not; rejoice in it or not; it is just true.

Then why not *choose* the life that you *want*? Why not deliberately and intentionally create, and lead, the life of your dreams? Because you have *already* done that, so far.

The life that you are currently living - exactly the way it is right now - was only a *possibility*, say, five years ago. There was *nothing* that dictated how your life would go in the future, from a point in time five years ago. Well, nothing other than your thoughts, and your choices based on those thoughts.

If you were to just look, the proof of what you have created is all around you and not only that, it *is* you! It is who you are and what your life has become, isn't it? If it is not to your liking, then change it. Choose new thoughts, and new end-results that you want. "You can do it!" (This is a "running" phrase repeated in many comedy films, and as Rob Schneider often says in many Adam Sandler movies.)

You *can* do it because those end-results that you would like for yourself are only *possibilities* just like any *other* end-result. And because there is no such thing as time, they all have already come into existence, or at least, you can think of it that way, if it helps you. It's just that whatever you *choose* to experience *as* your reality will be the only thing that will remain or that you will actually experience. All the other possibilities will simply fall away.

As I said before, when you add deliberate intent to *maximize* the Observer Effect, instead of just having an "effect" on an unwanted reality that was going to come into existence anyway, you would actually be creating the reality that *is* wanted. In other words; i.e., the much more succinct and wise ones of my idol, Dr. Dyer, "When you change the way you look at things, the things you look at change."

God=mc²?

So, become an *active* Observer of your own life. This active observation will have an effect on your life, the Observer Effect. This, in turn, will maximize the effect on your life.

(We are treading on the verge of another spiritual/scientific phenomenon called Parallel Universes, which we won't go into right now. However, here's a brief description of what this is. This idea says that there are parallel Universes, or Multiverses, created at each juncture of each choice made by each conscious entity, and therefore would represent truly infinite number of worlds, all in existence at the same time.)

Coming back to our world of the Universe from the possibility of Multiverses, let's say that you got laid-off from your job earlier this year due to this tough economy. And then things just started to unravel, and one thing led to another, and now you are homeless. You saw this book in a bookstore that you had been walking by, and you used your *last* $25 to buy this book because the title, the subtitle and the motto of the book gave you hope.

According to this book - your remaining homeless for the rest of your life, and your living in a multi-million dollar mansion of a home within the next few months - are both *equally* plausible and possible scenarios. Why? Because these are only two of the possibilities in this infinite list of possibilities. And you do have the power to choose any one of those infinite possibilities and therefore, to make it an actual reality. Knowing this to be a fact, what would you choose? Choose the scenario that you would want to see play out, not the one that you would not want to see.

Some might argue that even though both of the scenarios mentioned above are equal possibilities, the fact that a person may be homeless already makes the possibility of their *remaining* homeless *more* plausible (i.e., more likely to happen) than their ending up living in a multi-million dollar mansion. In other words, just because two things have *equal possibility* of coming about does not necessarily also mean that they have *equal plausibility* of coming about.

Ironically, I would say that they are right and wrong, at the same time. Sure, it is "easier" to *remain* homeless, if one were to be

Quantum Possibilities!

unfortunate enough to have been there, than to entertain the thought that one will have a huge mansion to live in. And so, here's the crux of this issue. It is *only* in our thoughts one thing is more or less plausible than any other. It is only the *perceived* ease or *perceived* difficulty of some task that makes us think of its plausibility or the lack thereof. In other words, I really do believe that all possibilities that exist are also equally plausible. If they weren't, they would not even exist *as* possibilities. Period!

Ask any person who has had the experience of, quite literally, going from rags to riches, and you will realize that it is true. And you know that these people exist because you have heard about them, or you know somebody like that. (How about the *true story* of multi-millionaire Chris Gardner, as portrayed in the movie *The Pursuit of Happyness*?)

So, I say this: Expect the best, and be ready *for* the best! Don't expect the best, and then be ready for the worst, just in case the worst were to come along. You might have heard that line which suggests adopting a "cautiously optimistic" view of life or towards something that you may have been looking forward to doing; e.g., an accomplishment or achievement of some goal.

In my humble opinion, expecting the best and being ready for the worst is, in more than one way, expecting and causing the worst to come along. And why would you ever want to do that?

(Now, please don't get me wrong, this is not always an easy and natural thing to do because of the way we have been programmed to think, and I do struggle with this some time. However, I just remind myself that I should only think about the outcome that I want and that it makes no sense to think about the one that I don't want.)

In other words, make a deliberate choice for the best to come along, and simply, by your having done so, *it will!*

SECTION IV: Action - What Should We Do, Exactly, To Lead The Life Of Our Dreams - The Kind That We Are Meant To Lead?

This is the Action Section of the book. This is where we will learn to apply, practically, the theories we have learned in the previous chapters. In order to truly transform our lives, we will have to do *something new*. If we continue to do the things we have always been doing, and if we continue to think the way we have always been thinking, then we will continue to get the results we have always been getting, right? You might have heard that many times before.

Well, the things that which we need to do are discussed, in detail, in this section. And it is not just physical steps that we need to take. We need to change the way we think, first and foremost. And then, there will be some very minor and subtle changes in physical behavior that we will be making, or we may notice that some of these changes have even started taking place automatically. Pretty soon, we will have a transformed life.

Do keep in mind that anything, including life-transformation or achieving Self-Realization is as easy as we believe it to be, or as difficult as we believe it to be. So, choose to think that this is easy, and it will be.

Chapter 24
"Science is truth!"

That is what an ex-convict said on a TV show, I think it may have been The Daily Show with Jon Stewart (but I am not sure of that). Regardless of what show it may have been on, the gentleman, who was being interviewed by the host of the show, had been acquitted of a crime because of DNA evidence pointing to him being innocent. Considering this scenario, I can certainly see why he would say that science is truth.

But otherwise, why do people, when they are told that something is "scientific" or "proven scientifically," take that to be Gospel? Please do pardon the play on words here, but interestingly, and ironically, nowadays even the Gospels are not taken as such unless there is scientific proof of the existence and effectiveness of what was said in them, and of the Gospels, themselves.

Pluto, the ninth "rock" from the Sun (not Mickey's dog) was a bona fide planet until about three or four years ago. Now it's not.

God=mc²?

Aspirin used to be bad for you; now it is good for you and not only that, it is so good that it might actually save your life if you take it when you might be having a heart attack.

(Of course, if you even *think* that you might be actually having a heart attack, the first thing to do is call 911! I would recommend that you check with your doctor regarding getting clarification about what to do, exactly, in the above mentioned scenario of a suspected heart-attack. However, from what I know, one should take an aspirin tablet and bite into it, chew it and swallow it, and not just swallow it whole. Again, I recommend that you check with your doctor regarding the strength of the aspirin tablet that one should take in such a scenario and other such important details.)

That was an obvious digression, but I hope that it was a welcome one, and at the same time I also hope that you never end up needing the information above. Anyhow, what I would like to say is that science is not the truth, at least, not the *whole* truth. Sure, science has gained valuable knowledge in a lot of fields. It can save human lives by using medicine and surgery. It has made it possible to communicate wirelessly with somebody half the way around the world. A huge cylindrical tube of aluminum, with fixed wings, and weighing tons can fly hundreds of people to places thousands of miles away, within a matter of hours. The list can go on and on. Pretty much everything that we see is man-made, and therefore, developed by science.

However, we don't know *all* there is to know; we don't have all knowledge that is in existence. In fact, as former Defense Secretary, Donald Rumsfeld, has so famously said, and I am paraphrasing here, "There are the *Known* unknowns; i.e., things that we know that we don't know. And then there are the *Unknown* unknowns; things that we don't even know that we don't know!" Sounds like a very confusing and funny statement, doesn't it?

(Gregg Braden, another one of my idols, who is an author of books that bridge science and spirituality, had mentioned this above

"Science is truth!" example of Donald Rumsfeld's speech in his book, *The Spontaneous Healing of Belief*, making a reference to the state of scientific knowledge today. By the way, I do recommend all of Gregg Braden's works, which include *The Divine Matrix*, and *The God Code*.)

An example of a *Known* unknown would be whether or not there is life anywhere else in the Universe. Well, it is a known *scientific* unknown, but it is surely *my opinion* that there is life elsewhere in the Universe, as I have mentioned in the chapter about Extra Terrestrials. And as I mentioned in that same chapter, now, there is a new science called Astrobiology. It is established to study just that, the possibility and the nature of life on other planets. So, in other words, science *is* advancing towards knowing the whole truth. In this specific example, Astronomy, and now, Astrobiology, which are sciences, are moving towards the whole truth about the nature and existence of life in the Universe.

To give you an example of an *Unknown* unknown, I would have to use something that was previously unknown, but now is known, because of the very nature of this knowledge. Before we came to find out that matter, i.e., all physical things, was made up of microscopic building-blocks called molecules, atoms and sub-atomic particles, we just did not know that. And even that knowledge, as we now are finding out, may not be completely accurate, based on what Quantum Mechanics is finding out.

Another example, and probably the only real example of a current *and* future *Unknown* unknown is this: How much knowledge, out of all there is to gain, have we really gained by now? There is absolutely no way to answer that question, scientifically or by other physical means. Do we know 80% of all there is to know? Or is it more like 8%? Or is it 0.0008%?

(Well, spiritually one *can* not only know how much there is to know, one can actually come to know and learn it all. That is what Enlightenment is – the true and complete knowledge of all there is to know.)

God=mc²?

There is true knowledge and truth to what science is revealing to us about the mysteries of life and about the existence of God; however, it has only been able to uncover a supposedly small part of that bigger mystery. (As you might recall from the Definitions chapter, science is defined *as* "knowledge.")

Regardless of how much of the whole truth has been discovered, we can be sure of one thing, and it is that not all of it has been found yet because we continue to keep uncovering new knowledge and truths. Anyhow, the point is that science is surely advancing *towards* the whole truth, but it is not quite there yet. However, there should be nothing stopping us from using those scientifically validated truths. That is exactly what technology is, anyway.

This book talks about how we - *any one of us* - can apply this new-found scientific validation and practicality of ancient spiritual knowledge and do it in a logical, step-by-step scientific manner to create and lead the life of our dreams - the life that we are *meant* to lead. (In all fairness, this scientific validation of spiritual principles is not "new" at all - the Vedas from the Hindu culture - have talked about the scientific aspects of these principles for *thousands* of years.)

I call this step-by-step process of creating your dream-life "Applying Spirituality scientifically, and practicing Science religiously." You will see the details of this process in the next chapter.

I have gone from being a believer to being an agnostic, and then to being a complete atheist, and then back to being a believer; and this time, with science backing my beliefs, a *devout* believer. So, I have been everywhere on the Spectrum of Belief. However, throughout my various phases of Belief, this process has worked flawlessly.

It did not stop working when I was not sure of God's existence, or when I was absolutely sure that He did not exist. It simply works. And now, I use it deliberately and consciously - to create my dream life. My faith, if you will, in knowing that this process will work came from scientific research and findings. It did not just come automatically.

"Science is truth!"

I totally understand what atheist, agnostics and/or scientists and even some believers (ones who are technically not agnostics, but who may be on the cusp of becoming "doubters,") mean when they say "Show me some proof, or at the very least, *some* evidence of the existence of God, and then we will believe." The reason I do understand is because, not too long ago, I was one of them.

They find it difficult, if not impossible, to have "blind" faith - in having trust in something that has not been proven, or at least not been proven scientifically. They find it difficult to have faith because some or a lot of things have not gone right in their lives despite their having prayed with all their might for those things. They also see all the things that go wrong in the world and they cannot see how God, if He really existed, would allow all of these things to happen. So, their conclusion is that God does not exist.

There is nothing wrong with that belief, logically. That's their rational and logical mind telling them that they need to only believe in something that they can experience or perceive by their five physical senses; i.e. with their senses of touch, taste, smell, sound and sight. And that if something bad happened or happens, then that must prove beyond a doubt that God does not exist or rather, *cannot* exist.

Science and Mathematics tell them that something can only be real if it can be *proven* to exist. Even more specifically, that thing would have to be perceived to exist by one or more of the five physical senses, and if it can be replicated or recreated (say, in a lab or in some controlled environment) at will, or that it has to be logical. And if it cannot be proven, it simply cannot exist, or the new idea that is being posited is simply false. And that events have to occur in a sequence; i.e., 1, 2, 3, 4, and so on and so forth. They *have* to. So, first it is the digit one and then the digit two. Two comes *after* one and not the other way around, or wherever it may decide to pop into the numerical series. And that time moves only in one direction; i.e., from the past to the present, and then onwards to the future. And ultimately, "stuff" makes up all the stuff that we see. That is, really

God=mc²?

small particles make up bigger particles, and then these bigger particles make up the physical things that we see.

The emphasis is on the physical, as all Materialists, almost always, do put the emphasis there. And I know that I sound lofty and sound like I have the classic "holier than thou" attitude when I say "those" Materialists but not too long ago, I was one of them, as I have mentioned before. At least, that was the case when I was going through that particular phase. So, I do have sympathy, in the true sense of the word, for them; I do really understand them. And using the very clichéd phrase - "If *I* can do it, so can *they*," - I really do believe that there is hope for the Materialists. Really!

And what I am talking about being able to do is to start using the Field of Spirituality in a scientific manner to create the life that they want to lead. And literally, *anyone* can do it, and not only that, *everybody* should do it because it was *designed* to be used that way. At the very least, everybody should know that it is very much possible to do so. Whether or not one does use this spiritual Field in the way it was designed to be used is a matter of personal choice.

Regardless, just for a little while - just for the while you read about this - I will beg and plead that you suspend your disbelief, suspend your prejudices, if you have any, and also suspend your belief of logic, because logic is overrated. Well, it is overrated sometimes. I know that this may be a little difficult to do because science and logic go hand-in-hand, but do try.

Please do not get me wrong. I am not asking you to abandon your affinity and liking for logic and your use of it to discern what can and cannot happen. I am just asking you to, *temporarily*, suspend your total reliance on it. Just suspend it. Temporarily. You can and *should* go back to it later on. And you should always trust it. (Well, other than when you are applying some of the principles laid out in this book.)

"Science is truth!"

Logic is logic for a very good reason. Logic, for a lack of a better word, is logical (as Spock, if he were playing the character of Gordon Gekko, would probably say in *Star Trek*). Logic just makes sense. But again, in certain cases, it *is* overrated! *Overrated* simply means that it is given a *whole lot more* importance than it *deserves*, and I am talking in specific situations or circumstances like the ones that I will be discussing.

I would like to reiterate here that I am not undermining science or logic at all by saying what I just said. In fact, all true scientists would agree with a lot of my statements in this chapter about how science is not an irrefutable truth, and how there are existent other such uncertainties about it. Also, I, myself, *am* a scientist, by nature, as I have said before. Another thing is that I would really be a complete fool to undermine science if that is what I were really trying to do. This is because I am using science and the scientific method to prove the benefits of spirituality and provide evidence for God's existence.

I just want to point out the fact that we have gotten to a point where science and logic have become overrated, and we need to realize that we should be giving these principles just the right amount of respect, and not more than they deserve to be given.

On the other hand, spirituality deserves *more* of our respect than ever before because it is proving to be equally, if not more, practical in creating the life of our dreams.

Chapter 25

You want to change your life for the better?

Then practice spirituality scientifically and apply science religiously

So, what do you think when somebody says that they "have got something down to a science?" Or that they practice something or do something "religiously."

We may all know that our friends are not scientists and don't really have anything scientific that they have accomplished when they say that they have gotten "something down to a science." It is just that they have perfected it or mastered it, whatever "it" may be that they are talking about. Isn't that the case? Unless, of course, they really *are* scientists, and in that case, we hope that they are talking about something other than their field of practice so that even we, the laypersons, can understand what they are talking about. Besides, if they are scientists, they will never actually say that they "got something down to a science." I think you get the point here.

(Not to brag, okay, maybe to brag just a *little* bit, I would like to mention that my dear friend, Dr. Vipul Chitalia, is not only a

God=mc²?

medical doctor, he is actually a research scientist, also. And that I am proud and honored by the fact that he wrote the Foreword to this book.)

In the case of someone doing something "religiously," it simply means that they practice it very regularly, and don't miss doing whatever it is that they do "religiously." That they are very disciplined about it. Whatever "it" is. For example, working out, watching what they eat, making sure that they watch a particular show on TV or whatever it may be.

And the funny thing is that it may have nothing at all to do with religion. It surely could, however, and they actually may be talking about going to church or a temple or a mosque on a very disciplined and regular basis. But for the most part, the mention of doing something religiously rarely has anything to do with religion. Just like in the case of getting something down to a science - it has nothing at all to do with science.

However, in my writing this book, I have done *both* - gotten spirituality down to a science, and actually proven that it *is* a science.

And if you really think about it, you will find that science *is* a religion, for all intents and purposes. Science has its extremely loyal following and they can really be very dogmatic about what they believe, couldn't they?

You all know exactly what I am talking about. We may all even agree that scientists have a typical look. When I say "scientist," don't you think of somebody in a white lab coat, wearing glasses and most probably with a beard or some kind of other distinguishing characteristic that would indicate that one was, in fact, a scientist?

And in 99% of the cases, you may picture this person holding a test-tube with a funky colored liquid, pouring some of that funky colored liquid into a beaker with yet another funky colored liquid already in it.

You want to change your life for the better?

(I think the lab container is called a "beaker" - because it has this beak-shaped area on the lip of this glass container that makes it easier to pour liquid out of it.)

All kidding aside, the way I prove that spirituality is, in fact, a science is by first proving that we are all spiritual beings and therefore not limited by the laws of Physics. Or, more accurately, not limited or governed by the laws of Newtonian or Classical Physics. The soul is governed by the laws of Quantum Physics! And this I have done already via the evidence provided in all the previous chapters.

(By the way, I had seen this ad on TV by Audi, the German car-maker, and I believe it was for the model called the A4. In the ad, it says that the Laws of Physics are really "mere guidelines" or "loose suggestions" when it comes to the particular automobile being advertised. I loved it! I would draw the same analogy to the soul. The laws of "regular" Physics are only suggestions that we can easily choose not to abide by.)

Furthermore, I will mention the real and very specific "scientific" principles that you can use to totally transform your life. Principles that you can use in a step-by-step, methodical, scientific way. If you take these steps, you *will* get the results that you have never gotten before. And these principles *can* and *should* be tested in the "lab" of your life! And upon putting them to the test, you will find that similar results can be created, and that too repeatedly so. (Write to me at **Prasann@GodEqualsmcSquared.com** if you are really curious to know why the results are "similar" but not "exactly the same." If this is a true science, as I claim it is, shouldn't the results be the same every single time the experiment is conducted, like it is supposed to be with any other science?)

In the rest of this chapter, you will find the details of the steps that I have taken and found to work very well for me. These will prove to be effective for you if you have previously tried to use the Law of Attraction, but found that the only thing you seem to "attract" is "failure."

God=mc²?

When you apply these principles, in a step-by-step, methodical way and get the results that you have been wanting, you will have unequivocal proof that these spiritual principles are thus scientific in nature also. Via your own direct experience, they will provide further evidence of the spiritual nature of our soul, and the fact that the soul does abide by Spiritual law.

Nine Simple Steps to "attracting" REAL success with the Law of Attraction and the One Simple Key that unlocks the potential of all of those steps

The One Simple Key to using these principles or steps is that they should ALL be applied, together! This is the most important part to really being able to tap the power of the Law of Attraction. However, you can learn them one-by-one, but the end goal should be to apply them all together.

And being the students of the teachings of the Law of Attraction, remember this one thing before you start applying these principles - life transformation is as easy or as difficult as you think it is. So, anticipate it being easy, and it will be.

Also, please try not to take things quite so literally. Some have said that the Law of Attraction does not work because they have thought it to be working literally, although, it surely *can* work literally. For example, they might have tried to use the Law of Attraction to manifest a Ferrari, one of the finest, fastest, and most expensive examples of Italian automobile engineering. In the process of wanting to manifest the car, they may have thought that all they needed to do was simply hold the thought of owning a Ferrari and that in a short amount of time - poof - a Ferrari would appear in their driveway, out of thin air. When that did not happen for them, they debunked this principle. Again, don't get me wrong - being able to do that is very much possible - spiritual masters such as Saint Jalaram, Jesus Christ, the Buddha, et al, were quite capable of manifesting physical objects out of thin air. However, in the journey of spiritual mastery, that state

You want to change your life for the better?

of being is not the first stage, but rather one that is reached farther down the road.

Having said that, here are the practical steps to take in order to achieve real success with using the Law of Attraction:

1) Faith First - Like George Michael sang in the album, *Faith*, from the late 1980's in a song by the same title, "I gotta have faith, faith, faith!" You gotta have faith! Why, you ask?

Because it really, really *is* the faith that provides the essential fuel for the ignition of this process, and nothing else. I will repeat: It is faith that gets this process started, and nothing else!

The "Creative Process," according to *The Secret* is, "Ask, Believe, and then Receive." In other words, ask for what you want, believe that you will get it - i.e., have faith, and then be ready to receive it - and then you will actually receive it.

Well, I say that we have to Believe *first*, before anything *else* can happen! Have faith first. And if "faith is a blessing you have yet to receive," as Robert Langdon, played by Tom Hanks, says in the movie version of *Angels & Demons*, then that does not necessarily mean that you are condemned forever; that you will *never* have faith because you were not blessed with it already. Well, unless a "miracle" occurs, and now, suddenly, you are blessed with faith.

The fact is, if you are not already "blessed" with faith, you can *learn* to *acquire* it.

You can, and should, *develop* faith, if you don't have it already. And I am absolutely not talking about having "blind" faith. I am also not talking about faith as in a *religious* Faith, meaning to have faith in a religious Deity or God, per se, and following the tenets of that particular religion. If you like, you can think of it in terms of having faith that the Law of Attraction works.

I think it was President Reagan who said, "Trust, but verify." I am saying, "Have faith, but get proof, too."

God=mc²?

I am talking about a faith that is based on and backed by scientific evidence. I would even go as far as saying scientific "proof."

If I could prove to you, scientifically, and without a doubt, that God *does* exist, and that He/She/It *wants* to answer *all* your prayers, would you then believe in God's existence and have faith? Would you then believe that, yes, as a matter of fact, God does exist and wants to answer all our prayers?

If so, get ready to believe, to have faith, if you dare! Because I am about to deliver the proof to you. Once you learn to develop the faith, and start applying all of the principles mentioned here, the proof will be delivered to you.

I know, I know - it is like the chicken and the egg, which should come first? What I am saying is that if you can develop the faith, or already have it, *and* you start to apply all these principles - your being able to create the life of your dreams will be the proof that this works.

However, again, I would like to emphasize that I am not asking you to have "blind" faith; please see the special "Note" at the end of the description of this first principle. In the meantime, know that the kind of faith I am asking you to have is truly based on scientific evidence.

In order for you to develop this faith, I beg you to look at your own life and examine how it became what it is today. That is exactly what I did with my own life, as I have said elsewhere in this book. I used that to determine that the Law of Attraction, Law of Karma, and the Law of Dharma were 100% in effect and were, in fact, responsible for what my life had become.

For example, one of my jobs was working at a bank as a Sales and Service Associate. (Incidentally, that reminds me of the shorter version of the word *Associate*; maybe you have seen it too, and thought that it was absolutely appropriate for a particular person in that position. Or maybe not.)

You want to change your life for the better?

Anyhow, I used to open new accounts for the new and existing customers of the bank and do the paperwork at the closings of their car or home-equity loans, and such. I remember that one of my regular customers was a car mechanic, who owned this garage right down the street from where I used to work.

Once, I had gone to his garage to get my car repaired since he was one of my regular customers and, because of that, a friend of mine. I had brought my car to his garage to have the rotors of my wheels replaced. I remember being there and having this particular conversation with him.

He had the car up on the lift and had just started working on removing the old, worn out rotors. Somehow our conversation had drifted towards the subject of annual income. We would pause our conversation every time he used the pneumatic torque-wrench to remove the lug-nuts from each tire so that we were not yelling over the very familiar loud noise of the wrench working. I remember telling my mechanic friend about what I thought one had to earn to lead a comfortable life.

I said, "Jim, I really think that somebody needs to make at least $50,000 a year to live comfortably. Otherwise they are just barely making it, and that's no way to live." I must have been making less than $25,000 a year at that time. I genuinely believed that this amount of $50K would be the perfect amount for an annual income. This would allow somebody like me to lead a comfortable life. That is what I wanted for myself. Even though this amount would have been *double* what I was making then, I never had a doubt or any conflicts in my mind about the fact that I would soon get such a job.

A few weeks or a couple of months later, a co-worker of mine from the bank, "Stacy," who had applied for and gotten a great job at a utility company, had come by the branch where I worked. At that time, Stacy told me all about this "great job" she had gotten at the Phone Company and how excited she was about the pay and the

God=mc²?

benefits that this position offered. She vehemently insisted that I should look into it also. (By the way, most Phone Company employees call it that - "the Phone Company" - they don't use the actual name of the Company, because it was just not necessary because not too long ago, there was only one, and everybody knew what its name was. I just "love" monopolies, don't you? Also, being a utility company, it was the *Phone* Company versus being the *Gas* Company or the *Electric* Company.)

Interestingly, another one of my customers at the bank had a daughter who had been working for the Phone Company for a few years, and she had just gotten a promotion to a Management position and secured a nice increase in salary and benefits and other such perks. He had mentioned this job to me before. A similar one to the one that Stacy had now secured. Since I had never done anything about getting myself into this much-coveted, high-paying job, I made a decision that I was not going to let even a single day go by now. So I called up the Phone Company (ironically) and scheduled myself to take the mandatory test that all prospective employees had to take in order to qualify for an open position there.

A few weeks later, I had gotten an offer for the job. Although it did not start with a very high pay, within a matter of months I would be making close to $50K a year.

The point to this story is that when you keep the faith, the thing, event or circumstance that you wish to see transpire *has* to do so simply because you kept the faith, and did not let go of it.

Die-hard Red Sox fans can tell you a little bit about "keeping the faith." And we can all learn from them!

By the way, after a few years in that job, I had been feeling that one needed to make at least a $100,000 or so, per year, to live a comfortable life. ("Greed, for a lack of a better word, is good!" No?)

I will let you take one guess at what happened to me and my annual pay a short time from then.

You want to change your life for the better?

(Note: In the Phenomena Section of this book, there has been a lot of the scientific evidence presented already. Quantum Physics, "traditional" science, and many, many other "spooky" and mysterious phenomena are discussed and explained in a very easy to understand language in the chapters in that Section. However, you absolutely don't *need* the evidence if you *already have faith*. In this and the next chapter, you have all the practical steps you need to make the Law of Attraction work for you. And yes, regardless of whether you believe the evidence or not. Again, I am assuming that you already know the basic principles of the Law of Attraction, and that you do believe, at least, somewhat, that it does work. Just that it hasn't worked for you......yet.)

2) Repetition and Discipline - I am absolutely convinced that we need to hear this message - the message that it is our thoughts and beliefs that create our lives - over and over and over again. Why? Because we have been bombarded with the opposite message over and over and over again. And really many millions of times over - if you consider all the sources of this opposite message - well-meaning parents, siblings, relatives, friends, schools and teachers, the media, etc., etc.

This erroneous message is the one that suggests that the world is an objective place, and that there are no subjective elements to it. That it *is* what it is. How we may feel or think about something is not going to change that something. And that our thoughts and beliefs are created *by* our reactions to our surroundings and the way our life is unfolding.

But here's the great thing - we don't need to listen to the correct message a million times over to undo the damage that this type of wrong thinking has caused. The reason is that, deep down, we already *know* the truth! It's just that it has been kept from us by this message that the opposite of what we truly believe is true, and by the fact that it has been brought to us countless times.

God=mc²?

And in fact, we did fight this wrong learning. And we fought valiantly! (Anybody hear of the "Terrible Two's?")

We persisted as long as we could, but in the end, it was too much pressure; it was all just too much to take. So we succumbed to it. Like everybody else before us, and everybody else contemporary to us. Well, *almost* everybody else. And those very few who didn't; well, you know their names. Quite literally, you *know* their names! Those are the famous people in any and all fields of endeavor, and maybe you have not heard about some of the other ones because it is still not "their time" yet, or it is their choice not to be famous. The ones who are well-known are so because they are extremely successful at what they do. (Now, I am not suggesting that you *need* to become famous to prove your success. What I *am* saying is that when you are super successful, the fame will come automatically. And what would you need to do to become successful? Think correctly, and to develop a knowing that your thoughts and beliefs create your reality.)

But what about the rest of us; are we fools? Are we lemmings who go along unquestioningly with the popular opinion? No, we are super-smart. In fact, we are geniuses! We know that what we know, deep down, is right. Ironically, we just need somebody else to reiterate and reinforce to us the truth that we already know. Of course, that somebody has to be one who is not following the popular opinion. The source of this reinforcement could be a *guru*, a true spiritual teacher and mentor. Regardless of where the reinforcement comes from, the truth, as it is, has to be validated by our own selves. It simply cannot be otherwise.

So, undo the wrong learning. But please do remember that it was never *our* fault that we did not get the right teachings in the first place. However, it *is* our choice to learn the right teachings *now*. So, *choose* to learn them and validate the truth that already exists within you.

And once that happens, you will make it a way of life. Watch the magic happen when that happens. The outcome of every situation or encounter will be predisposed to be in *your* favor.

You want to change your life for the better?

In the car, I had a copy of Dr. Wayne Dyer's CDs; his seminar related to his book, *Being in Balance*, and also later on, the audio-book version of *The Secret*. I listened to them over and over and over and over again. At least 60-70 times - each! There was a time when I could have recited the whole audio-books, by heart. Before I knew or realized it, I had genuinely learned the lessons, techniques and principles taught in these materials.

So, if you are a good auditory learner, then I suggest you listen to such material on a repetitive basis. Or if you like to read, then read, over and over again, your favorite book on the principles of the Law of Attraction. Or read any other book on practical spirituality, preferably one that you know, for a fact, has valid principles, and ones you know will work only if you could apply them.

Like this one that you are reading right now! (How about *that* very "subtle" hint!)

If you are a better visual learner, meaning you can easily pick-up on material that you see - as in a movie or a video, or via the process of using other visual aids - then use those to immerse yourselves in these teachings.

Listen to, read, or watch these principles until you know them by heart, and then keep listening, reading or watching even after you feel you know them very well. Let them become who you are!

What will happen is that you will start to apply some, or all, of these principles in your life automatically - without your even knowing that you are doing it. Or you may become so aware of them that you may start using them with your conscious knowledge. It doesn't really matter because your goal is to *start* applying them. If you find that you haven't been applying them, make a conscious effort to do so. There is just no way around that. As I like to say a lot, there is no other short-cut; this *is* the short-cut.

Repetition and building up a discipline about it, and then starting to apply what you have learnt are two of the basic steps that

God=mc²?

are necessary to get the Law of Attraction, or any other spiritual principle, working for you.

And this you may not have heard anywhere else, however, is crucial to your success!

3) Obsession – It's not just a men's fragrance from Calvin Klein. I know, I know, other than as the name of a famous cologne, the word *obsession* has a very negative connotation. However, I beg you to think of it as a very good thing, at least, in the context of what we are trying to do here; which is, of course, create the life of our dreams.

You really do have to make this goal of life-transformation a *healthy* obsession of yours. This is not something you can just dabble in, and have success at. You really have to dive in, head first, and immerse yourself in the thoughts of what you want to create for yourself.

However, nobody has to know this; it can be our little secret. In fact, it will be better if nobody else knows about it. Otherwise they will think that you have gone crazy. If you tell them *after* you have done what you wanted to do or after you are already on your way to creating the life of your dreams, and have manifested some tangible results, then, at that time, they will think that you are just so very dedicated and committed to what you want, and how great that is. It will be an ideal that others will want to emulate.

Here's some evidence that this is something that if you do, you will achieve success: Do you know any doctors, lawyers, engineers, accountants or any other professionals? If you do know them, do you think that they were *not* obsessed with what they wanted to do or become, in terms of their professions? Do you think that your personal physician woke up one day, a few years ago, and decided that he/she wanted to become a doctor, and now is one because of just that one decision? You know, for a fact, that they had to have been obsessed with what they wanted to achieve, right? It would not

You want to change your life for the better?

have happened otherwise because we have a perception that just the education necessary to qualify to practice some of these professions is so very lengthy, and difficult to get, not to mention expensive. Also, once done with that education, there is the new challenge of actually being good at what they have learned. Of course, we all also know that these professions can be very worthwhile and rewarding, personally - in terms of career satisfaction, and professionally - in terms of monetary rewards, not to mention the prestige and respect that comes along with being, say, a doctor or an attorney. So, even after considering all the benefits of some of the professions I mentioned above, relatively few people get into these fields of work. And this is because we all know what it takes to get there.

Another set of examples would be professional athletes or professional artists of any kind – painters, dancers, singers, authors, musicians, actors, etc. Or any other successful person in any field or any type of business, and it does not even have to be a *super* successful person. But of course, it is easier for us to look at the mega-star, and so I will use them as examples.

Do you think Tiger Woods is not obsessed with the idea of golf? (Of course, this is after the scandal, the one about his numerous extra-marital affairs, was exposed to the media. So we can say that there were *other* things that he *was* obsessed about also. However, on a personal note, I do wish him well, especially because I really do believe that his remorse is genuine.) Do you think Roger Federer does not think about or play tennis all day? Do you think that Robert DeNiro only focuses on acting once a month or so, and the rest of time focuses on, well, playing golf or tennis? Do you think that Bill Gates, now that he probably makes tens of millions of dollars each day, only thinks about computer software once every few years? Do you think Donald Trump does not have real estate as his top priority? Do you think stock-market guru, Jim Cramer, does not think about Stocks every second of the day, and probably even dream about them at night?

God=mc²?

How about Mahatma Gandhi – do you think he just thought that he will *try* to win India's independence by peaceful and non-violent ways – something that had *never* been done before?

So, are you starting to see the picture? Are you starting to see that obsession is simply another name for complete and total dedication and commitment? And that without it, it would be impossible, or at least, very, very difficult to achieve anything at all. And with it, it is almost a guarantee.

How badly do you want what you want? Develop a *positive* obsession about it, and watch what happens. Make it a part of who you are, and think about it consciously and deliberately, for at least a few minutes every day. Longer, if it is possible to do so without actually hindering your life. I am talking about having a laser-like focus on, and thinking concentrated thoughts about, say, a profession that you want to be involved in, or if it is some artistic endeavor you want to engage in – whatever it may be.

I do want to clarify that I am not advocating becoming an obsessed "stalker" of a person, if it is a desire of yours to be in a relationship with a person of your liking. I am not suggesting developing *that* type, or any other type, of an unhealthy obsession! I am just suggesting that if you do want to be in a relationship and it happens to be the most important priority for you, then the *idea* of the relationship should have "top of mind" status for you. You cannot be focused on career, and simply not think about the relationship that you wish to create for yourself, and then expect to create it. It simply won't happen. You may, however, find yourself in a relationship even if you may not have been focused on it, but it may not necessarily be the kind of relationship you *wanted*. And in most cases, and for almost all of us, isn't *that* the bigger problem?

If it is not something specific like that, and if it is just a general goal of life-transformation, then think about your end-result, at least once a day, for several minutes.

You want to change your life for the better?

Some of the things you will want to do to create that commitment and dedication is in the previous step; i.e., of repetition and discipline about your thought habits. Others things associated with creating the dedication are in other steps, for example, visualization, gratitude, and taking action. As you read about them, you will see why that is the case.

4) Knowing that you deserve it - Another very important thing in this whole process is knowing that you deserve whatever it is that you are wanting. I promise you that you might come very close, but you won't actually get what you want if you truly don't believe that you deserve it.

I know, because I have been so very close to a lot of things that I have wanted but truly and genuinely never believed that I deserved them. And because of that unconscious belief, lost whatever it is that I wanted. In my case, mostly this was in regards to relationships. I have always done pretty well with money or career, friends, etc. Even before I had conscious knowledge of the Law of Attraction, I had been using it to create what I wanted. But relationships were the area of my life where I always stumbled. I would attract the woman of my dreams, and there would be a connection, and then the feelings of my not being deserving enough of a relationship with her would drive her away. I would never actually say that I truly believed that I was not deserving or worthy enough, or even think that, consciously; however, my sub-conscious thoughts were contrary to what I really wanted in my life.

To give you an example of what I mean, there was this girl that used to work in the same office as I did. Let's say her name was "Jennifer." So, Jen was the woman of my dreams! She was so beautiful and she had such a gorgeous smile that I used to say that she had the best smile this side of the Milky Way galaxy. She was Meg Ryan-esque in her looks and in her demeanor; she was so sweet and so nice. She was perfect! She was the kind of girl that you would bring home to meet your mother because she was the one. The one

God=mc²?

that you wanted to marry, and spend the rest of your life with. And, in case you haven't been able to tell by now, I was head over heels in love with her. Or so I thought! I was definitely infatuated with her.

(There was another girl at work, "Karen," whom I was *actually* in love with, but I was just too stupid to recognize that fact, and blinded by my infatuation with the lovely Jen, as mentioned above. To use another movie-star simile, rather a combination of two; Karen looked like a person whose looks happened to be the perfect combination of Charlize Theron and Scarlett Johansson, to give you an idea of her physical beauty. And she was not just pretty to look at; she was genuinely a nice human being. One of the nicest that I have ever met. Yeah, even nicer than Jen! And as I said before, unfortunately, I was just too moronic to realize the truth about how I felt about her. I let her get away. And she was, truly, "the one that got away!")

Has this ever happened to you? You might have thought that you were in love with one person, but were actually in love with another? Or, maybe you were in love with two people at the same time? Anyway, I will wipe away my single tear, and get back to the story that I meant to tell you.

One Saturday, I had been working a rare overtime shift, when I realized that Jen was in the office also. So, I thought to myself, "This is my chance. I have to ask her out tonight. It is now or never!"

So, I went up to her and after making some small talk, I asked, "Hey, if you don't have any plans after work, would you like to join me for a drink?" Two or three seconds elapsed before her sweet reply made it past her lips, but those moments seemed to last a few million years. Although, I could have waited a *billion* years if that's what it would have taken to hear the words.

She said, "Sure! I don't have any plans." On the inside, I was ecstatically happy, and doing "cartwheels" in my mind, but I did not let that show. Nonchalantly, I asked her what time she was going to be done for the day.

You want to change your life for the better?

The evening went pretty well and I felt that it may have been a *beginning* of something special.

Then, a few days or a couple of weeks later, I asked her to join me to play a game of pool with a friend of mine. It was meant to be a casual outing, nothing to indicate a serious connotation. I did not want to rush things and scare her away as I knew that I tended to do. We got together and had a good time, but at that time my insecurities and self-esteem issues started to resurface. My beliefs of not being deserving enough of a romantic relationship with this beautiful woman started to manifest in unforeseen ways.

We would be at the pool table, and she would keep asking me how to hold the cue stick, and how to play pool. Despite my stupidity and naiveté in these matters, I did think that she may have been *pretending* not to know how to play pool and such. She may have wanted me to wrap my arms around her, and show her how to hold the cue and to take aim and hit the cue ball. Just so that we could be close to each other. But my "issues" prevented me from doing so. (At the very least, she may have wanted to enjoy the fragrance of the cologne that I used to wear, which she always used to compliment me on. And no, the cologne was not Obsession, by Calvin Klein; it was Emporio, by Armani!)

Also, as far as I know, my "friend" did not help my case, either. I think he may have said a nasty thing or two about me when I might have stepped away from them to get drinks for all of us. With friends like these, who needs enemies! Right? Of course, I don't know that for sure, so that is just conjecture from me. And I think that it may have just been "normal" paranoia on my part, and maybe there may have been nothing to it at all.

However, there was no denying that my own feelings of not being deserving enough did very little to attract Jen towards me. In fact, they did just the opposite. They repelled her! Now, that is what I would call the Law of Repulsion. And apparently, I was skilled masterfully in that art!

God=mc²?

Come to think of it, this may have been the same reason why I failed to realize or accept my feelings for Karen, also.

So, the moral of the story is that you really have to get yourself to the place of believing; every fiber of your being has to *believe* and *know* that you deserve that great relationship, that great job, perfect health, a fabulous body, great friends, or *whatever* it may be.

And when you do believe, there will be a whole different kind of confidence about you. You will *feel* the difference! And others will feel that about you too. You will genuinely feel deserving, and then, you won't even have to try to attract what you want, it will be automatically attracted *to* you.

There are two things you can do that will get you to the place of believing that you do, in fact, deserve those things that you so dearly want. And like with everything else, this is something you need to do daily, if possible.

One of them is simply realizing that you are a spiritual being, a soul, and that you are a part of the Primary Spirit, Universal Mind, Source or God. You are perfect (as a soul). And being a part of God or as Dr. Wayne Dyer says, a "piece of God," how could you *not* deserve anything that you desire? So, repeat to yourself on a daily basis, if it is possible for you to do so daily, "I am a spiritual being. I am perfect. I absolutely deserve everything that I desire because I am a piece of God."

You have to realize that you are, in fact, perfect, regardless of how "broken" or "damaged" you think you might be. Regardless of what you may have done or what kind of person you might have been or still are. Regardless of what kind of a past you may have had. Regardless of the state of your life in the present moment. Nothing; absolutely nothing changes the fact that you are a spiritual being, first and foremost. Nothing you can do or have done will *ever* change that fact!

You want to change your life for the better?

And I know, in the beginning, it won't even sound right, especially if you have been holding a chronic belief that you are not deserving enough; however, in a matter of days, you will start feeling good when you say those words. And in a matter of a few more days, you will start believing. And that is the point you want to get to, in order to start creating the "miracles" in your life.

5) Doing the "180 Dance" - And this "dance" is nothing like the Macarena. We have been trained, by now, to think more about what we don't want, then to think about what we do want. People who may be familiar with *The Secret* know about this (or if they are familiar with other Law of Attraction teachings).

What is the exact opposite of what we don't want? The 180 degree opposite of what we *don't* want would be what we *do* want. I have to give credit to my friend and now, ex-colleague, "Ayyub" Mark Bailey for the phrase "Doing the 180," which is a technique of reverse psychology that he often uses to create a desired outcome in various difficult situations in his life.

(Sorry, Ayyub, maybe my mentioning this is going to alert everybody else about your technique, and thus render it useless. Or maybe not, because you could always do a 360, if that is the case. Also, they may never know, for sure, when you are using the technique. So, I guess, it is still safe.)

Anyway, I just added the "Dance" at the end of that phrase. This has also been called "pivoting," I believe, by Esther and Jerry Hicks.

But how do you get yourself to do that?

(Note: Please know that it's not that you should have no negative thoughts at all - you will get them, from time to time - but know that you will eventually *decrease* the number of negative thoughts you get as you train yourself to only have positive ones, and eventually, you will completely eliminate them.)

God=mc²?

Now, that is the thing that we have to learn, don't we? Well, you can use any and all tools available to you. First, you can start by using things like the most powerful tool in business - 3M's genius of a simple creation that helped transform my life - The Post-It Note! Also commonly, but venerably, known as the "yellow sticky."

Stick them anywhere and everywhere (well, as long as they don't inhibit your work or life). For example, I had a sticky on my computer monitor at work. It said, "What do you want for yourself? Focus on that!" Simple, right? It absolutely brought my mind back to where I wanted it to be; i.e., focused on exactly what I wanted. You can write your own message that is pertinent to you. It could be "I am wealthy and abundant." "I am in a perfect relationship."

In other words, if you want to be wealthy, you don't want to focus on the lack of wealth by saying "I don't want to be poor," or even "I *want* to be wealthy." What you want to say, think, and focus on is this idea that you *are* wealthy already. Or to use the other example of wanting to be in a perfect relationship, you don't want to say or think "I don't want to be alone," or even "I want to be in a perfect relationship." The former is the worst possible thing you can reiterate to yourself. The latter is a move towards the kind of thinking you want to develop; however still, that is only a better way of stating what you want, but not quite the best yet. The best way to do it is to say "I *am* in a perfect relationship!" And try to generate the feelings of how that would feel or be like. And then give thanks or feel genuine feelings of gratitude and happiness for this having happened. The reason, I believe, that you would, at least, have an idea of how it is going to feel like when you get what you want is simply because you know you want it.

To give you an example, let's say that you are not in a relationship currently, but you do want to be in one. Well, even if you have never been in a romantic relationship before, you have an *idea* of what it is going to be like. You know that the feeling of being in a relationship is going to be better than the feeling of being alone.

You want to change your life for the better?

I know, for a fact, that you have this idea of how it is going to be like, because if you did not think it was going to be better, you would not want to be in a relationship. Simple as that.

So, go to that *feeling* you expect to have when you are actually in the relationship, and try to feel it *now*. And don't forget to say "thank you" for it.

I do understand how and why some of you who may have understood the principles of the Law of Attraction very well, and even understood these practices of thinking thoughts of only the things or events you want in your lives, and of visualizing and feeling gratitude, however still, you just seem to struggle with it. What I would suggest is to not give up because these efforts do build upon themselves and they might have been right on the cusp of this thing taking off, and you might have ended up giving up just before you were going to start seeing results. So, I do beg of you to stick with it, and I guarantee you that if you learn to apply all these principles in your life, you will see *measurable* results in your life. And in your being able to actually measure the positive changes, ironically, you will also find that they are immeasurable in terms of what they bring into your life.

Anyway, this surely has worked wonders for me. Almost two years ago, I had been sick and tired of my job, and it felt like torture to me every day. Every time I felt that somebody or something was bothering me, I looked at my sticky note on my computer monitor - because it was right there - staring at me; I could not ignore it, even if I wanted to. It forced me to think about what I wanted, which was freedom from this "prison" of a job that I had, and then I would imagine that I had already been granted that freedom, and give thanks for it. After doing that, I would immediately go from being frustrated or angry, to being calm and patient, and even happy.

Within a matter of only a few months (it doesn't have to take months or even weeks - it can be done in days - it all depends on

God=mc²?

you), I had been offered a Severance Package if I were to accept a lay-off. My "prayers" had been answered. I was free!

(By the way, in this economy, a lot of people might want to use this technique to *create or manifest* a job, and not to lose it. But that's the great thing about this - you can use it to do *whatever* you *want* it to do. I used it to manifest a lay-off with a great Severance Package. When I was still at my job, I had thought, hundreds of times, that I should just walk away. Just quit! But I did not. Instead, I manifested something even better.)

So, start using this or other tools as a reminder of what you want to think about. Put a sticky on your fridge, on your dashboard in your car, on your mirror in the bathroom, maybe even on your favorite credit or debit card - so every time you use the card - you will be forced to see the message. The same applies with any place that you see or visit daily. Make these a part of your life, and they will help transform it.

6) Emotion based visualizing - Visualizing is absolutely essential to creating the life of your dreams. However, you have to make sure that you are visualizing while feeling the emotions of the thing you are visualizing. It cannot be just plain ol' "seeing" in your mind's eye - you actually have to "feel" it in your heart too. You have to feel the joy that you would feel if you were exactly in the time and place that you are visualizing.

Another extremely important thing is to actually "see" through your own eyes when you are visualizing. So, if you are visualizing owning a huge mansion of a home - visualize that you are sitting in the office, or any other favorite room of your palatial mansion - and envision staring out the window of that room - as if you are seeing out the window through your own eyes. Do not see yourself sitting in the chair in the office, as if you are watching a movie starring you. This is an important distinction. So, actually "see" through your mind's eyes, when visualizing. Also, as the teachers in *The Secret* have

You want to change your life for the better?

said, try to create physical movement in your visualizations. Have it be as if you are moving around and doing things. Mike Dooley, my favorite teacher from *The Secret*, says to incorporate as many of your physical senses as you can while you visualize. "See" through your eyes, "hear" beautiful music playing in the background, "feel" the kiss of your lover, "taste" the wine, "smell" the fragrance of the roses, etc., etc.

There are no limits to what you can fully experience when you are visualizing. Just remember to *feel* the ultimate feeling that you are after, happiness and joy. "Fake it, till you make it!" You might have heard that one. Or "Dress for the job that you want, not the one you are in." Well, those are ways to help you with your visualizations, and therefore, to get the Law of Attraction working for you.

In order to help you with visualizing, a Vision Board is a great tool; however, you don't absolutely *need* to have a Vision Board. You can and may want to use it in the beginning. It is only a tool, as I said, to help you hone in on what you want to focus on, and therefore, create in your life. And to help you create the *feelings* of being in the place or having the thing you want.

If you can get yourself to "feel" the feelings without a Vision Board, go right ahead. I, myself, have a Vision Board with a picture of my dream mansion and dream cars, and also a few fake million dollar bills. However, I don't use it anymore because my visualizations have reached a level where I don't need to actually *see* the Vision Board with my physical eyes anymore. And I promise you that you will also get to that place, if you visualize regularly.

Just like Mike Dooley does, I visualize (and meditate) every single day.

7) **Gratitude** - Hand in hand with the above principle of emotion based visualizing goes this principle of emotion based gratitude expression. It absolutely works.

God=mc²?

Again, as I say about any of these principles is that they all have to be applied together in order to have maximum efficacy and efficiency in manifesting your creations; however, you can learn them one-by-one.

I found this slightly difficult in the sense that, first, how do I visualize something as if it is already done, and then to generate the feelings of having it already done, when I know, intellectually, that it is not done? And on top of that, how do I express genuinely felt thankfulness or gratitude for the event as having transpired already?

It really does get easy if you practice. I promise you! And before you know it, it is second nature. Pretty soon, this will be how you think about anything and everything you wish to accomplish. I promise you that too; however, provided you do take these simple steps.

Think about it this way - anybody can, very easily, feel the feelings of having won the lottery if they have actually won the lottery, right? And anybody can express gratitude for having won. In fact, they cannot help but react that way, right? They start jumping and yelling and screaming in ecstasy and gratitude when they first find out that they have won the jackpot.

The challenge (and it really is *not* a very difficult one) is to feel how it would feel to win the lottery *and* to give thanks for having won the lottery *before* even having bought the ticket.

Now, I know that I used to do the following: Every time the jackpots on the Mega Millions or the Powerball lotteries went up into the hundreds of millions of dollars, I would buy a few tickets, and then daydream about what I would do with the money if I were to win the jackpot.

I am absolutely positive that every person who has ever bought a ticket for a lottery offering a major jackpot has done just that. Have you? I think you may have.

You want to change your life for the better?

Do you remember how that felt? It felt good, right? Even if it had been for only a few moments that you had done that. In your fantasy, you might have bought a fancy car, and a very nice mansion of a house, you might have quit your job, paid-off any debt that you might have had, "taken care" of your friends and family, and even given a lot of money to charity, and then, sailed the seas, or done whatever you wanted to do, right here in your private "paradise" of a life. Right?

I know that my daydreams depicted a scenario exactly like the one above.

Now, if you can learn to do that exact visualization with anything and everything that you want to accomplish, achieve, or possess in your life - it will be guaranteed to happen for you. The key is to make it a "place" you "visit" regularly. Daily, preferably.

Oh, and by the way, it can work with the lottery too. But you cannot just do it once, and expect it to work the very first time (although, it surely is possible); however, if you persist in that thought to the point where there is no evitability other than your winning the lottery, and you believe it with every fiber of your being, and not only that, you believe that you deserve it and give heart-felt thanks for it, you *will* win the lottery.

The counter-point here is this: After having that fantastic daydream about what we would do with all the money that was won, all of us who had that "winning" ticket in their hands also believed, deep down, that the odds are way against us winning (for example, in the case of the Mega Millions - the odds of winning the jackpot are 1 in 175 million), and that the "reality" of this is that, most probably, we are *not* going to win it. Another thing, and I read this somewhere, is that winning the lottery entails all the other players, the ones who also bought tickets, losing *their* chance to win, so that *you* can win.

God=mc²?

Also, even if you do win, the other thing that I have heard is that the energy "stored" in the money won is very negative. Again, this is because all the many millions of people who also bought the ticket now envy you and don't like the fact that you won, instead of them, and so this new wealth carries within itself a negative sort of energy. This negative energy will, in turn, one way or another, lead to the destruction of your life.

And that has, indeed, happened to many a jackpot winner. You may have read or heard stories of how the lives of these lottery winners took a drastic turn for the worse shortly after their having won it. However, still, I do believe that ultimately it depends on the person who has won it, and can make their life what they want it to be, lottery or no lottery.

The thing about creating or manifesting the life of your dreams - which is, undoubtedly, an extremely positive endeavor - is that it works the best when your intentions are in harmony with the intentions of others, or if your thoughts are about benefiting others as well. This happens to be an extremely positive endeavor, in and of itself. In other words, if your goals are for the highest good of everybody involved, of course, including yourself, they will have a super power unto themselves. And I do absolutely believe that!

What you can create using these principles in all aspects of your life will be much more exhilarating and exciting than simply winning the lottery, as Mike Dooley has said, I think.

Again, as I said before, I used to buy lottery tickets, and quite frankly, I still buy them. In fact, I have been buying them from when I was a little kid, six or seven years old! Back in India, there was a lottery shop near my dad's oil store in downtown Vadodara. So, whenever I was visiting my dad's store, I was sure to ask dad to have our accountant escort me to the nearby lottery shop and make the payment for the tickets of my choice.

(On a related note, my *other* favorite money-related activity for when I was at my dad's store was to insist on sitting near my dad,

You want to change your life for the better?

putting me within an arm's length of a reach of the very exciting and enticing cash drawer. I would separate all the currency, which totaled in the amounts of tens or even hundreds of thousands of rupees, into neat little piles of the same denomination notes. I would make stacks of a 100 notes each, and make sure that the bills were facing the same way and right-side up. I was a big-time stickler about that. Then I would apply an elastic band around each one of the stacks, getting them ready for deposit at the bank. I used to enjoy that thoroughly.)

Regardless, it seems that I may have digressed a bit. So, I have always believed in the possibility of my winning a major lottery jackpot and I will continue to believe that. However, if I were given a choice to simply "win" a jackpot versus "earn" the many millions of dollars (the caveat being that it might take a year or two before I see *any* money coming in with this latter choice), I would still choose the latter just because I know that the fruits of my labor would taste much, much sweeter than the one's of dumb luck.

However, contradicting what I just wrote, I also have come to a realization that there is no such thing as dumb luck, or for that matter, plain ol' "luck," - "dumb" or otherwise, or "coincidence," or "accidents," because *everything* - every circumstance, every person, every living being, every event - absolutely everything has a purpose.

So having said that, go ahead, create the life of your dreams - regardless of whether you want to win the lottery or to create the perfect career or to have the perfect partner or whatever else your brilliant mind can conceive.

Whatever it is, it is waiting for you to connect to it. Just don't forget to give thanks for it in advance.

8) Taking action - This step may seem obvious or, on the contrary, *not so obvious*, as some Law of Attraction students have erroneously thought to be. Regardless, there are specific things you should do, in terms of taking action.

God=mc²?

I beg you to pay attention to this: Thinking a certain way is more powerful than acting a certain way if your thoughts are not congruent with the actions you are taking. Think about *that* for a while! Have you ever done all the right things; taken all the correct physical action in order to achieve some desired end-result, and yet the result had not been what you had intended it to be? In that case, I can promise you that your thoughts had not been in harmony with the result that you wanted to achieve. You might have even believed that "it would be nice" to have that result, and you might have really wanted that particular result, but then, you truly did not *believe* that it could happen, for various reasons.

We already discussed that principle; it is about feeling deserving or worthy of the desired end-result. However, it points to the fact that you could act in accordance with what you want, but if you don't add the power of your harmonious thoughts to it, you may not create what you want. And that, ultimately, the thought can prove to be more powerful than the actual action.

So, first and foremost, the action you plan on taking should be in accordance with the dreams that you wish to realize. Once that is the case, you should apply all the principles mentioned above. For example, you should have absolute faith that you will get what you want; you should keep reiterating your goal to yourself, verbally, in written form, or mentally; you should be dedicated and committed to achieving the end-result; you should genuinely feel that you deserve what you desire; you should visualize the end-result as if it has already been achieved; you should give thanks for it as if it is already done; and lastly, take the physical action that you think will get you to the achievement of your desired end-result.

I know, I know – it sounds like a *lot* of work! A lot more than just taking the required action, right? You might be thinking that it is not worth putting in all that effort and mental work. I promise you that it only *sounds* like it, and not only that, I will prove to you that you have been doing all of those things *already*. So, there is actually no *extra* effort required here.

You want to change your life for the better?

It is just that we, you and I, have already been doing all of those things but with a negative attitude or with a possibility of a negative outcome in mind. Haven't we? Think about it! When we first think about a new goal or a desired end-result, what do we do? We have doubts or worries about whether we will get what we want or not; we keep reiterating the scenario of things not working out and *why* they could possibly not work out; we find ourselves wavering as far as a commitment to seeing something through; we try to find "legitimate" reasons for our not being worthy of the end-result; we see ourselves failing; we then proceed to blame ourselves, others or circumstances for that failure. We may have already started to take action before thinking about all of these, or we may start to then take action, which, at that moment could be defined as half-hearted, at best.

I am not saying that we might have done this with *all* the goals that we want to achieve; only that we may have done the above with *some* of them that we did not achieve or in cases in which we found the achievement of some goal to entail a lot of boring, tedious and even soul-quashing work. And that is a perfect segue to my next point.

Which happens to be a very important one specific to the action part: The action you are taking should not feel like a chore or "work." It should not feel like a burden to you. So it is exactly counter-intuitive and contrary to what I mentioned above in terms of all these things sounding like a lot of work. In fact, you can use that feeling as a gauging tool - if something feels like a burdensome chore or tedious and boring work - then it is simply not the right thing to be doing.

Now, please don't get me wrong. I am not saying that there won't be any effort required; just that the effort expended will not *feel* like *work*. Instead, it will feel like play. And it *will* be play, well, as far as you are concerned.

God=mc²?

Anyhow, I cannot tell you what, specifically, the action is that you should be taking because I don't know what you intend to create for yourself. However, I *can* tell you that if you are using a talent or faculty that you know that you already have, you will feel alive and passionate about it. And whatever action you take while using that talent and moving in the direction of that dream will not feel like a chore or work to you. It won't feel like something you *have* to do, but like something you *want* to do.

Let that feeling of knowing that it is something you want to do be the guide to the action you should be taking.

(I know that this might be something that you may have heard many times before, but it really does work, and I beg you to, at least, think about this and see what you come up with, as far as a talent or skill that you may have, that you could make a career out of. Just please think about it.)

So, let's say for example, that you wish to create a career of your dreams - a career where you will make a lot of money, have the freedom to express yourselves, and to feel fulfilled, in every possible way, and even help others, and therefore, be very happy. And in this example, let's say, your current job is with the Phone Company, but your passion is writing, then you should simply *start* writing, if you weren't doing so already. If you write poetry or if you want to write a book. Take action. Start writing. *Just do it!* As the famous Nike tag-line and trademark says.

(By the way, this above example is based on a true story - *my* story - and I go into a lot more detail about it when I provide the definition of the Law of Attraction and how I used it to create this book, and the importance of action in having done so. This is at the end of this chapter, as an Epilogue to it.)

And if you were already writing, but were not giving the attention, time, or effort that you knew you should be giving it, then *start* giving it the attention, time, or effort that you should have been

You want to change your life for the better?

giving it. Don't feel guilty or ashamed that you have not done so yet. Those are negative emotions, and are not needed and won't help you. Simply start doing the thing you know you should have been doing. As soon as you start doing so, you will be inexplicably inspired to do something more.

Let's continue with that example of your being a budding writer. Well, in that case, you will be inspired to write some more. Maybe to write about something that you had not thought about before. You will feel excited and enthusiastic.

This process is a "virtuous cycle," as opposed to that other nasty one we so often talk about. This is a good cycle, and it will feed itself. You will be inspired. As you may have heard a lot of the self-help and spiritual gurus, including my favorite one, mention that the word *inspired* means to be "in-spirit." And when you are in-spirit, you don't need to get motivated by an outside force, you are self-motivated.

Dr. Amit Goswami, Ph.D., a featured scientist in *What the Bleep do we (k)now?!* and author of several books, says in his latest one, *God Is Not Dead*, to alternate between the states of *doing* and *being*. He says to "do-be-do-be-do." We can even sing that.

So, in the state of doing, of course, you are taking action. But then stop, and turn to a state of just being. And according to Dr. Goswami, you will be inspired in these moments of "being." Then you can go back to taking action based on the inspiration you received while you were in a state of being, and go back to a state of doing. And back and forth; so on and so forth.

I have found this to be the absolute truth, and I do agree with Dr. Goswami, wholeheartedly, on how this process works.

9) Become a SOP, don't remain a POP - You might be saying, "Huh? Become a *what*?" Become a Spiritually Oriented Person; SOP, and not a Physically Oriented Person; POP. If you are not a SOP, simply *becoming aware* of the intention that you *want* to become a spiritually oriented person will move you towards that.

God=mc²?

Repeat to yourself, "I am a SOP, and not a POP." I really did think (and still do think) that this *mantra* that I have come up with is a hokey one, and especially since the word *sop* has a negative connotation. It sounds silly and even funny. However, here SOP is, obviously, an acronym. You don't have to use the acronym; you can say the whole thing. Regardless of how it sounds and how you decide to use it, I beg you to realize that it works.

All of the things that I write about in this book are, as a matter of fact, ways of becoming just that - a SOP - becoming a spiritual person or becoming a spiritually *oriented* person - which is really our orientation anyway - that is our point of origination – Spirit or God. So, in accordance to that, we have to learn to stop being physically oriented, and move towards being spiritually oriented. At the very least, start being less physically oriented and start being more spiritually oriented. Tip the balance in favor of the spiritual. And as I mentioned before, this whole process of Self-Realization is really about just that.

Again, if you feel the need, have a yellow sticky with that saying, in your own handwriting, "I am a SOP, and not a POP!" posted wherever you are going to see it multiple times every day - as I previously mentioned - on your fridge, on the bottom of mirrors in your home. On the dashboard of your car, on the side of your computer monitor at work and at home. Maybe even inside your wallet - have the sticky wrapped around your favorite credit or debit card. Think of all the places you are forced to look at or your attention has to be drawn to, and strategically place these stickies there.

Here is a very important note of caution: You will have to work on actually paying attention to these notes because in spite of the brilliant positioning of these stickies that you may have come up with, it is possible to get "used" to them, and stop noticing them. So, do make it a habit to look at them purposely - at least you will be looking in their general direction anyway - just pay attention to the words on them, and mentally reinforce the message to yourself.

You want to change your life for the better?

It truly does work. I know it! I have used, and am using, this and all of the steps mentioned here. I really do believe that learning all these steps and putting these principles into action; i.e., following this scientific methodology, is the "right" way to "pray."

So, welcome to the rest of your life which will be one dream after another, coming true!

And I will repeat what I started with:

The One Simple Key to using these principles or steps is that they should ALL be applied, together. This is the most important part to really being able to tap the power of the Law of Attraction. You can learn them one-by-one; however, the end goal should be to apply them all together.

And being the students of the teachings of the Law of Attraction, remember; life transformation is as easy or as difficult as you *think* it is. So, anticipate it being easy, and it will be!

Epilogue to this chapter

I would like to provide a definition of the Law of Attraction here, briefly, just in case some of you may not have heard about it. And then I provide you with a real-life example of how I used it to create this book. This law states that we can "attract" anything we want to ourselves by the virtue of our thoughts. In other words, whatever we think about on a regular basis will come into our lives, whether we really want that thing or not.

The crux of the idea of the Law of Attraction is that everything in the Universe is, ultimately, energy. And being energy, everything vibrates. This vibration can also be described to be "wavelike." Regardless of whether you consider things to have back-and-forth type vibrations or a wave-like movement, both could be represented as having a frequency. The frequency is the rate at which something vibrates. The frequency of any vibration is measured in Hertz, represented by the acronym Hz. Which is, simply put, the number of times the particular thing vibrates in a second. So, for example, if something has a frequency of 1 Hz, it vibrates once every second. If something has a frequency of, say, 50 Hz, the rate of vibration is 50 times per second. And similarly, one of 2000 Hz has the rate of 2000 times each second.

So, just like sounds have vibrations, our thoughts also have a vibration unto themselves and therefore, they have a frequency at which they vibrate, too. When we hold a thought of something in our mind on a regular basis, we start to tune the frequency of that particular thought to the frequency of whatever we may be thinking about. Since everything in the Universe is energy, ultimately and at its core, and so it vibrates, anything that we can possibly think about is also going to have an inherent vibration, and therefore a particular frequency.

In other words, the frequency of the vibrations of our *thought* of a particular thing, and the frequency of the vibrations of that particular thing become exactly the same. And then we physically attract that thing into our life experience, because at the level of vibrations, like attracts like.

All of this you may have heard about, but you may not have heard about why, exactly, vibrations attract like vibrations. This is because the Universe always wants to "be more"; it wants to continually expand. And this applies to any and all things, living or non-living, in the Universe. This is the reason why we have the *physical* law of attraction (if I may call it that), meaning the attraction between the opposite sexes which leads to their mating, and thus results in offspring. Two of a particular species unite to create more of the same. Life begets more life!

(There is a continuation of a more technical; however, still very easy to understand explanation of how and why the Law of Attraction works, on my website. If you are interested in learning more, please check it out at **www.GodEqualsmcSquared.com**)

You want to change your life for the better?

However, more than our thoughts, it is really our feelings that actually attract whatever we are thinking, and therefore feeling about, into our experience. However, the feelings are closely associated with and result from thoughts. And thoughts held for a long time are defined as beliefs. Beliefs, in turn, shape our attitudes, and our attitudes dictate how we act. But please be cautious here - as you read these words - you could easily come to the conclusion that, ultimately, it *is* the *action* that brings something into our experience. And that in the above chain of events, if we simply left out the last part; i.e., the one of action, then *nothing* would happen.

I don't want to undermine the power of action; however, I also don't want to overrate it. Your thoughts (and when I say thoughts, I mean a regular way of thinking about things, your mentality about something specific, or even about life, in general), feelings, beliefs and attitudes - all of these sans action - can and do bring things, events, people and circumstances into your life. The action you may or may not have taken in the past may have affected the outcome of some event or circumstance in your life. However, that outcome was affected by your action, or lack thereof, to only a certain degree!

The rest was brought to you by all the other aspects of how we "create" our lives - thoughts, feelings, beliefs, and attitudes.

Hopefully, this real-life example of how this book came into being may shed some light on this process: Almost three years ago, this book that you are holding in your hands did not exist. Not even an idea of it existed in my head. Sure, the idea of it existed as a potentiality. But the idea was not a "real" idea in my mind yet. And suddenly, one day, a thought popped into my mind that I should write a book about bridging science and spirituality, and about providing scientific evidence of God's existence (and that God wants to answer all our prayers, and how to ensure that the Law of Attraction works for everybody so that they can create a life of their dreams, too). Of course, I did not think about it that way, exactly. I just thought that I should write a book based on the general idea of what science was

God=mc²?

saying lately about spirituality. The rest of the related concepts came to me later on.

So, first and foremost, this physical book with over 97,000 words in it, and printed on approximately 325 pages was "only" an idea. An abstract, non-physical thought in my head. Other than having a *general* idea of the overall subject of the book, as I listed above, and the one very specific idea of God being Divine Energy, I did not have a clue of what, exactly, I would write about, what the chapter titles would be, what the sub-title and motto/slogan of the book would be, or how it would be broken down and other such minutiae. Initially, I did come up with the title of the book as $God=mc^2?$ Regardless, I held onto the thought that I wanted to write this book, and the fact that I could actually accomplish this never-before-done task (for me, that is), became a firm belief.

Then I started experiencing even more feelings of inspiration and feelings of accomplishment. You could say that the initial thought that I had gotten about writing a book was of an inspirational nature, and I would agree with that. Anyhow, these feelings started to drive my thought processes all the time, thereafter. The goal of writing this book became very important to me and all of my thoughts started to center around this idea of becoming a published author and having this become my career, eventually.

Mind you, at this point I had not even written a *single* word. However, since the predominant thoughts in my mind were about this subject, I started getting ideas regarding what to write about. I started getting inspiration from anywhere and everywhere. It was like magic. And quite frankly, it *is* magic! And it is also a miracle!

Now came the part that required me to "take action." What I would do is just write down whatever came to my mind, and that which I remotely felt would be material I could use in my book. I would write a word, or a sentence or a phrase on a yellow sticky or in a notebook. Sometimes, I would write a few paragraphs using the word processing software on my computer. The point was that the

You want to change your life for the better?

book started to "come to me" in bits and pieces; in words and phrases. And the only thing that I had to do was record those thoughts somewhere.

That was all the action that I needed to take. (Well, there was other action needed to secure a publisher and to develop the artwork for the cover and such. However, to physically write the book, all I had to do was record the inspirational thoughts that I got. I got an indication that all the rest would be taken care of later.) So, of course, action is important, but as I just demonstrated to you using this example, all the other aspects - starting with thoughts - are more, if not equally, important. At the very least, one can reach a solid conclusion that thoughts are the first step to any creation, and therefore they are the originating source of all creations.

In other words, I used the Law of Attraction to create this book. I have done precisely the same in creating anything else - thing, event, circumstance or experience - in my life. And guess what, so have all of you. Without exception.

It may be just that you might not have been using this principle deliberately and purposefully to create the life that you want. Just know that - with or without knowledge of it; or with or without deliberate intent - you have been using the Law of Attraction to create your life, and you will continue to do so. However, you do have a choice to use it deliberately and intentionally to create the life that you want.

(The Law of Attraction is *one* of a *few* other Laws or principles one can use to create the life of one's dreams. The others being the Law of Causality, also known as the Law of Karma; and another being the Law of Self-Responsibility, or as I like to call it, the Law of Dharma. I described and defined them in chapters 9 and 10, respectively.)

Chapter 26
Specific applications for specific situations

As I have mentioned before, we want to lead the life of our dreams in *every* aspect of our life. And for us to do that, we have to analyze where we are currently, in any or all spheres of life, and then decide where we want to be.

Then we can apply the Law of Attraction, while keeping in mind the Law of Causality (Karma) and the Law of Self-Responsibility (Dharma), to create the life that we want for ourselves. We would also want to apply other specific practical principles such as meditation; ego dilution; charity of thought, word, and deed; anger control and modification of other negative behavior via mindfulness; conscious awareness of the impact of our existence on the whole world; and living a spiritually oriented life. Some of these principles and laws, I have already discussed in previous chapters; however, there are other ones that we haven't talked about yet. We will do so, in detail, in the next few chapters.

God=mc²?

Another very important point is that the new life that we want to create has to be in accordance with our ultimate good, and also with the greater good of the world. If we do apply these principles, it will, in fact, be so. Not only that, we will we able to manifest the life of our dreams in no time at all.

Having said that, here are *some* applications of those spiritual principles in some very specific situations or for achievement of specific goals. However, do always keep in mind that these principles can truly be used to achieve any goal, and in any situation. As long as you apply the nine specific steps we learned in the last chapter, along with the other general spiritual principles mentioned throughout the book - to *any* situation - it *will* turn out in your favor. These principles can be applied universally. Anyway, as I mentioned, here are some specific examples of where you can apply them (and they are mentioned in no particular order of importance because we know that all of them are important):

1) Wealth/Money/Abundance - We all want material abundance. Without exception. Sure, some of us can live on less than others, but we still want that "some," whatever the quantity may be. In other words, we want our own ideal amount of money or material wealth so that we can lead an ideal life of comfort and convenience. It doesn't have to be a life of a king or a queen. It surely can be, but it does not have to be.

Please keep in mind that among many principles of spirituality you will find that a sense of irony reigns supreme. In the Law of Attraction, as soon as you stop running after the wealth, and start thinking the thought and start generating the genuine feeling within yourself that you already have, in your possession, all the abundance that you want or need, and give genuinely felt thanks for it being in your life, the wealth actually starts to flow into your life. (This does not just apply to wealth; it also applies to everything and anything that one would want to attract into one's life.)

Specific applications for specific situations

In the practice of meditation, one should focus on non-thought *not* by forcing the mind not to think, but by being easy about it. Not resisting the thought, but acknowledging it when it does come, and releasing it.

As it was mentioned in the teachings of *The Secret*, "What you resist, persists." Or as I think I may have seen printed on a T-Shirt, "It is all bass ackwards!" We think that in the dogged pursuit of something or by going after something relentlessly, we will get it; whatever it may be.

Or conversely, by putting all of our efforts in stopping or resisting it, it will stop – if it happens to be something negative or something unwanted. However, from the principles and steps mentioned in the previous chapter, and throughout the book, you may be realizing that it is simply not the case.

So, when it comes to money, simply *imagine* that you already have the amount that you want. Imagine and create the feeling of *happiness* associated with having that money, and give heartfelt thanks for it. There is also another trick, if you will, to this if you are finding it difficult to create that feeling of happiness associated with having the money, when you know intellectually, that you don't have the money. Think about something – *anything* – that you know for sure that you do have, and you are genuinely thankful for having it and it makes you happy just thinking about it.

The trick is to immediately go to that feeling of happiness or joy at the very moment you start getting worrisome thoughts or feelings about money or your relationship or whatever it may be. (The way to learn to do that was discussed, in great detail, in the last chapter. Also, the way to make this your very nature; i.e., to do that automatically, was also discussed there.)

In other words, you *don't have to* create the feelings of happiness associated *specifically* and *only* with having money in order to manifest money. You can generate the feelings of happiness about

God=mc²?

anything at all, and still manifest money or a great relationship or better health, etc. It just works.

Happiness is the antidote to the poison of worry, and at the same time it is also the magnet for more happiness.

As you might have noticed, there is a lot of repetition. The basic steps to create whatever you want are the same. Hence, the repetition.

Before I go any further, there is another thing I want to mention about the Law of Attraction. It is a clarification about the thing that people seem to bring up a lot when I define or describe the Law to them. They mention that it seems that the Law of Attraction is a process of our becoming a lot more aware of the things that were already around us, and not the fact that one starts to actually attract *new* things; viz., people, events, circumstances, opportunities or knowledge, to themselves. Obviously, "new" meaning that they weren't already present around us, waiting for us to discover them.

I would like to clarify and say that, absolutely, that phenomenon *does* occur; i.e., the one of our becoming *aware* of things that may have *already* been around us, but we were just not aware of them before. This is a very common phenomenon called Reticular Formation, created by the Reticular Activating System in the brain. This part or system of the brain is involved in filtering incoming external stimuli to discriminate irrelevant background sensory data.

Think about it this way: If we were to take in all of the data coming in through all of our senses at any one moment in time, we would be so confused that we won't be able to do anything at all. We won't be able to function properly just because there would be too much information pouring into our perception, all at once. The Reticular Formation filters out the so-called useless data, and only gives us the stuff that is truly useful to us.

Who determines what is "useful" and what is "useless" to us? We do! The Reticular Formation only obeys our commands to it regarding what we consider useful and useless.

Specific applications for specific situations

A perfect and often used example is the one of a particular car - either a particular make and model, or a color of the vehicle - becoming so important to us that we start noticing that particular car everywhere. If memory serves me well, it might have been the Self-help guru Tony Robbins whom I had first heard mention this. However, as I mentioned before, people have brought up this phenomenon to counter the other *real* effects of the Law of Attraction, so I did some research online to find out how this phenomenon of Reticular Formation works.

To give you a clearer example of it, let's say you might have been thinking about buying a new car and you have had your mind set on a Silver-colored Nissan Altima. You might have gone into a Nissan dealership to test-drive the car, or you may have been doing research online about where to buy one, and about the prices and other options that you might consider when buying your Silver Nissan Altima.

What you have done by actively and consciously researching the details of this car is that you have told your RAS, Reticular Activating System, that a Silver Nissan Altima is very important to you, and now the Reticular Formation "knows" that. So now, instead of considering the visual stimulus provided by a Silver Nissan Altima to be useless background data and filtering it out, it "allows" that data to flow into your perception. Simply put, it allows you to see it.

And Voila! You start noticing all these Silver Altimas on the road, and you start to think that there sure are an awful lot of them around. However, you know, *logically*, that there was always the same number of them on the roads before you started noticing their vast numbers somehow.

So, this Reticular Formation *does* get activated when you start using the Law of Attraction. It gets activated because you start to actively focus on what you want; e.g., if you want wealth in your life, you would have started to focus on wealth. Instead of doing the usual, which was to focus on the *lack* of wealth, now you are focusing on the abundance of it and the inevitability of the wanted wealth coming into your life, or better yet, you are focusing on the "fact" that it is *already* here. Now that you have told the RAS that wealth is important to you, the Reticular Formation will "allow" the stimulus provided by all things that could be considered wealth related, or wealth itself, into your perception.

This wealth, information about wealth, or anything at all related to the creation of wealth – all of these – were already around you, but you had been blocking them from the perception of your physical senses because you had specifically, however unknowingly and unwittingly, "told" your RAS to block it. And you had done so by telling your RAS to focus on the *lack* of wealth, and thus only allow, into your perception, all the things associated with lack of wealth, and how to create it. Since it is not the boss of you, you are the boss of it; the RAS simply obeys your commands to it!

So, again, the RF, Reticular Formation, does get activated; however, we also really do start to attract *new* events, people, places, things, circumstances, opportunities or whatever is going to get the "event" that we have been meaning to manifest with our thoughts, to actual manifestation. This is the Law of Attraction working at the vibratory energetic level, and thus, magnetizing and attracting wanted things to you.

As you might have already surmised, the Law of Attraction *and* the Reticular Formation were working before also, and not only that, but also that they are always working. It's just that now both of these forces will be working to bring *wealth* instead of bringing the *lack* of wealth; i.e., *poverty*, to you. (Or any other thing that you want.)

Also, the activation of the Reticular Formation is the necessary precursor to the activation of the Law of Attraction. Again, since we know that both of these principles are always in action, this "activation" is really a "re-activation," but now in the direction of what is wanted, as opposed to what is not wanted.

Specific applications for specific situations

Before I moved on, I hope that I was able to clarify the difference between the Reticular Formation and the real effects of the Law of Attraction, as I wanted to do.

Anyway, I hope that you will use all the tools and principles mentioned in the previous chapter to bring wealth and prosperity into your life. Do not worry about *how*, exactly, you are going to get that money. As Mike Dooley says so wisely, "Don't mess with the cursed *how's*!"

To give you an example of this, here's something that happened to me very recently. There are many, many other similar stories that I could share with you, but this one is the latest.

About a year ago or so, I was starting to reach a point where all the money that I had received from my Severance Package was exhausted. I still had a few thousand dollars, but I had invested that money in the stock market. I did not want to sell the shares of the stocks that I owned unless I really had to do so, because the stock market was showing signs of recovery and I had faith that my investment will be worth a lot more in the near future.

By the way, I am a big fan of the stock market and financial guru, Jim Cramer, and I am a student of his teachings. I really do believe that one of the ways of creating financial wealth in our lives is by investing in the stock market. Of course, one should do their "homework," as Cramer suggests. I do have a set of his books listed in the Recommendations and Sources section at the end of this book. Please do check those out if you are even mildly interested in becoming wealthy. They are, truly, recommended reading from me, and they will change your financial life for the better. You may also want to watch his very entertaining and educational show, *Mad Money w/Jim Cramer*, on the highly esteemed financial news network, CNBC.

Anyway, since I was not planning on liquidating my stock portfolio, I started to think about what I would do when the money ran out. You could even say that I started to worry a little bit. But then I started to remind myself, everyday, when I did my meditation and visualization, that all I needed to do was have faith that I already had the money that I was going to need. Again, I did not have a clue as to how, exactly, that money would materialize, just that it would and I would not have to sell my shares of stock.

It was the beginning of the month of May, and I got a disturbing call from my former co-worker. Little over four years ago, at the height of the Real-Estate Boom, my co-worker and I had formed a business partnership and via that partnership, decided to buy this parcel of raw land in hopes of developing it or getting it ready for development, and then "flipping" it for a decent profit.

Well, we never ended up being able to sell it because our asking price for that parcel of land had been tad bit too high (it was not an outrageous one; in fact, it was smack-dab in the middle of the range of the prices that the market was supporting at that time). However, since this had been right after the real-estate market had peaked, and there was a huge "inventory" of properties for sale, the parcel stayed on the market and we never ended up being able to sell it.

So, fast forward to that day when I got the call from my business partner in May of 2009. He had gotten fed up with the fact that we had not sold this land yet and he was really antsy about doing something about it.

On that call he said, "Either you buy me out of my share or I buy you out of yours. We have to do something with this! My money is stuck in this deal, and I want it out. If you cannot buy me out, I will buy you out and have the freedom to do what I choose with this land."

When we had initially purchased the land, he had put in a lot of cash, up-front. I was only making monthly payments to him to help pay for my share of the initial cost of the land. I had made other investments into this deal, for example, for the engineering expenses

Specific applications for specific situations

and attorney's fees, etc. However, it was fractional, when compared to his initial investment. In short, if I wanted to buy him out, I would have had to come up with around $50,000. Conversely, he could have bought out my share by paying me approximately $16,000.

I, being the eternal optimist, still had hopes that we could sell this land and make a profit now that the real estate market had bottomed and was showing signs of a resurgence. My wife is a licensed real estate agent, and does real estate sales on a part-time basis. So she knew what was happening in the market as far as the movement of inventory in terms of homes and land was concerned, and the prices at which this inventory was moving.

My business partner had given me plenty of opportunities and ample time to dispose off the property, but nothing had happened yet. And so when I went to him, once again, with a request of giving me some more time to see if I could sell the land, he was not very receptive to the idea. However still, he gave me a couple of weeks to see what I could do. I almost found a buyer, but the deal did not come to fruition.

On May 27, 2009, my business partner ended up cutting me a Cashier's Check in the amount of $16,358.93 and buying me out of my share.

I ended up with the money that I needed!

2) Relationships - Whether it may be a romantic relationship or relationships with your family or friends, or even business partners or associates, the "rules of engagement" are the same.

Give to the other first what you wish to get for yourself *from* the other. You want your spouse to be more understanding and supportive; well, then be a more understanding and supportive spouse yourself. (I know, I know, this can be very difficult to do; I am married too! But do try, at least.) You want the young children in your family, whether they may be your children or grandchildren, to be more respectful, then give them the respect that they deserve.

God=mc²?

Mahatma Gandhi knew the Law of Attraction very well. One of his quotes that is very famous is "*Be* the change that you would like to see in the world."

In the case of your searching for a perfect romantic partner, quite literally, *become* the kind of person you would want to attract to yourself. If you want a genuinely loving and caring person as your mate, then become that way yourself, if you are not so already. If you want a spiritually oriented person as your boyfriend/girlfriend, then become a spiritually oriented person yourself.

Sometimes the other person that you may have been wanting to create a relationship with just may not be the person for you. And we all do get a "gut feeling" about this anyway. A feeling that although you want somebody to be in your life, there is just something not quite right about the person or the situation. But somehow we tend to ignore or override that feeling, and in due time, we find out that we were, in fact, right. In that event, you will know that there is somebody else who is just right, waiting to come into your life. You just have to be open and receptive to the fact that this person you currently want in your life is not the kind of person you truly want, and that the one that is perfect for you *will* come along. This could apply to somebody who may already be in your life, and you might realize that they are not right for you.

Or if your family members simply don't approve of what you are doing or wanting to do; for example, choose a career path that they don't agree with or marry a person whom they don't approve of, in that case you just have to know that whatever you are doing is right for you. You don't have to be disrespectful towards them, even if they are that way to you. And I know that this can be very difficult to do, and sometimes you may feel that you just don't have a choice but to react in the same way. Try to do your best in being kind in your response.

3) Health - This can be a tricky subject to talk about just because so much can go wrong if we don't know what, exactly, is the source of our illness.

Specific applications for specific situations

Again, I do reiterate that I am not a medical doctor, or for that matter, a doctor of any kind. So, please seek advice from a licensed professional in the medical field regarding any and all medical conditions that you may be suffering from. Having gotten that disclaimer out of the way, regardless of what you may be suffering from, you can always *add* the power of your soul to the power of medicine to heal whatever may be ailing you.

Even if there may be an identifiable physical source or reason for an illness, ultimately that physical reason can be attributed to some sort of an ill-thinking. Scientists have proven that stressful and negative thoughts do lead to high blood-pressure and ulcers and other such physical ailments. Nowadays, doctors and other medical professionals, and scientists, have no problems acknowledging the mind-body connection.

Poor diet, alcohol and tobacco abuse, the use of other narcotics and other such self-destructive habits do have their negative physical and non-physical effects on the human body. This is not news to us. These habits, and in most cases they are addictions, have the capacity to destroy perfectly healthy bodies and minds. They cause debilitating, life-threatening, or downright terminal diseases, don't they? Lung cancer or emphysema from smoking; liver damage from drinking or drug abuse; Diabetes and Hypertension from poor diet, and lack of physical exercise. These are just a few of the several maladies that are attributed to a poor life-style. One would think that most of these would be caused by physical problems or deficiencies; however, I think that they are caused by spiritual deficiencies or lacks. Or at least a combination thereof.

So, of course, an addiction-free lifestyle, proper diet and exercise are obvious ways of maintaining a healthy body and mind. However, having a positive attitude towards life and living a spiritually-oriented one are also essential requirements to creating a healthy, disease-free mind, body, intellect, and spirit. And of course, also in moving towards creating and leading a life of our dreams, and becoming blissfully happy, a goal that this book is dedicated to.

God=mc²?

In an unfortunate event of your suffering from an ailment of any kind, of course, apart from getting the proper medical attention from a doctor, imagine yourselves as already being healed from that ailment or disease. Try to feel, as much as possible, as you would feel if you were your healthy self again, and give thanks for being healthy. This process will help the medical treatment to work in an even better and faster way.

In late November or early December of 2009, I happened to catch this particular segment on my favorite cable network, you guessed it, CNBC. The topic of discussion was that the big pharmaceutical companies are really concerned about the growing prominence of the Placebo Effect and how, during clinical trials, these Placebos - Sugar Pills or pills that have no medicinal qualities or value - are actually beating out the effects of specialized pharmaceutical drugs. In other words, the test subjects who take these Placebos are experiencing a *bigger* benefit versus the test subjects taking the actual medical drug meant to treat whatever ailment they may be suffering from.

You might have heard about this famous Placebo Effect and how it shows us the true power of our minds and the true power of our thoughts and beliefs. Scientists have recognized and acknowledged this effect for years, or maybe even decades. And as per this program that I was watching, this Effect is *increasing* in frequency and intensity. This increase is an alarming one to the drug companies, and it is making them take notice of it. And quite frankly, I was glad that they were admitting this on national TV, for everybody to see and hear.

This can only mean one thing: More and more people are realizing the genuine power of their thoughts and beliefs! This is just gravy, as they say, as far as the scientific evidence that I have presented so far and am trying to present via this book. To use another food metaphor, it is just icing on the cake!

Specific applications for specific situations

However, based on this *proven scientific* phenomenon, I do have a rhetorical question to ask: If we all, including scientists and doctors, can agree that this Placebo Effect does take place as far as pharmaceutical drugs are concerned, why cannot we agree that this same effect of belief works with anything and everything else in life?

Like I said, it was a rhetorical question. It absolutely *does* work with anything and everything else!

4) Physical attractiveness, physique and weight-loss - There is a lot more of a thought element to these things than one would think. (Sorry about that pun.)

You might have heard this before that when somebody is really confident, they just *seem* to be more attractive, don't they? Also, when somebody is genuinely comfortable "in their skin," that also seems to make them more appealing. Even more so than somebody else who may have a better looking body and may even be more beautiful or handsome, or more accomplished and successful.

To be comfortable with who or what one is and to be confident in oneself are not too very different from each other. The only real difference may be that sometimes confidence can be mistaken for arrogance, whereas the level of comfort that one feels "being oneself" comes across more so as a cool, low-key demeanor.

So, just having or developing a certain attitude about yourself can lead to your being more attractive.

However, let's say that you don't want to just *seem* attractive; you actually want to *be* as physically attractive as possible. What do you do then? Well, you apply the same principles here as well. You see yourself, in your mind's eye, as having the physically attractive body that you want. You feel the feelings of that. You imagine that people are noticing you, admiring you, and complimenting you on your perfect physique or figure. You give genuine, heartfelt thanks for this. Before you know it, you will be doing the physical things that will bring about those changes in your body. You will find that

God=mc²?

you are eating a healthier, leaner diet. You will find that you are inspired to exercise. All of these inspirations will lead you to becoming the person that you want to become, physically. All of this will only lead to the increase in your self-confidence, and that, in turn, will only add to your attractiveness.

Also, your feelings and thoughts about exercising; i.e., simply your conscious awareness about the fact that you are engaged in physical activity will turbo-charge your work-out routines. In other words, and to use a more concrete example, let's say that you already have a work-out regimen. In that case, think conscious and deliberate thoughts that you are, in fact, working out and imagine getting even more of a beneficial response from those work-outs. (A "beneficial response" could be one or more of the very reasons why you started to work-out, to begin with - fitness and endurance, weight-loss, muscle-development, greater flexibility, decrease in blood-pressure, lower cholesterol - any and all health benefits one expects to receive from exercise.)

By your adding what I like to call a "Thought Work-Out" to your already existing physical training or exercise routine, you will start seeing better results without doing anything more, physically. And if you don't have a formal and set routine, but you do engage in some physical activity every day, then simply start thinking of it *as* "exercise." By your doing so, you will start getting the benefits *of* exercise from that non-exercise physical activity. Again, I am talking about benefits that you were *not* getting before, even though you were engaged in the physical activity.

For example, I live in a four-story townhouse-style condo, with three living levels, with the main door on the first floor or ground level. This door leads to the staircase to the second door which is the entrance into my living room on the second floor. On an average day, I am climbing up and down the stairs, from my living room located on the second floor, to the third floor where two of our bedrooms are located, fifteen to twenty times. Often, I am also

Specific applications for specific situations

climbing up to the fourth floor loft. Ever since my wife and I moved into this condo, which was a little over five years ago, I have always held the conscious thought that these climbs, up and down the stairs in my home, are, in fact, exercise.

And now, for over two years, since the birth of our son, I am doing so while carrying him in my arms many times. So, in my mind, I have added weight-resistance to increase the intensity of my exercise. Oh, and by the way, we have cathedral ceilings on the second floor, so they are nine or ten foot ceilings, and the ceilings on the other levels are also higher than the normal seven foot ceilings. Which means that the flight of stairs between the floors is longer than usual; there are three-four more steps than a staircase in a normal townhouse-style home; i.e., one with multiple living levels but with normal-height ceilings. You may not think that this is significant, but had mine been a home with regular height ceilings, then I would have climbed 82,125 *fewer* steps in the last five years. That is a *lot* of exercise that I would *not* have gotten.

(I arrived at the number this way: 15 climbs per day, on average X 365 days in a year X 5 years X 3 extra steps in the staircase = 82,125 *extra* steps climbed in the last 5 years.)

Okay, in all honesty, it sounds like a lot because it is spread out over five years, but it is a fact that every little bit of physical activity helps. And every little bit more helps at least that much more.

This talk about engaging in more physical activity is a little bit of a diversion from the point that I am actually trying to make; however, I decided to take the detour because I wanted to emphasize the point made in the previous paragraph before saying what I am about to say.

I genuinely believe that by my simply *thinking* that I was engaging in exercise every time I climbed up or down the stairs in my home, I actually *received* the benefits *of* exercise. And if I had not thought that, I would not have gotten any benefits from the stair-

God=mc²?

climbing. It would not have been more beneficial even if I had ten extra steps in the staircases of my home, and even if I had been climbing them 25 times a day *if* I did not believe that it was exercise.

So, believing or thinking of any and all physical activity as exercise provides the body with the benefit of exercise, and if you engage in even a little bit more of an activity, your mind will provide the added benefit of that added activity.

You might have seen the TV commercial for a wonderfully simple yet brilliant product from Philips called the DirectLife Activity Monitor. In the ad, they show this guy sitting on an exercise ball, while he is in his office, working. Then they show a lady doing a body-stretch while she is filling water into a pitcher, and lastly, they show another person jumping over the turnstiles and climbing down the stairs instead of taking the escalator down, or something to that effect. This monitor works because it makes you actively think about all your physical movement. In other words, it adds the power of your conscious awareness to the already occurring physical activity, which, in turn, makes you think of that movement as exercise. Then, of course, you actually get the benefit of exercise. Also, now "knowing" that all your activity is, in fact, exercise, you tend to do more of it. This, in turn, only makes this process work that much better. (For more information on this great product, please see www.directlife.philips.com.)

As I mentioned before, this process of adding your conscious awareness to receive an increased response to exercise works with all types of beneficial categories including weight-loss goals. You want to imagine what your perfect weight is, and think that you are at that weight already, and give thanks for it.

I have never really had a problem with body-weight all my life, and I have never really worried about it much. Well, up until maybe a few years ago. I don't know how, but I had picked up on thoughts that had made me think about certain foods or drinks, especially beer,

Specific applications for specific situations

that they will give me a paunch. Consequently, I developed what is popularly known as a "Beer Belly." (I don't know if *popularly* is the right word.) And so I tried to avoid these foods and drinks. However, now, I have realized that my thoughts are the culprit for my paunch and not what I have been consuming.

Dr. Dyer says "You are not what you eat; you are what you believe about what you eat!" So, you could change your thoughts and drop these erroneous beliefs or you could do whatever you think is going to get you to your ideal weight, and in that case, the only things left to do would be to exercise and eat a healthier diet.

In other words, if you come to a conclusion that the reasons for your physical weight-gain are only and exclusively physical - food and/or lack of exercise - then you don't have a choice but to work on manipulating those physical sources or reasons.

The ideal combination, in my opinion, would be to stop *thinking* that food is responsible for your weight-gain and at the same time focus on eating healthy foods, and also engaging in physical exercise. (Notice that I did not say "focus on eating 'non-fattening' foods." Again, you don't want to focus on the aspect of the food that you attribute to your weight-gain, rather you want to simply focus on eating "healthy" foods, and therefore, on having a healthy body, at an ideal body-weight.)

I would also add that, ultimately, one is concerned about one's own body-weight - the actual number of Pounds or Kilograms one weighs - *only* because of the assumption that the higher the weight, the less physically attractive the person is, and not to mention, also less healthy he/she is.

Let's say that you were a woman weighing 170 Pounds. Before you rip me to shreds for having said that, let's also assume that you were also pronounced the sexiest woman on the planet! Would you care that you weighed 170 Lbs?

God=mc²?

Well, you actually might care very much about it. About how, exactly, you could *maintain* that weight! Wouldn't you?

That example was only meant as that, an example. *Generally* speaking, a person who is overweight is also generally less healthy than somebody who is not. Again, this says nothing at all about their attractiveness.

When you see yourself as what you truly are, primarily a spiritual being, you will have a completely different outlook on life, and about yourself. These erroneous beliefs and assumptions about yourself and for that matter, about others also, will simply fall away. Again, I am not saying you won't want to be physically attractive anymore; it's just that you won't give it the *false* importance that you used to give it. On the other hand, you will give a lot more importance to being healthy because this body is the vehicle; a conduit; via which you can do what you came here to do.

This works. It simply works!

5) Achievement in career or business - You *can* enjoy a non-competitive "winning streak" in your business or career. You may be wondering, "How is a *non*-competitive winning streak possible in any competitive endeavor?"

If you want to achieve a goal in your career, job or business, you can do it without wishing or causing harm to your so-called competitor. Competition is only created when there is an erroneous belief prevalent that there is not enough of whatever is being competed for. (You may have heard this before in *The Secret* and elsewhere.)

In order to accomplish this, you should focus only on what your own goal is. Let the others do what they want to do or what they must do. This does not mean that you don't defend yourself if and when attacked in any way, shape or form. And this could mean being attacked competitively by a negative ad campaign, or somebody else coming up with a product or service that they claim to be better than

Specific applications for specific situations

yours, but it truly isn't. It just means that you, yourself, don't do the attacking. However, ultimately, do the thing that feels the most right to you. I have confidence that you will know what that is because you will be a person who is truly guided by his or her own conscience. And when you do that, career success will search for you and find you. You won't be able to hide from it; not that you would ever want to hide from it.

Obviously, this specific example goes hand-in-hand with achieving wealth or abundance because we normally associate how we make our money with what we do; i.e., the business we engage in or what our career is in terms of a job, profession, or vocation. So, if you know, for sure, what you would love to do, then simply do it. That will be the best way to achieve success in whatever you do.

You might have heard this phrase said about somebody who might be a little arrogant or boastful, and generally, it is a guy: "He is a legend, but only in his own mind." Well, you do have to become a legend in your own mind, in a way, for the Law of Attraction to kick in. Just be careful about whom you share your thoughts with. If they don't know enough about you, they may start to think that you are suffering from "delusions of grandeur," and that there was something seriously wrong with you, emotionally or mentally. (I am sharing from personal experience because I have been laughed-at and ridiculed by some folks close to me for having shared my goals and dreams with them.)

Again, please don't get me wrong. I am not talking about becoming over-confident or arrogant; I am talking about developing genuine self-esteem and a genuine sense that you are quite capable of accomplishing anything at all. (Because you are!) And not only that, you have already accomplished it (in your mind, that is). As we now know, what is true now in physical reality, *had* to have been true in the spiritual realm first. So, it is the same with achieving success in your career or business goals also. And quite frankly, with anything and everything else. The end-result has to be true and real in your mind first.

God=mc²?

Having said that, I would like to move onto what I have heard the super-successful real estate mogul, Donald Trump, say several times, "Do what you are passionate about!" I agree with him wholeheartedly. It is the same thing as I have mentioned before a couple of times, just in different ways. When you are passionate about something, first of all, you will be naturally good at it. Secondly, if you are not that good at it, you will be genuinely inclined to get better at it. Thirdly, you will just love what you do and enjoy doing it, and therefore, will be happy doing it, and so you won't care if you have been doing it for too long - whatever your measure of time may be - hours, days, weeks, months, years, or even a whole lifetime. And fourthly, since this will be something that you just love and enjoy, and it brings you success, and money and happiness, you will *want* to do it forever. And finally, as we all know how this works, all of these positive results will only end up being cause for more of the same. Happiness is a powerful electro-magnet that attracts even more of the other good things along with it - more success and money - and even *more* happiness. Isn't *that* interesting?

It will end up being a virtuous cycle, and you will love being spun around in it.

6) Sports or other competitive situations - Sports and business have both been compared to war often. You may even have heard the invoking of *The Art of War*, Sun-Tzu's principles of military dominance, as they may relate to competitive business and sporting situations. And the analogy is a good one, in terms of a competitive business or in case of a sporting event, the opposing team being one's adversary. However, this analogy can, and does lead to one seeing the other as their "mortal enemy." Now, *that* is not so good!

There are, in fact, some similarities in this item when compared to the previous item; i.e., the one related to achievement in career or business, and so I won't be redundant and repeat the points that may be common to both. Just like in the achievement of business or career goals, one can still achieve great success in sports; however,

Specific applications for specific situations

one should only focus on what one's own goal is, and not worry about being better than another person or another team. The concern should be about being the best *one* can be. There is a difference between wanting to be the best that one can be, and wanting to simply be better than another person. Just because you may be better at something than another person does not necessarily mean that you are the best that you can be.

Sports, or I should specify, *spectator* sports, are *more* a form of entertainment than anything else. This is not like the gladiators of old; one does not have to kill the other, or perish themselves. The physical survival of one person (or team) does not depend on the opposing one's demise.

However, nowadays, there is more boasting about how superior one's team is as opposed to another's. This bragging can come from the team members of a particular professional sport or it can come from the loyal and even not-so-loyal followers of a team. Sure, this generates more furor and more ticket sales, and ratings on TV for the broadcast of these sporting events, and therefore, ultimately, more money for the teams, and their owners, and the players and the sponsors, and so on and so forth. Mostly, this is in regards to professional sports; however, certain amateur events such as college football and basketball generate the same kind of a response from the fans.

There is nothing wrong, per se, with what I just mentioned; however, there used to be this honor and respect prevalent and expressed among sportsmen. A Code which used to be called the Sportsman's Spirit. It is probably still called that, but I just don't see it expressed much, nowadays.

Again, if there is genuine cause for celebration; i.e., for the victory of one's team, sure, one *should* celebrate. And that includes not just the team members, but the fans also. However, the celebration should be appropriate. Is there a need for riots and looting, and

God=mc²?

burning and turning cars over and such? Is there *ever* such a need, regardless of whether it is a celebration of victory or the mourning of a loss? What would doing these things prove, anyway? I just don't get it, but maybe I am just naïve.

Don't get me wrong, I am very happy when my beloved Red Sox are winning in any game at all, forget about it being the Playoffs, the ALCS, or even the World Series. I remember that I cried happy tears when they finally won, after an 86 year drought. And I have only been a fan for a handful of years! Before that, when I was growing up in India, I remember being passionate about the Indian Cricket team, and especially how the furor reached a "fever pitch" in the stadium when India was playing against their arch nemesis, the Pakistani team. The situation was very similar in every single household with a television or radio set in either of these neighboring, yet feuding countries; the combined populations of which would have been at least a billion people, even at that time. And these were countries which had *actually* gone to war, militarily, three times!

Anyway, back in our good ol' U.S. of A., when the Red Sox won the World Series in 2004, I do remember, very clearly, that they played Etta James' song, *At Last*, on TV as part of a promo, and I balled my eyes out. But I was not out there on the streets throwing debris around and turning into a pyromaniac.

As you have read my words before, I am surely not against making money. I am, obviously, not a prophet of anything, but if I were to be one, I would be the "prophet of profit," as Jim Cramer would say, I think. In fact, I am in favor of *unlimited* profits. Just profits earned in a righteous manner. And that is absolutely possible.

Anyhow, this is more of just a personal commentary on what I think may be wrong with the world of competitive sports today. I just don't see the genuine Spirit of the Sportsman anymore. Players being rude to each other, and engaging in "Trash Talk." Baseball players taking anabolic steroids and other illegal substances to

Specific applications for specific situations

enhance their performance and resorting to other such unnecessary measures. Do we really need to watch muscle-bound barbarians ripping each other to shreds, so to speak? I thought *that* was a Medieval thing to do, no? Maybe there is some "animalistic" need for that; however, I can assure you that there can be no *spiritual* need or benefit from it.

With the degradation and deterioration of the Sportsman's Spirit also comes the degradation and deterioration of the Everyman's Spirit. One does not have to be the reason for another, necessarily. However, causality, if it were a factor, would probably be active in the reverse direction. Meaning that the deficiency in Everyman's Spirit has led to the same in the Sportsman's Spirit, also.

(Here when I say "Sportsman," or "Everyman," I don't just mean the male human; I mean it in the more universal and unisex kind of way. I hope that this reference reminds you of an episode of the super-hit show *Friends* where one of the characters uses the word "guys" to refer to a few of the other female characters in the show, and then clarifies that she does not mean that to be just "men.")

Anyhow, I really do feel like Tom Cruise's title-character, *Jerry McGuire*, at this moment, and so what I am going to do is print out copies of this "Memo"; no, no; this "Mission Statement," and send it to all the owners/shareholders of all the professional teams, and also to all the executives in charge of making the decisions regarding the broadcast of sporting events on TV and other media. Hopefully they will see that we have all, collectively, "created this monster" and we can all take action to tame it.

Whether it is sports, arts, business or a job-based career, I hope that we can all come to a place of realization about one thing, and that is that there *really* is *more* than enough to go around. In fact, there is *infinitely* more than "more than enough!" Just imagine what that phrase means. Let go of all competitive thoughts or feelings in your mind and your heart. And now try to feel how it feels. If you

God=mc²?

just knew that there was nothing you needed to compete for, then wouldn't there be a sense of a calming relief that you would allow yourself to feel? That you can just live, just feel, and just be.

I had heard Self-help guru Tony Robbins say that we are not "human *doings*," we are "human *beings*," so just "be!"

So, there, these were some of the examples of specific situations that in which you could use the spiritual principles mentioned in the last chapter, and as a whole, mentioned in this book. Do keep in mind, again, that you can use the same process to create the result that you want, in any situation, in any endeavor, for any reason, whatsoever, because it simply works.

Chapter 27
Meditate; don't medicate!
(Well, medicate to heal your body; meditate to heal your soul)

In the late 1980's, The C + C Music Factory sang, "Rock & Roll to please your soul." Well, I have a better, more permanent way to please your soul. It is called meditation. (I have nothing against Rock & Roll, by the way.)

Please let it be known, again, that I am not a medical doctor and medication should be taken to heal physical and even mental/emotional disorders. But the soul, well, that needs meditation.

Like with everything else we have talked about and examined, we will do the same with meditation and find out really what it is, once and for all.

About 25 years ago or so, I had first heard the definition of meditation. I had gone to Mumbai, and had been visiting the home of one of my paternal aunts. I have a very vivid recollection of this particular conversation with my cousin, Vipul Majithia. Although I

God=mc²?

don't remember how and why the topic of Yoga had come up, but it had. That led to the topic of meditation, and since he was very much into Yoga and meditation and other breathing exercises at that time, I asked him, "What is meditation, and how do I do it?"

He replied, "Meditation is *thinking* about *nothing*."

After hearing that, I do remember being a bit baffled, and thinking to myself, "How would I do *that*? I am *always* thinking about *something*. I cannot think about nothing. It's impossible." My 10-year old brain could not fathom how that could happen. Then, I remember asking my cousin, "How can we, when we are awake, have no thought at all? How is that even possible?!"

He told me that it was, in fact, very possible and went on to explain in detail, how it was possible. The following few paragraphs will clarify how.

Thinking about "nothing" is possible because there is a gap; a space; a time when there is really *no* thought in our mind. And that empty space exists *between* any two distinct thoughts that we may have. In terms of time, it is extremely small, maybe millionths of a second or thousandths of a second, but at that level, does it really matter? Our minds are not sensitive enough to know the difference between those two vastly different - a thousand times different - durations of time. I am talking about a thousandth of a second vs. a millionth of a second.

Regardless of the details about the exact time durations, the fact is that there exists this gap between our thoughts. And our goal, as we start to meditate, is to expand that gap - to make that chasm of "non-thought" progressively bigger. And not only that, but to eventually, with practice, be able to get to that mind-space of non-thought at will - whenever, wherever, and for however long - we may want to do so.

The way to specifically think about nothing is to first start by trying to focus and concentrate your thoughts on two, and only two,

Meditate; don't medicate!

specific things. The quantity of *two* is extremely important because we want to really hone in on the mind-space between the two. You can work with images or words in your mind; however, try to learn to focus on those two distinct images or words. You want to be able to "see" them clearly, in your mind's eye. You could use the words "Jesus" and "Christ" as two *different* words, as long as you can see the actual words and not the image of Jesus Christ in your mind's eye.

If you prefer images to words, then use two different images. In that case, you could use the image or picture of Jesus Christ as one image, and the other image could be of Lord Krishna. Of course, they do not have to be religious images; they can be images of anything at all. One could be of a boat, and another could be of a car! If and when using words, you would want to focus on the actual spelling of the word "car" in your mind, and then immediately go onto to focusing on the word "boat" in your mind.

What you want to do is focus on the first image or word with all your attention, and you can keep mentally repeating the appearance of the first word or image in your mind. You could think and focus on the word "car" repeatedly. "Car, car, car, car, car." And then switch to focusing on the word "boat" and keep repeating that. Ideally, if you can simply "hold" the first word or image, without actually repeating it, that's even better. And then, switch to focusing on and holding the second word.

When you switch from focusing on the first word to the second one, you will realize that there really is a gap between those two words, when there is no thought in your mind. If you don't "find" the empty mind-space when you go from the first word to the second one, then try to go backwards from the second word to the first one. Sometimes, that works.

Please do realize that the first time you do find the space between your thoughts, it may seem to last for only a fraction of a second. However, that feeling of being there will be unmistakable! There is no way for me to explain to you how that would feel like; you will just know, with certainty, that you are there. Try to just "be" there. As soon as you get an actual thought that says, "Whoo-hoo, congratulations! You are now in that place of non-thought," guess what, you just had a thought, and so now, you are no longer in the place of non-thought. But with practice, you will stay in this place of non-thought longer and longer.

So, what I suggest is that while you are doing this, be very easy about the whole thing. This should not feel like a lot of work to you. In fact, it should not feel like work at all. Indian spiritual leader and humanitarian, and founder of The Art of Living Foundation, Sri Sri Ravi Shankar, says that meditation should be effortless. And if you don't feel that it is, it will *become* effortless, eventually, but for this to happen you have to, ironically, start with that feeling first. While meditating, if another thought or another image, one that you had not "planned" on thinking or seeing in your mind's eye pops up, don't resist it. Let it appear, and let it be there, and then let it go. This may happen again, and may happen several times. Just know that it is perfectly okay.

This is perfectly okay and completely normal because we are so used to thinking all kinds of different thoughts throughout our day. So, until you have trained your mind to gently block other thoughts that you don't intend to think deliberately, they will pop into your mind here and there.

It is like muscle building - once you start working out a muscle - it gets progressively stronger, and physically bigger. A bicep can allow you to lift heavier and heavier weights and for longer and longer durations of time as it slowly grows stronger from exercise.

There is really no short-cut to learning how to meditate! We just have to practice meditating. We just have to work out, just like it is with physical exercise. It is the same with meditation. The only

Meditate; don't medicate!

way to, first, learn how to meditate and secondly, to get better at it is to *start* meditating.

I would recommend a wonderful book, aptly entitled *Getting in the Gap*, by my self-proclaimed spiritual guru, Dr. Wayne Dyer. He explains, in detail, not only the process of learning how to meditate, but also the myriad benefits of doing so. In the book, Dr. Dyer defines meditation as "making conscious contact with God."

I have also heard another very similar thing about meditation. That when we are meditating, we are in vibrational harmony with who we really are, which is a spiritual being. This is because when we have no thought at all, we don't have any negative thoughts, by necessity, because we are not thinking about anything at all, positive *or* negative. When we have negative thoughts we are in a vibrational discord with who we are, because who we really are is a part of God. There is no negativity in God! God is only positive energy. And so, while we are being negative, we are not being god-like.

Esther and Jerry Hicks say, while channeling the spiritual entities called Abraham, that they would prefer us to have pure positive thoughts all the time than to have no thought at all. However, that is a very difficult thing to achieve, and so they would settle for us having no thought for *some* time of our day.

At least this way, they would say, we can ensure that we are not having negative thoughts *all* the time. Of course, the next goal is to have more positive thoughts, and then eventually *only* have *positive* thoughts.

As it may be clear to you by now, meditation is simply a way to control one's mind and one's thoughts. And as we understand some of the concepts of practical spirituality, we understand that learning how to control one's mind is the single most important thing one can learn to do, in order to realize the ultimate goal of creating a life of one's dreams.

God=mc²?

Apart from thinking about nothing at all, we can actually meditate "on" something specific. We can have very focused and concentrated thoughts about something we would like to accomplish or manifest in our life. We can meditate on a *mantra* or visualize scenarios which depict specifics of the life of our dreams. For example, we can simply meditate on the mantra of "Om," or "Aum," which is considered to be the primordial sound of the Universe; i.e., the sound that existed even before the Universe came into existence, the sound of God. As I will discuss in much more detail in the next chapter, we can also meditate on the chakras in our body in order to remove blockages of energy located there.

Or we can think and see mental pictures of the life that we would like to create. For example, you could see yourself with your perfect life-partner, walking, hand-in-hand, with him or her on the beach, or you could imagine yourself driving a Porsche. In other words, we can even visualize during a meditative session.

So to reiterate, meditation is simply a way to control one's mind and one's thoughts. Or learning how to focus concentrated thoughts on a thing, event, *mantra*, or chakra. Learning how to control one's mind is the single most important thing one can learn to do because all realities that we choose to manifest first start in thought.

Chapter 28
Kundalini Rising!
How you can use the power of this evolutionary energy to change yourself and the world

There are these chakras in our body, as you might have heard about lately. *Chakra* is a Sanskrit word meaning a "wheel." Or a circle, or a center. Here, in the context of our bodies, it represents a center of energy.

And it is absolutely true that we have these centers of energy in our body. And this is scientifically verifiable!

Here are a few lines from a wonderful book entitled *Chakra Meditation*, by Swami Saradananda (and I recommend this book very highly): "Today, the term is usually associated with seven focal points of radiant power, or vital energy, within the subtle body. These are centered around the base of your spine, lower abdomen, solar plexus, heart, throat, forehead and crown of the head."

God=mc²?

"Someone with medical training might understand chakras as energetic centers approximating the nerve plexuses in the physical body. A clairvoyant might regard chakras as vortices of energy. A yogi would define chakras as centers of spiritual consciousness. And psychologists use the chakra system to map the development of the human personality. Each is correct."

So, as mentioned above, we have seven chakras of energy in our body. And they match up with, or pertain to, certain propensities and tendencies that we may have, or demonstrate. They are also essential to the proper functioning of bodily organs. In other words, chakras have an effect on the body, mind and as you will read in the next few paragraphs, also on the spirit.

At the base of the spine resides this infinite spiritual energy called *Kundalini*. It lies dormant there as a "coiled serpent," as that is what the Sanskrit word *Kundalini* means. It is akin to a metal spring pushed or squeezed down so that there is no space between its coils. Imagine the potential energy in that spring and what would happen when it is let go or released!

In this case, it is infinite *spiritual* energy that is "squeezed" into a "spring" and this spring sits at the base of our spine. As we practice meditation and also learn to become more spiritually oriented, this energy starts to make its move upwards through the chakras in our body, and it eventually reaches our Crown chakra, and breaks through it. Since *Kundalini* is a conscious spiritual energy, it expands our consciousness and awareness into the entire Universe. This is when we have the experience of Enlightenment and Bliss.

(In chapters 29 through 33, we will discuss, in much more detail, how changing ourselves by engaging in these spiritual activities not only brings benefits to us, but how it also does the same for the whole world.)

Therefore, meditation on the chakras, and the resulting removal of energy blockages at each of the chakras, is essential to our advancing on the path to higher consciousness.

Kundalini Rising!

Having said that, I would like to say that there is a lot more to the chakras and the proper meditation techniques associated with them. The discussion of these details is not possible within the scope of this book; however, I did want to make a mention of the chakras and *Kundalini* energy, in case you had not heard about them, or if you had already heard about them, to give you some clarity as to what they are. I strongly recommend and suggest that you get the book, *Chakra Meditation*, if this is of even mild interest to you.

Chapter 29
Pro Bono
(Hint: This does *not* mean "being in favor of the band U2's lead singer")

"For the greater good" or "for the good of the public." Pro bono - Latin in origin. Of course, the pronunciation of the name of the lead singer of U2, Bono, is different from the phrase that I am quoting here, but in writing, it is the same. (Incidentally, U2's Bono does do a lot of pro bono work, and that is very admirable.)

You might have heard the phrase, *pro bono*, being thrown around in movies and on TV, especially on legal dramas like Law & Order and Boston Legal, etc.

"Why do only lawyers get to do pro bono work?" you might think. Or you might think that they are the only profession that has simply thought about doing such work - at no charge, and for a greater cause - for something that is greater than a profit or a wage. For the good of the community, or school or city or whatever, in order to earn good Karma. Of course, doctors and nurses and people in many other professions do pro bono work all the time, and that too,

God=mc²?

without ever hearing a single word of appreciation or mass publicity of their work. So, it's not just lawyers who do pro bono work, and it is great that so many people are engaged in such work.

However, we have to be aware of the true motives behind somebody doing pro bono work. The motives are not always so innocent or innocuous as they may seem. I should say that in *most* cases, they truly are, but just that not in *all* of them. The not-so-innocent motives might include gaining publicity and notoriety in order to, ultimately, profit from this new-found exposure, and the resulting increased interest in a particular person of a particular profession doing the pro bono work. And to a lesser harmful degree, in order to mitigate guilt felt due to having done other "bad" things (not necessarily to mitigate the bad actions themselves, i.e., the bad Karma of those bad actions, but simply to "feel" better by doing a good act, and there certainly is a difference between the two).

On *Nip/Tuck*, the highly provocative and stylized show on the FX channel that had its series finale just recently, the lead characters of the show - the two best buds from college - these two hot-shot plastic surgeons would often take on a very difficult and highly publicized case, on a pro bono basis just to further their careers.

Well, to be totally accurate, the character in the name of Dr. Christian Troy, played by Julian McMahon, was the one into the profit potential of such publicity. Whereas Dylan Walsh's character, Dr. Sean McNamara, was truly interested in doing good, without getting anything in return except for the satisfaction derived from having helped somebody.

Again, please don't get me wrong; even these things are not bad as long as nobody is being exploited for profit. However, that is rarely the case; somebody is always being exploited. There is nothing at all wrong with profit; what is wrong is the exploitation of people or circumstances to achieve profits.

Pro Bono

You might hear about some big movie star or some other type of celebrity claiming that they donated millions of dollars to charity. If you are a celebrity and you are talking about your donations or other acts of charity publicly because you want others to take the same initiative - well, then you are definitely worthy of praise! This is because you are *helping* the cause, and not *hurting* it, or trying to take advantage of it. And the same with anybody else trying to help the cause, whatever the cause may be.

If it is meant to get others to be inspired to do the same, then kudos to you; celebrity or not.

Other than the exception just mentioned, my thought has always been that the amount of the donation should be unknown and the donor anonymous. Then, and then *only*, is it *true* charity! Otherwise the donor is giving just so that they can be known to have done so. So that adoring fans can shower them with adulation and admiration, not to mention, "free" publicity (it is not really free because they did pay for it by the amount of the donations).

So, no different when it comes to pro bono work, or volunteer work - which is just charity of a different kind - the donation of your time and your talent and/or effort.

Why am I talking about the "greater good" here? Because humans possess the consciousness that allows them to empathize and sympathize with somebody when that somebody is in pain. The pain felt could be of any kind - mental, emotional, physical or spiritual.

Humans can sympathize with someone else who is going through a situation similar to what one may have gone through. Meaning that they have already experienced what the other may be experiencing, and therefore know, first hand, what that feels like. Also, humans have this unique capability of empathizing with somebody else. Without actually having gone through the same exact experience as someone else, we can *imagine* what it may be like to go through the experience that somebody else in pain might be going through.

God=mc²?

Of course, sympathy is normally stronger than empathy; however, I think of it this way - I don't absolutely *need* to be homeless to know how it might feel to be without a home. I don't *need* to be so poor so as to be starving to know what lack of food, and therefore, insatiable hunger, might feel like.

(In a way, I can tell you what that may feel like because I have experienced it, although it was a self-imposed fast due to my hunger strike against God.)

Humans can put themselves in the sufferer's shoes, so to speak, and imagine how that might feel, and then try to mitigate that pain somehow. And often, at the neglect of one's own profits or comforts.

Of course, we all are also woefully aware of "Schadenfruede," as the Germans call it, gaining pleasure from seeing another in misery. The *opposite* of sympathy. Taking guilty pleasure in another's pain. And in some cases, actually being the *cause* of the pain to begin with, so that later on, we can see the other in pain and relish it. Which, by the way, is the true definition of *envy*.

We have been taught to think that envy is a lesser evil than jealousy, however, the vice versa is true. Any wonder why envy, and not jealousy, is one of the "Seven Deadly Sins?"

Well, Karma is like a boomerang, it comes back, doesn't it? Okay, *only* if the boomerang is *perfectly* thrown and actually does not hit something in its trajectory, as my "mates" from Down Under would agree.

I am sure you have heard another version of that about 50,000 times, haven't you? Well, here it is, 50,001st time: You reap what you sow! We can all say it in unison - what goes around, comes around. Just like a perfectly thrown boomerang!

Karma is impartial - it just delivers what you deserve - good or bad. It is like Newton's third law of motion, "Every action has an equal and opposite reaction." Except, in this case - it is a *similar* reaction - good reactions for good actions, and bad reactions for bad actions. So, the reaction is equal in intensity or force; the direction is opposite, meaning if you were the "giver" or the "doer" of the action, then the reaction is being *received by* or *done to* you, and it is of the same type, good for good; bad for bad.

So, if you are at a place in your life where you have decided to do some good deeds to mitigate your bad Karma, then, first and foremost, stop doing the bad deeds that you may have been engaged in. Of course, that is only if you had been engaged in those bad deeds, whether they may have been in actions, words, or thoughts. That, right there, will stop the bad Karma from building up, which is what you do want to *begin* with.

"First, do no harm," to paraphrase a part of the Hippocratic Oath that new doctors take as part of becoming doctors. (Not to be confused with the Hypocritic Oath a few people seem to abide by, "Do as I say, not as I do," or "The rules apply to you, but not to me!" By the way, hypocrisy is a major contributor to the accumulation of some very bad Karma.)

So, if you are engaged in Schadenfruede or doing other harmful things to others, you are exercising your *choice* to build up bad Karma, and at the same time, you are not building up any good Karma. Now, that's a double-whammy, as they call it, to the advancement of your soul!

You do, after all, have the Free Will to choose; i.e., to choose to enjoy another's misery, to mitigate it, or to remain neutral. Just know that you will have to pay for it later; assuming that you have or had chosen to enjoy their misery. Unless, of course; or really, if you are *off*-course from where you wanted to be in your life because you are asleep at the wheel. And since you were not on-course, you have been rudely awakened by the alarm of "a series of unfortunate or unwanted events" happening in your life. And now that you have woken up and realized why those unwanted things were happening,

God=mc²?

and so, in the meantime, have actively been working to mitigate your own accumulated bad Karma.

In other words, if you have any kind of suffering in your life, or things are not going the way you want them to, even though you are being a good person, and not currently engaged in any harmful activities, you have to realize that the suffering is due to some other built-up bad Karma.

And truly *selfless* pro bono work is a sure-fire way of mitigating one's bad Karma. A perfect, but very simplistic, example is in the show *My Name is Earl*. (Sadly, now a cancelled show - I wonder, what did they ever do to deserve *that*, and to build up that kind of Karma?)

In the show, the title character, Earl, if that was not abundantly clear from the title of the show, had made an extensive list of "bad things" that he had done and the names of the people he had done them to. He had decided to, one-by-one, "make things right" by doing something that his victim would say would undo the damage caused to them by Earl. In this way, Earl would earn the right to cross them off his Karma List, and thereby undo the bad Karma that he had earned by "doing them wrong," initially.

That is a very good example of how bad Karma does come back to bite you in the butt, and what can be done to mitigate that. However, it is also a very simplistic example, and in reality, Karma does not work exactly that way – that good deeds don't *directly* mitigate and nullify equally bad deeds, as discussed in the chapter on Karma.

I do have a disclaimer about the word "selfless," as mentioned in the paragraph above the last one. I know that there really is such a thing, but it is extremely difficult to act truly selflessly or at least, act selflessly most of the time, unless you are a true Saint. Earl, as mentioned above, is no Saint! (As the viewers of the show might know.)

However, he does genuinely want to be a good person; much better than he used to be; but at the same time, he wants his life to be better also. In the Pilot episode of the show, Earl, a petty thief, wins a lottery jackpot, and then immediately gets hit by a car; ends up losing his winning ticket and also ends up in the hospital. If memory serves me well, while in the hospital, he happens to watch an episode of the Carson Daly show and hears him mention Karma, and how it works. As soon as he decides to make the Karma List, he finds his lost winning ticket! Thus, he makes the connection of good or bad events happening in his life to good or bad Karma, and comes up with the conclusion that, from that moment on, he will only do good deeds because he wants only good things in his life (as we all do).

So, he is not being truly selfless by making the Karma List and making things right for the people on the List. He is creating good Karma, and he may be mitigating his bad Karma. Again, I want to emphasize that he *could* be creating good Karma, and at the same time he *could* also be mitigating his bad Karma, but just that it is not necessary that he would be doing so by the same acts that are meant to be mitigating his bad Karma.

Not that there is anything wrong with that, as Jerry Seinfeld would say. In fact, there is everything right with that! It should be our goal to be just like Earl; even though he is no Saint, he is a good role model.

So, what I would suggest is that you see an act of supposed selflessness (and I am talking about your own act) as really a *selfish* act. The only difference being that you are doing that act for a much, much higher purpose; i.e., for the attainment of Self-Realization. And therefore, it is, ultimately, a "selfish" act.

Mike Dooley, my favorite teacher from *The Secret*, as I may have mentioned before, has said in his wonderful audio program called *Manifesting Change: It Couldn't Be Easier*, that even Mother Teresa had done what she had done for a selfish reason. As far as I know, Mother Teresa has not yet been canonized, although, she has been officially "beatified," i.e., declared as "blessed," meaning that there is a belief that she has ascended to heaven, and that she has the

God=mc²?

capacity to intercede on behalf of people who may pray in her name, as per the Roman Catholic Church. In other words, since she has not gone through the last process of canonization, and therefore, not yet deemed to be a true Saint, I would have to agree with Mike. However, even if that is the case, it does not take anything away from what she has done in her life, which, I think we all can agree.

Anyhow, coming back to our world of non-sainthood, as much as possible, try not to think of the end result; i.e., that you are going to be getting something in return other than simply the satisfaction of knowing that you helped somebody who needed the help. Just let it go. There is an old Eastern Indian saying that I have always remembered. Directly translated, it says "Do a good deed, and then throw it in a well."

The direct translation may not make sense; however, the meaning is that once you do a good deed, simply forget that you did it, and move on. Don't dwell on the implications of it for you other than the good feeling you may be experiencing. And then move on, preferably, to doing many other good deeds. "Don't dwell, just throw in a well." That's a better sounding and even rhyming new mantra that you may want to adopt.

Now it might be a little bit clearer as to why all of the religious and spiritual traditions teach us to "be a good person," to "do good deeds," and "think good thoughts," etc., etc. And of course, to think about and do something for the greater good. They have only said so because that is really the only way of bringing our own good to us.

Well, at least, the only lasting, truly satisfying *and* spiritually advancing way of doing so.

And these spiritual traditions truly wanted that for us.

Chapter 30
Can we *ever* afford to *not* be nice?

"Be nice. I want you to be nice until it's time to not be nice!"
- Patrick Swayze, as Dalton, *Road House*

The late Patrick Swayze said those words as a bouncer at a night club in the cult-classic of a movie, *Road House*. That sounds like sage advice, doesn't it? However, we have to realize that there is *never* a point when we can afford to *not* be nice.

Is it difficult to remain calm, and cool and maintain a good demeanor at all times? Of course it is, and it can be not just plain ol' difficult, it can be very difficult at times. Well, it is difficult, at first. With practice, like with anything else one would like to master, it becomes fairly easy. And then eventually, it becomes second nature. And then primary nature. It becomes who you are!

It is a matter of re-wiring the "circuitry" of our brains. Our brains have nerve cells called neurons. Neurons physically "wire" with each other to form "circuits" that "remember" things, events, names, places and are also responsible for us learning new motor skills or forming habits and addictive behaviors. More than that, these circuits

God=mc²?

also learn a particular reaction and also learn to form a pattern of behavior. This collection of circuits that form all memory, skill or behavior is called a "Neuronet." It is who we are, mentally.

(I first learned about this "Neuronet" from the hybrid film, *What the Bleep do we (k)now!?* Which, by the way, if I have not said so expressly, is the one movie/documentary you *must* watch! It will change your life; at least, that is what it did for me.)

When we first try to learn to do something new, for example, we try to learn to ride a bike, the neurons in our brains try to figure out how our body can learn to balance so that we can ride the bike without falling; i.e., the neurons try to successfully learn to ride a bike. As we repeat a motion over and over again, the neurons that need to interact with each other in order for us to be able to learn to balance now form a connection with each other which is relatively permanent (as in the case of riding a bike or learning how to swim - you never "forget" or "unlearn" how to do those things).

Neuroscientists call that process "neurons that fire together, wire together." And this process works for not just physical or motor movements, it also works for modification of emotional or mental reactions.

For example, I used to always have a tough time with Road Rage, as so many of you may be having also. I used to get so angry when somebody would cut me off on the highway or not follow some rule of the road, and therefore, it would end up being something that I would be forced to do; a maneuver that I would have to make in order to avoid ending up in an accident. That would make my blood boil!

Road Rage is a "disease," in a sense. I have heard about how some of the genuinely nicest people that you may know turn into "nasties" when they get behind the steering wheel of a car. You might have seen that yourself. In fact, you might be one of those nice people.

Their anger originates from their need for perfection in manners and behavior. No wonder that they are bona fide "nice people." They follow rules on how to be good human beings. This same need for

Can we *ever* afford to *not* be nice?

perfection is exhibited while driving, in terms of following the rules of the road. They apply this stringent rule not only to themselves, but to other drivers on the road equally. And when others don't comply, it makes these nice people very angry and agitated.

After learning about this principle and this specific way that I could change my behavior or reaction, I decided to start practicing it. At first, it was difficult, and I found myself getting enraged, but then I started making a conscious effort to *not* get angry. As I did this, I found that I was able to control my anger more and more. I would still get upset on the road sometime, but most of the time, I was able to keep calm.

Now, I rarely get upset when somebody is driving extremely slowly in front of me, and there is no way to pass them and I am stuck driving behind them for a long stretch of the road. I just know that now I have more time to enjoy the music on the radio or to listen to the CD of one of Dr. Dyer's seminars. I don't mind a traffic jam now, for the same reason. Unless, of course, I absolutely *have* to get somewhere on-time, and I know that this jam is going to prevent that from happening. However, interestingly enough, now I seldom find myself stuck in those kinds of traffic jams. I don't think about yelling obscenities or flipping the "bird" to the person who may have cut me off in traffic, or tapping my brakes so that the car behind me which is tail-gating mine would have to slam on its brakes to avoid a collision. I just don't engage in such passive-aggressive or even downright aggressive behavior anymore.

I have, effectively, learned to tame my Road Rage. Well, for the most part! So, this can and should be used to make any and all changes within ourselves - physical, mental, or emotional - and it can lead to spiritual changes as well. We can use this process of creating a new Neuronet, and thereby, becoming a completely new person. The kind of person that we want to be.

Chapter 31
Leggo my ego!

All spiritual and religious texts or material; all spiritual and self-help gurus; all books on this subject of achieving higher consciousness and bliss; all of them teach us that the ego is the most egregious of culprits as far as the reasons why we all seem to suffer so much in life.

There must be something to it, don't you think?

So, what, exactly, is this thing called the "ego" and why is it such a menace to society, and the self? To demonstrate how dangerous the ego can be, I would like to share an incident that happened with me not too long ago. I want to do this *before* we discuss the nature of this beast because, in a way, this incident will help shed some light on the very definition of the word. This event will show the manifestation of my own ego in a very negative way; however, it will also show how it led to the eventual dilution of my ego, later on. It was one of the most important and powerful lessons that I have learned in my life.

God=mc²?

For this, I have Providence to thank.

(Singer Alanis Morissette, in her song entitled *Thank U*, sang "Thank you, Providence," but did not provide clarification regarding which "Providence" she was expressing gratitude towards. Unlike her, I will clearly explain that it is, in fact, the City of Providence, Rhode Island and Divine Grace, which is the meaning of the word *Providence*, both that are responsible for my life lesson.)

I used to work in a building near downtown Providence, RI. It used to be my and a friend's routine to go get a cup of coffee at the Dunkin' Donuts location right across the street from our building. Each day we used to take our break at around 3:30 PM, or so, and make our "Dunkin' Run."

It was a day in May of 2006. I don't recall the exact date, but if my memory serves me correctly, it was early May. It had been a little bit later than our usual time; it must have been 4:30 PM; I and my co-worker/friend, Rick Gauvreau, had stepped outside of our building, and since it had been a little bit later than usual, I lit up a cigarette as soon as I was out in the open. According to my normal routine, I would have waited to have that cup of coffee in my hand before I lit up that smoke. (I have quit smoking since January of 2007, but back then I was still a smoker.) We walked up to the coffee shop, and since I was in the middle of smoking my cigarette, I did not want to put it out and "waste" half of it, and so I requested my friend to go into the coffee shop, and to get me my usual cup of coffee. He obliged, and stepped into the store.

As I was standing outside this Dunkin' Donuts store located on Empire; a one-way street in Providence; enjoying my cigarette, three guys were walking by. Almost as soon as they had passed by me, one of them turned around and came straight towards me and said in a very demanding voice, "I want a cigarette!"

Mind you, he was not requesting a smoke; he was demanding it as if he was entitled to it! As if I was simply holding a pack of

Leggo my ego!

smokes for him and he could ask for and get one, on-demand, because in his mind, they were his cigarettes.

So, I instantly said no or that I did not have any more to spare. As he was walking away, he blurted out angrily, "What a cheap [expletive deleted]!" (That expletive rhymed with "mother trucker," as the censors would edit it on the cable TV networks of TNT or TBS.)

That just set me off like a bomb! I was offended beyond all belief! The "storm" of electrical impulses brewing in the Neuronet of my brain, and thus resulting in thoughts in my mind, was yelling at me and pointing me to the absurdity of this situation. A guy who was walking on the street, who himself was a smoker, but did not have enough money to feed his own bad habit, was saying that I was the one who was cheap. How ironic! And how dare he! So, I cussed back. I said something that would be translated by the censors as "forget you!"

(Just in case you might be wondering, this was *before* I got started on my way to transforming myself and onto the path of higher consciousness.)

Hearing this, another man from this group of three people, not the one who had initially asked me for a cigarette, but this other guy, came back towards me, and immediately got "all up in my grill," and asked rhetorically, "Why did you have to say that to my friend?" As he was too close to me for comfort, I raised my arm, and with my forearm right in front of me, as if to block him from head-butting me and to, simultaneously, move him away from me. Before I knew it, he had taken a swing at me.

A fight was then underway. I swung back at him, and think I hit him, and there were a few more punches thrown, back and forth. One landed on the left side of my face, between my left eye and ear. In the meantime my friend Rick, who was in the store, must have seen what was going on outside the glass doors of the store, and rushed outside.

God=mc²?

At this point, I don't recall exactly what was going on, but my friend said that he had pulled this guy away from me. I do remember not being engaged in fisticuffs with this guy anymore when I noticed the first guy, the one who demanded the cigarette initially; I saw him running back towards me. I also took two or three running steps towards him. After there were a couple of punches thrown, we were wrestling each other to free our arms to throw more punches, and we both fell to the ground. It was onto the sidewalk, but before we knew it, we were both on the street, but in a marked parking spot.

It was a sideways angled parking spot, not one that is parallel to the street and to the sidewalk - it was not the kind of spot where you would have to "parallel park," as would fit a whole car-length. It was one that would fit the width of the car, and once a car would be parked in that spot, it would be almost perpendicular to the street, but with a slight angle, length-wise.

In our wrestling, we almost went out of the area of the parking spot and into the street with the oncoming traffic; with fast moving buses and cars barreling down this one-way street.

I remember having one of the most fearful impulses of my life, "I am going to die today!"

We could have wrestled our way, while still rolling around on the ground, onto the middle of the street and been crushed by multiple numbers of buses and cars before anyone could have done anything to prevent it. Or, at the very least, a driver of a car could have easily decided to pull into the "open" parking spot that we were in, and quite possibly ran us over because we would have been below and out of his line-of-sight due to the car in the next spot, and also because it was an angled parking spot.

Of course, none of those things happened, obviously, otherwise I would not be in this physical realm anymore.

Anyhow, my friend pulled this other "dude" away from me, and I was still lying on the ground when the first guy that started the fight

Leggo my ego!

came back from nowhere and started to kick me, quite literally, when I was "already down."

Again, I am sort of foggy on the exact sequence and quite frankly, even the exact details since the whole thing, from beginning to end must have lasted 20 seconds, at the most. I am relaying the information based on the combination of details that I can recollect and from what my friend had said had happened.

While this must have been going on, a few of my other co-workers, whose shift had ended for the day, were in a restaurant next to the Dunkin' Donuts shop. They must have heard the commotion and had stepped out of the restaurant to see what was going on. As soon as these "street punks" saw a whole bunch of my co-workers step out, they realized that now they were the ones who were outnumbered. And so they started to run. A few of my co-workers, among which were the gentlemen by the names of Bob Couming and Kerry Morrissey, ran after them and caught two of the "perps" from the gang of three, and turned them over to the police.

(By the way, if I have not expressly done so already, I want to thank Bob and Kerry and anybody else who helped me in any way at all, including calling the paramedics and the police, helping me fill out the police report, making sure that I was not seriously injured, and such. Of course, I owe a debt of gratitude to my friends, Sarah Santagata and Rick Gauvreau, among others.)

Anyhow, by this time, which was a few minutes later, a crowd had gathered around us. My friend, Rick, had helped me up and onto my feet, and was asking how I was doing. Needless to say, I was not doing well.

My left ear was ringing from the punch to the face, and I had an awful headache. You know how in comic books and animated films, cartoon characters are depicted as "seeing stars," when they get hit with something. I was seeing stars too! My back was hurting from being kicked repeatedly when I was down on the ground. Also,

God=mc²?

I had a huge gash on my left elbow, which I must have gotten when I landed on the ground, when I first fell down. I had a concussion, and was taken to the hospital to be checked out.

All this transpired because I could not handle the fact that somebody had "dared" to brand me as "cheap," which I surely wasn't. Well, at least in my own opinion, I wasn't. If I truly believed that I was not cheap, and not only that, if I saw myself as generous, then it should not have mattered what another person thought of me. But the fact that it did proved it to me that it had been my ego that had played a major role in what had happened.

Ironically, the very ego that is, supposedly, the one responsible for the preservation of my life would have been the one that could have led me to my demise.

If I could have just let go of my ego, and said "So what if some guy that I don't even know called me something that I am not, so what?" In retrospect, it seems so easy and simple to do, doesn't it? But if one is not conditioned to respond that way, it is not easy at all. In fact, it is a whole lot easier to respond in the way that I did.

They say that smoking cigarettes can kill you. I agree; however, inhaling the noxious fumes of our own ego can do a better job at it, as I almost found out.

So, what is this thing, this beast, called the ego? The ego is the part of us, and more specifically, a construct of our mind, that tells us who *it* believes *we* are. I said that it is a construct of the mind because it could not be a construct of, or a part of our soul, because if that were the case, the ego would not be a problem at all. It would already identify ourselves as who we really are, which is primarily, and foremost, spiritual beings; eternal and infinite souls, with temporary and finite bodies.

Instead, the ego identifies ourselves simply and solely as physical beings. Sure, we have these "minds" which produce or have thoughts, however, the ego justifies those non-physical thoughts and

Leggo my ego!

this non-physical mind as the only necessary things for the physical body to exist and to seek out what the body wants or needs, as a matter of physical survival. The ego makes us believe that if the body did not exist, there would be no thoughts or mind, and therefore, the person would not exist.

In other words, the ego has come into existence out of *perceived* necessity. Even though it is a construct of the mind, and is only existent there, it bases all its beliefs on the physical world. And therefore, this perceived necessity that the ego feels is the reason for its existence is, necessarily, of a physical nature. And how, meaning through which media, is the physical world perceived by us? You might have guessed it - through our five physical senses. So, we have to go beyond the physical senses to overcome the ego.

When we start realizing and then believing the truth that we are not separate from God, we start to realize that we are getting all the things that we truly want, because we are truly deserving of them.

And in order to realize that truth we simply have to let go of our ego. The concept is simple, but there is really no simple way of letting go of our ego, we just have to practice humility, and we have to try to remember to do it as much as possible. If we cannot let it go completely, as least, we should begin the process of "diluting" the ego. That is the only way.

The hallmark of the ego is the importance of self that it makes us die-hard believers in. When somebody insults us, in any way at all, for example, calls us "stupid," or "cheap," or some other pejorative term like that, it is the ego that is insulted and hurt by those unkind words. It is from the ego that we respond to those words.

However, I can truly say that it can become much easier to *not* respond from the ego; not respond like I had done; if and when we have started to apply all the other principles that we have examined. One of the major examples of a principle that can help dilute the ego is that we should humble ourselves by, and when, we put our faith in a Higher Power to bring us what we want. And when that Higher Power does bring us what we want, we cannot help but know that it was, in fact, that Higher Power which brought us what we wanted, and not our efforts alone that did it.

In other words, we can start diluting the ego when we start taking less credit for the good things that happen in our life, and start giving more credit to God for them. Of course, this Higher Power, God, *will* bring us what we want if we have learned to pray the right way. (As we have learned to do very specifically in Chapter 25, and generally, throughout this book.)

This process makes us re-think our notion of our self-importance. More specifically, the importance of the mind and the body.

That, in and of itself, is what can inspire humility within ourselves. We will simply learn to give credit to the Higher Power, which is, ironically, located within us. This, in turn, leads to the dilution of our ego. And by purposefully and deliberately doing this several times, we will develop a new "Neuronet" which is now very easily capable of repeating the previous behavior, as we discussed this process in much detail, in the last chapter.

Another way to effectively dilute our ego is to think about the labels that we put on others and ourselves. This is discussed a lot more in detail in Chapter 13 already. When we re-examine the ways we define ourselves, we can stop doing it in ways that make the ego even bigger, and therefore, even more bothersome.

We have to learn a new way to define ourselves. Which, as you might well know by now, is as infinite and eternal spiritual beings, first; and then as these "carbon-based, electromagnetic 'suits' called bodies," second. (As a Near Death Experiencer had told Ms. Atwater, and as she had mentioned in her book, *The Big Book of Near Death Experiences*).

Contradictory to the *physical* reasons for the existence of the ego, there is even a *spiritual* reason for the ego to become active.

Leggo my ego!

When a person is on a spiritual path, and has made some headway in terms of reaching progressively higher states of consciousness, there is a very real danger of that diluted ego resurfacing and starting to reclaim its hold on him or her.

The way it starts to exert its importance is by pointing to the fact that now he or she is "better" than others because he or she is closer to God. Or is a highly advanced soul, or has experienced higher levels of consciousness. This is the classic and quite literal example of one suffering from the "Holier Than Thou" superiority complex.

One would think that by the very nature of this experience, one would have diluted the ego even more; however, sometimes it can have the opposite effect. It is an ironic or paradoxical phenomenon, and I am not quite sure why this happens, but it does. I do believe that when we achieve the highest form of enlightenment that we can achieve while still being physically alive, the ego is annihilated. Gone. Once and for all!

However, until that happens, constant vigilance, or an "ego watch" may be called on for all such times. Also, it might be a good idea to have, mentally handy, the *mantra* of "leggo my ego," which was inspired by the very famous and clever "Leggo my Eggo" slogan of the yummy Eggo® brand waffles made by the Kellog's Company. (Eggo waffles are, of course, very delicious, and nutritionally good for you, too. In other words, they are good for you all around! Whereas the ego is *none* of those things - it leaves "a bitter taste in your mouth," and is hazardous to your health!)

By the way, doesn't this make you want to dig into the freezer and get your own Eggo waffle or two? Oh, none left? You gotta make a run to the super-market and get some. I know I do!

Chapter 32

Do you think that the world would be *any* different if *you* did not exist?

Have you ever thought of *that*? Have you ever thought about how different, if *at all* different, the world would be if *you* never existed? Well, I think I know the answer to that - it would make a *world* of a difference to *me* - because you would not have bought my book. Okay, all kidding aside, did you think that it would pretty much be the same, well, except only *without* you? Or did you think that it would be different, but not much. Or did you think that it would be a *lot* different? And if so, in what way?

I think that the world would be radically and totally different if you had never come into existence!

(Think about the following scenarios by thinking about them as if they pertain to you, however, I am going to use my own self as the example.)

Similarly, I think the world would be radically and totally different if I did not exist. And not because I am somebody special;

God=mc²?

it's simply because I do exist right now - and because of my having come into existence - I have altered the state of the whole world in the most radical way. Every single person that I ever came into contact with, or interacted with, on any level or in any manner, and thereby was influenced by me, in a positive or negative manner would not have been influenced so if I had not existed. (I would like to think my influence was *only* positive, but who am I kidding - oh, wait - I am kidding myself.)

Everything would have been radically different for everybody on the planet. Starting from my parents, of course, because they would have never had me as a child so all of their decisions would have been very different, and so would their lives. Of course, the same for my siblings - they would have gotten more of the goodies - my share of the goodies; darn, I hate to think about that! (Then again, I would have never gotten their hand-me-downs, so I guess that would have been okay.)

My wife, my son, every person that I went to school with, every teacher, every professor, every driver on the road that I might have cut-off - sorry - I truly mean it, every person that I ever worked with, every customer that I served, every cashier that I was upset with because I had been "waiting too long," in the line (or as the British call it, "Queue"), every DMV employee, every boss, every ex-girlfriend, every friend, every author or book publisher etc., etc. You get the point. I had to make it visual - to give you an idea about how and why our existence is not *just* our existence.

(So, have you been visualizing yourselves in this role instead of me? And have you been thinking about how things would have been different for those people that you would never have come into contact with?)

And I have only mentioned people that I have been in *direct* contact with, and therefore shaped their lives. What about the Second Degree of Separation? What about all the people that *they* have ever

Do you think that the world would be *any* different....

come into contact with, at any time, on any level? Do you think that their life would have been different? Then, what about the Third Degree of Separation, and so on, and so forth.

And guess what, this "ripple effect" is not just determined by space, meaning whom you come into contact with, in this physical realm, at a particular place. It is also determined by time. Meaning, some of these interactions, obviously, have a time value and component to them also. I will give you an example of what I mean. My grandfather, my dad's father, passed away a few years before I was born. So, as a child, I never got a chance to play with my grandfather, as most grandchildren get to do, and almost always, love and remember that experience very fondly. Now, if I had gotten that chance, I might have been deeply influenced by that positive experience, and maybe my life would have been completely different.

So, the effect of having made contact with or connected with somebody a long, long time ago still continues to have an effect on the world, and it will continue to do so, forever. This is true for every being on the planet, which has ever lived, or is living, or will ever live. As I had mentioned in Chapter 7, quoting English poet John Donne's line, "no man is an island."

Again, this is not about being a *good* different or a *bad* different, it is simply stating that the whole world would have surely been different. This is the world-famous Butterfly Effect. A butterfly simply flaps its wings somewhere, and that results in a hurricane elsewhere, thousands of miles away.

Of course, we could also say, conversely, that the flapping of the butterfly's wings may have *stopped* a storm from brewing elsewhere!

Now, knowing that, my dear fellow-butterflies, I beg you to be careful about how, when, and where you decide to take flight and flap those mighty wings, because you just don't know what kind of an effect you might be having on the whole world.

God=mc²?

You just never know what effect your deeds, words or thoughts may have on one person or the whole world. A smile; a kind word and maybe one of encouragement or hope to somebody who may have been feeling hopeless; just a small thoughtful gift to brighten up somebody's day; or a very generous act of simply listening to somebody talk can sometimes save a person's life. You never know what kind of a difference a few words, within a few seconds, from a bus driver could make for a kid - one who may have run away from home, and may have been sleeping on a bench at a bus station - ready to end his life. Or how simply maintaining your "cool" while driving your car on the highway may prevent a 50-car pile-up.

So, I urge you to apply this rule, if possible, to everything that you do: *Overestimate* the damage that you can cause with your actions, and *underestimate* the good that they can do.

Having said that, if you do want to change the world, I am very sorry to tell you that you and I are too late for that party. We have *already* changed it. However, we can rejoice in the fact that the world is changing perpetually. And that we absolutely have the power to change it for the better. And we can do it anytime that we choose to do so. Of course, right now would be the best time to start changing the world for the better, but only if we feel ready.

The point is that regardless of what life "throws" at us, we can always *choose* to react in a certain way, and nudge the effect we have on others, in the positive direction.

And here's the secret to changing the world: We should change ourselves! Like the late Michael Jackson sang about our wanting to make the world a better place and how to go about doing it, "I'm starting with the man in the mirror!" If every person on the planet endeavored to change *just one person* - themselves - what we all would be doing is changing one, single person. The result would be almost seven billion people who would have changed, and hopefully, for the better. So, quite frankly, we can *start* with the person in the

Do you think that the world would be *any* different....
mirror, and even *stop* there! We don't even have to try to change anybody or anything else.

A good example of a perfect oxymoron is: This *change* being *constant*. Meaning that the only thing in life that is constant *is* change. Everything is always in flux. Everything is always changing, isn't it? Since that is the case, we should endeavor to perpetually reach for higher and higher levels of consciousness for ourselves, making this perpetual change a perpetually positive one.

Chapter 33
How will you see yourself and everybody else after this?

After a person "becomes" spiritual, he or she starts seeing people in a different light. And I have the word *becomes* with the quotes because I would like to point out that it is a process of *becoming aware* that one *is* spiritual already. In other words, we don't become spiritual; we just *realize* that we are spiritual.

What ensues when that happens is what I like to call the "Shallow Hal Effect." As you might recall in the movie, the title character, played by the versatile and very funny Jack Black, is truly a very shallow guy. He is a playboy that only cares about a woman's physical beauty, and is not really interested in finding out whether or not a particular physically attractive woman is also beautiful on the "inside." After he has a run-in with the amazing self-help guru Tony Robbins, in an elevator, and after Robbins hypnotizes him, Hal starts seeing the real "inner" beauty of the people he meets, especially, women. Although he is able to see the real inner beauty of everyone, being true to his playboy nature, he just notices the women more.

God=mc²?

Likewise, when one becomes spiritual, one starts to see others not as physically beautiful or ugly, man or woman, Democrat or Republican, old or young, Pepsi lover or Coke lover, right or wrong, Easterner or Westerner, Red Sox Fan or Yankee Fan (well, maybe *that* distinction always remains obvious), Scientist or Spiritualist, etc., etc. You get the idea.

You simply don't see these distinctions - you really start seeing people as what they really *are* - as souls; infinite spirits; or as Dr. Wayne Dyer calls us all, "a piece of the Divine." And when you start to do that, you also start to *treat* everybody else differently. Of course, that is a *good* differently, not a *bad* differently.

At least, that is exactly what has happened to me, and I sincerely hope it happens to you also.

Along with seeing everybody else as spiritual beings, you also start to realize that everybody else has the same exact basic wants and needs. We all want to love and be loved. We all want to feel like we are important and an integral part of the world, which, as I described in the last chapter, we *are*. We all have the same exact basic struggles and we all rejoice the same way when we triumph over life's obstacles, whether the obstacles may be perceived or real.

We all want to live the life of our dreams. We all really do want the same basic things; viz., peace, love, health, happiness, freedom, joy, abundance, satisfaction, longevity of life, to name a few.

We don't want just quantity; we also want quality in regards to all of these things mentioned above. And we all want these things regardless of who we are in the physical realm; i.e., regardless of our age, gender, race, profession, educational background, socio-economic status, country of origin or of current residence, sexual orientation, personal preferences, political persuasion, religious faith or spiritual beliefs (which includes Atheists and Agnostics), or any other distinction you can think of. In other words, we all want *one* thing - to feel perpetual bliss.

How will you see yourself and everybody else....

When we practically apply the theoretical principles of science-based practical spirituality, we will see everyone as who they really are - spiritual beings seeking their own bliss, and therefore there will be a new-found respect and love for one-another. (Incidentally, by practicing the principles discussed in the last few Chapters, we can express our love for God; i.e., to love *Love* itself.)

And having that respect and love for another will lead us to treating another in a much better way, and thus lead to making the attainment of this spiritual goal even easier - for them, *and* for us.

Moral of this chapter: Try to see everybody as spiritual beings trying to seek their own bliss, and if possible, help them do that. In that way you will make it easier to seek your own bliss. By the way, this is another great example of a virtuous cycle.

Chapter 34
"God wants spiritual fruit, not religious nuts!"
- A church sign

I thought that this sign, from outside the Attleboro Advent Christian Church, which is a church in my native city of Attleboro, MA, was a pretty funny and a totally appropriate one for this book; I think you might agree with that opinion. So, I *had* to mention it!

I have said elsewhere in the book that, ultimately, the purpose of religion is to steer us towards spirituality. And that, interestingly enough, it seems to be what science is doing also, however, it may be doing so inadvertently.

So, God wants us to enjoy these "fruits" of spirituality. He does not care so much about religious or dogmatic "nuts!"

Again, as I have mentioned before, just not in those words exactly, I am in favor of religion - *any* religion - that moves the Faithful *towards* God, and does so in a non-judgmental and non-dogmatic way. However, one does not absolutely *need* religion to

God=mc²?

become more spiritual and to have a direct connection and relationship with God. One can do it by following a non-denominational spiritual path that respects *all* religions, however does not specifically follow any one of them. One can do it by walking that path of non-denominational spirituality by incorporating some or all of the principles laid out here, and in other material that may be of interest.

I have a new-found respect for the fundamental teachings of *all* religions, and specifically, for my own, Hinduism, based on what I have learned while researching this book. I have developed respect not only for the basic principles but also for the myriad rituals, rites, and ceremonies deeply rooted in those religious and spiritual traditions. I used to be so bored and jaded in hearing about, or worse, for having to endure some Hindu ritual. I never knew or, for that matter, cared, about why some ritual was being performed.

Now, I try to learn as much as I can about the symbolism *behind* the ritual because there always was some deep meaning and reason of a symbolic nature behind the physical actions of the ritual.

And not only that, there was and still is a *scientific* or a *practical* reason for performing a certain rite. So, for example, in a Hindu wedding ceremony, which is *hours* long, a couple is considered wedded only after they have walked around a holy fire seven times. Well, each of these rounds made around the holy fire symbolizes a promise or an oath of performing certain duties and living a virtuous and faithfully married life. I never knew that! I was 25 years of age, and had attended twice as many weddings as the number represented by my age, until the time I learnt that.

I want to tell you a short story about how that happened:

It was around Easter time in the year 2000. I had gone up to Toronto, Canada, to attend my cousin Sunny Thakrar's wedding.

I was unpleasantly surprised when I first saw the *mundup*, which is the mini-stage set up for the wedding ceremony. This *mundup* is a gazebo-type construction, with four metallic or wooden

"God wants spiritual fruit, not religious nuts!"

poles which are decorated by traditional Indian designs. There is, generally, also a beautifully adorned dome or roof to this mini-stage. There are also lots of flowers hanging from the top, and all around this stage.

Similarly, this was a beautiful *mundup*, if memory serves me well; however, memory does serve me well about another thing; I do remember clearly that I could not help but notice the very conspicuously placed microphone in front of the priest who was to conduct the ceremony. I had never seen one placed on the wedding stage, in front of the priest for him to speak into - in an Indian ceremony.

And I wondered if that was to annoy us even more than he possibly could have with the monotonous drone of the unintelligible Sanskrit *mantras*, or if there was some *other* unfathomable reason for it being there. Maybe the purpose was to lull us into a gentle, trance-like siesta! At that point, I could only pray that it was just that because I could not consciously sit through another one of these painfully long and boring ceremonies. Don't get me wrong, please. I was very happy to be present at my cousin's wedding; it is the actual wedding ceremony that I was a little bit chagrined about.

Well, the priest, as he started to recite the holy *mantras* necessary for the marriage to take place, also started giving us a play-by-play, if you will, in *English*, of what those Sanskrit mantras meant and what the particular rite that may have been going on at that time symbolized. That was the first time in my life, ever, that I actually enjoyed a wedding ceremony, with all its rituals. I have to give some major kudos to my Neema aunty (Sunny's mom) for her genius in coming up with that unconventional idea!

While growing up, whenever I had attended a wedding with my parents and the rest of my family, the highlight and the only good reason for my having been there was the food. Nothing else! Well, okay, maybe a close second, when I was still a kid, would have been getting to play with other children at the wedding who were equally

God=mc²?

uninterested in the wedding ceremonies. Later on, as I grew to be a teenager and older, that second position was replaced by the joy of seeing and meeting pretty girls at those weddings. Other than those exceptions, everything else was something to be tolerated and endured, just so that I could get to the best part of the whole wedding: The scrumptious feast! I think a lot of us can relate to that, Hindu or not.

Now, of course, things have changed a little bit. Now, I care about the wedding rites and rituals as much as I do about the yummy meal. I enjoy both, equally!

In mystical Judeo-Christian tradition, the practice of Baptism was supposed to be full-body immersion in water until death by drowning occurred. And then the person was "brought back to life." As you might imagine what this process may have caused - a Near-Death Experience - an actual realization of the Holy Spirit or something to that effect. This is as per a quote from *The Big Book of Near Death Experiences*, which further featured a quote from another book, *The Meeting of Science and Spirit*, by John White.

Most, if not all, experiencers of NDEs develop a deep spiritual belief after their NDE, even if they had been "die-hard" Atheists (please pardon the pun there) before their experience. So one can clearly see the practicality of this type of a Baptism, in terms of providing *experiential* proof of God's existence. In other words, one can see the practicality of this religious ritual; however still, it is not necessary to go through this process to have an experience of God. Any mystical experience that can be created using physical means can also be created using spiritual means alone!

Again, don't get me wrong, please. I am *still* not a big fan of religious rituals; it's just that now I try to understand them, and do respect them. However, my appeal to you is to try and inquire about your own religion and religious rituals and to learn as much as you can about the symbolism *behind* them. Most rituals, if not all of them,

"God wants spiritual fruit, not religious nuts!"

have a hidden or indirect symbolic meaning that may or may not be clear to us, upon initial observation. A particular ritual may even seem silly or inane or quite frankly, even insane! However, in a lot of cases, they simply aren't so. (As Robert Langdon, who is a Symbologist and a character from Dan Brown's famous novels and adapted feature films, *The Da Vinci Code* and *Angels & Demons*, would agree.)

A word of caution, though! Please do not take this to mean that you can partake in blind belief and start taking part in rituals or ceremonies of human or animal sacrifices and such. These types of sacrificial and other such violent or potentially harmful rituals (in any way) are, in fact, inane, insane and unnecessary. Well, at least that is my humble opinion. Do remain skeptical of any and all rituals unless you find no reason to be so anymore. Otherwise, you should have nothing to fear from, as far as any aspect of religion is concerned, and in fact, you may even feel the same kind of affinity for it as I have grown to do now.

However, again, *know* that you don't *need* to belong to, or practice, any specific religion, in order to enjoy spiritual fruits, and thereby, have a direct connection with God because that is how it was, and still is, meant to be.

In other words, you can enjoy spiritual fruits without becoming a religious nut!

Chapter 35
Closing time!

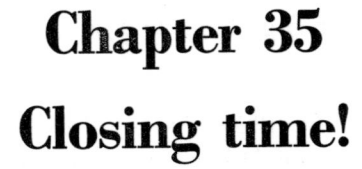

"Closing time; every new beginning comes from some other beginning's end"
- Semisonic, from the song *Closing Time*

The above is a line from a hit song by the band Semisonic. I don't remember, exactly, when this song was a hit, but I think a lot of us knew about it or heard it. It was at least eight years ago or so. No worries if you haven't heard it, though.

I think that it is a very poignant song because it talks about how the Universe works, both on the macroscopic level, as in with the formation of galaxies and stars and then their eventual end, and on the microscopic level, meaning in our lives. It points to the fact that all life is cyclical. There is *really* no "real" end to it. As the lyrics literally say, every new beginning comes from some other beginning's end.

There was the Big Bang that created the Universe, and then there will be the Gnab Gib - as scientists often joke; the reverse of the Big Bang, and of course, "Big Bang" spelled backwards. The Big Crunch, as it is also called.

God=mc²?

And then there will be another Big Bang, and the expansion of the Universe created by that gargantuan explosion will go on for billions or even trillions of years, and the contraction will go on for an equal amount of time, ending in an implosion, which in turn will cause yet another Big Bang, and so on and so forth.

In fact, well, I cannot prove it to be a fact, but chances are that there have been multiple universes in existence before the one we are existent in. I am not talking parallel universes; I am talking ones before ours ever came into existence. They were not contemporaries of each other. There is a mention of this in the ancient Vedas, if I am correct.

And of course, that also means that after ours ceases to exist, there most definitely will come into existence another Universe, with all of its splendor - its galaxies, stars, planets and all the various celestial bodies - and of course, living beings that will inhabit several thousand of the planets that will also come into existence.

There was another very important point that the song makes, and it reminds me to mention my interpretation of that point here. It talks about "gathering up our jackets, and making it to the exits…"

Well, when we leave this "joint" called Earth, we don't have to gather up our jackets. We leave them behind, to be replaced by brand new ones. Or none at all, depending on where we are headed.

Of course, a jacket is a metaphor for our body. Ultimately meaning that we are what? You guessed right; that we are spiritual beings and that we are not these bodies we have or inhabit. And that at the time of physical death, or if we have achieved much advancement in our spiritual journey, then by choice, our souls will leave these pieces of apparel behind. We will do so simply because we won't actually need them in the spiritual realms of existence since we will already *be* all that will be needed for us to exist there.

Closing time!

Other than the significant scientific and spiritual points made in the song (whether intentional or not), its mention is appropriate for another reason. Because it is "closing time" for this book also due to the fact that all things are cyclical, and as anything that has a beginning, it must also have an ending.

Chapter 36
Goodbye!
(For real now, I mean it!)

What else did you think I would end the book with? "Hello?" That just would not have made any sense! Why would anybody do that?

Anyhow, I do mean it, may God be with you, as He always is, anyway. I just hope that you can make it a *knowing* within yourself that He is with you at all times, because He *is* you!

You are God. Not god-like, or even "a" god; you are *the* God! Because there is only *one* God. And we are *all* part of that *one* God; therefore, we are that God. Energetically, everyone and everything in existence *is* God, as even science agrees! It's just that everyone and everything is in different states of consciousness, and therefore in different states of awareness and recognition of this fact.

You will start coming to a realization that this is absolutely true when you start understanding and applying the principles in this book.

God=mc²?

Then you will start living your life the way you *want* to. You will start living it the way God would want you to because by your living the life of your dreams, God is doing the same thing. In other words, what God wants for you, and what you want for yourself is the same. God lives vicariously *through* us, because that is the *only* way God can experience life. So, go out into the world, and do what you were meant to do - live the life of your dreams - and achieve perpetual bliss. Do it *knowing* that it is *by*, *for*, and *as* God!

God is always with and within you, and so you are never without God. The meaning of the word that is the title of the first chapter and this chapter, the final one, is not just its meaning or even a wish for another person. It is an absolute fact; as we now know it to be!

Will you ever say *Goodbye* to somebody and still remain unaware of the true meaning of what you are saying?

I know that I won't.

Goodbye!

ADDEDNDUM

People find it easier; much, much easier; to change a physical routine than to change a mental routine. They find it much simpler to change what they do, on a daily basis. They can change their routine, but what is a lot more difficult, or at least, what people find a lot more difficult to do is change the way that they think.

They may claim that they have changed their thought process, but that is the last of the things to change. Unless of course, they are hit with something tragic or so unexpected that it simply throws them off their normal, beaten path of thinking.

So, overall, this is a new way of thinking, more than anything else. You can continue to do what you normally do, as long as you now think in this particular manner, you will change the results of those same actions you used to do. Oh, and another thing; those actions - they cannot help but change in accordance to this new way of thinking. And you won't even know when your actions changed. It might be a while before you realize that you simply don't do those things that you used to do.

People approach wanting to make a change by changing what they do, physically. And it's not that it cannot happen that way. It can and does, but it's just too darn difficult, takes a lot longer, and with a lot of supposed "failure" in the process. It is taking the long road, when a short-cut is readily available.

Take the short-cut. And this is the short-cut!

RECOMMENDATIONS AND SOURCES

(R is a Recommendation; S is a Source; and RS is both)

Books:

    John Assaraf & Murray Smith, *The Answer*, Atria Books, R

    P.M.H. Atwater, *The Big Book of Near-Death Experiences*, Hampton Roads, RS

    Colette Baron-Reid, *Messages From Spirit*, Hay House, RS

    Gregg Braden, *The Divine Matrix*, *The Spontaneous Healing of Belief*, HayHouse, RS

    Dan Brown, *The Da Vinci Code*, Doubleday, RS

    Sylvia Browne, *Phenomenon*, Dutton, RS

    Rhonda Byrne (Featuring Various Teachers), *The Secret*, Beyond Words/Atria Books, (Documentary Film/Book/Audio Book) RS

    Jack Canfield, *The Success Principles*, Collins, R; *Key to Living the Law of Attraction*, HCI, R

    Deepak Chopra, *Life After Death: The Burden of Proof*, Harmony Books, R

    James J. Cramer, *Real Money: Sane Investing In An Insane World*, R; *Mad Money: Watch TV, Get Rich* (Jim Cramer with Cliff Mason), R; *Stay Mad For Life: Get Rich, Stay Rich* (Jim Cramer with Cliff Mason), Simon & Schuster, R

    Lama Surya Das, *The Big Questions*, Rodale, RS

    Mike Dooley, *Notes from the Universe* Series (3-Book Set), RS; *Choose Them Wisely*, Beyond Words/Atria Books, R

    Dr. Wayne W. Dyer, *Being In Balance*, RS; *Change Your Thoughts - Change Your Life*, R; *Inspiration*, R; *The Power of Intention*, RS; *Excuses Begone!* Hay House, R

Eknath Easwaran, *The Bhagavad Gita for Daily Living*, Jaico Books, RS

Dr. Amit Goswami, *God Is Not Dead*, Hampton Roads, RS

Esther and Jerry Hicks, *Ask and It is Given*, Hay House, RS

Christopher Hitchens, *God Is Not Great*, Twelve, RS

Stacy Horn, *Unbelievable*, Harper Collins, R

Linda Johnsen, *The Complete Idiot's Guide to Hinduism*, Alpha, RS

Debra Lynn Katz, *You Are Psychic*, Llewellyn, RS

Dr. Bruce Lipton, *The Biology of Belief*, Hay House, RS

Ainslie MacLeod, *The Instruction*, Sounds True, RS

James Van Praagh, *Ghosts Among Us*, Harper One, RS

James Arthur Ray, *Harmonic Wealth*, Hyperion, RS

Swami Saradananda, *Chakra Meditation*, Duncan Baird Publishers, RS

Mary Ann Winkowski, *When Ghosts Speak*, Grand Central Publishing, RS

Hybrid Films, Documentaries, and other Films:

Introducing Abraham: The Secret Behind "The Secret"? 2007, Hay House, RS

The Shift, 2009, Hay House, R

The Voice, 2008, Intention Media, RS

What the Bleep do we (k)now!? 2004, Captured Light Distribution/Twentieth Century Fox, RS

What the Bleep!? Down the Rabbit Hole, 2006, Captured Light Distribution/Twentieth Century Fox, RS

Feature Films:

A Few Good Men, 1992, Castle Rock Entertainment, RS

As Good as It Gets, 1997, TriStar Pictures, RS

Angels & Demons, 2009, Columbia Pictures, RS

Bruce Almighty, 2003, Universal Pictures, RS

Bulletproof Monk, 2003, Cub Five Productions, RS

Coming to America, 1988, Eddie Murphy Productions/Paramount Pictures, S

Contact, 1997, Warner Bros. Pictures, RS

Dumb & Dumber, 1994, New Line Cinema, RS

Flatliners, 1990, Columbia Pictures Corporation, RS

The Fly, 1986, Brooksfilms, S

The Fifth Element, 1997, Gaumont, RS

Ghostbusters, 1984, Black Rhino Productions/Columbia Pictures, RS

Hideaway, 1995, TriStar Pictures, RS

The Hitchhiker's Guide to the Galaxy, 2005, Touchstone Pictures, RS

Jerry Maguire, 1996, Gracie Films/Tristar Pictures, RS

The Matrix Trilogy, Various, Warner Bros. Pictures, RS

Mission: Impossible, 1996, Cruise/Wagner Productions/Paramount Pictures, S

The Pursuit of Happyness, 2006, Columbia Pictures Corporation, RS

Road House, 1989, Silver Pictures, RS

The Rock, 1996, Hollywood Pictures, RS

Shallow Hal, 2001, Twentieth Century Fox Film Corporation, RS

The Terminator, 1984, Hemdale Film, S

What Dreams May Come, 1998, Polygram Filmed Entertainment, R

Wall Street, 1988, Twentieth Century Fox Film Corporation, RS

Television Shows (and the Networks of their original or current airing):

Are You Being Served? BBC, RS

Dharma & Greg, ABC, S

Friends, NBC, S

Ghost Whisperer, CBS, RS

Ghost Hunters, SyFy, RS

Heroes, NBC, RS

Mad Money w/Jim Cramer, CNBC, RS

Monk, USA, RS

My Name is Earl, NBC, RS

Nip/Tuck, FX, S

Seinfeld, NBC, RS

UFO Hunters, The History Channel, RS

Audio Programs:

Being in Balance, Dr. Wayne Dyer, Hay House, RS

Manifesting Change: It Couldn't Be Easier, Mike Dooley, TUT Entp., RS

Songs (Song title, Artist, Album):

Here We Go, Let's Rock & Roll, C+C Music Factory, *Gonna Make You Sweat*, S

U Can't Touch This, M C Hammer, *Please Hammer, Don't Hurt 'Em*, S

Man in the Mirror, Michael Jackson, *Bad*, RS

Material Girl, Madonna, *Like a Virgin*, S

Faith, George Michael, *Faith*, S

Thank U, Alanis Morissette, *Supposed Former Infatuation Junkie*, S

What's The Frequency, Kenneth? R.E.M., *Monster*, S

Simply Irresistible, Robert Palmer, *Heavy Nova*, S

Closing Time, Semisonic, *Feeling Strangely Fine*, RS

Because The Night, 10,000 Maniacs, *Campfire Songs: The Popular, Obscure & Unknown Recordings*, S

Can't Get Enough of Your Love, Babe, Barry White, *Can't Get Enough*, S

Other Sources of Information (Internet):

www.imdb.com

www.wikipedia.org

www.artofliving.org

Other Mentions (M):

The Animal, 2001, Revolution Studios/Happy Madison Productions (Movie), RS

The Daily Show with Jon Stewart, Comedy Central (TV Show), RS

Ghost Adventures, Travel Channel (TV Show), M

Ghost Lab, Discovery Channel (TV Show), M

The Jay Severin Show, WTKK 96.9 FM Boston Talks (Radio Talk Show), RS

Party of Five, Fox (TV Show), M

The Power of Intention, PBS (TV Show - Special), M

Slumdog Millionaire, 2008, Celador Films (Movie), R

Star Trek, NBC (TV Show - Original), S

Street Signs, CNBC (TV Show), RS

Squawk on the Street, CNBC (TV Show), RS

Quantum of Solace, 2008, Metro-Goldwyn-Mayer (Movie), RM

ACKNOWLEDGMENTS

There have been several thousand people who have come into my life so far. These wonderful angels of a being have helped shape the person that I am today. I would really have to write a book dedicated to each of those individuals regarding how they have helped me; however, for now, I will name a few names, to begin with.

I will start with a couple of people completely and totally instrumental in my having written this book, and they don't even know that I exist.

The first one of these wonderfully inspiring people is my self-appointed spiritual guru, Dr. Wayne Dyer. As I just said, Dr. Dyer does not even know that I exist; however, he has absolutely transformed my life. I recommend all of his books, CDs, DVDs, Seminars and other related material. You can find information about them at www.DrWayneDyer.com, or you can also go there via the link from my website, www.GodEqualsmcSquared.com.

Thank you, Dr. Dyer, from the bottom of my heart and soul!

Another person who is oblivious to my existence is James J. Cramer. Yes, the "Mad One" himself - Jim Cramer - of the show *Mad Money w/Jim Cramer* on the highly esteemed financial news channel, CNBC, which, by the way, is the only network on 95% of the time in the Thakrar household. (The remaining five percent is reserved for shows such as *Barney & Friends, Mickey Mouse Clubhouse* and such – for my two and a half year old son.) Jim's show is what I derived inspiration from in terms of the format that I have followed in this book - one of using pop-culture references - in order to demystify complex topics in both, science and spirituality. (Well, in his case, he demystifies Stocks and helps individual investors successfully navigate the "Streets" of the Stock Market.) Thank you so very much, Jim! Also, many thanks to your nephew, Cliff Mason, and the staff of Mad Money, especially Candy Cheng and Regina Gilgan. By the way, everybody should tune into Jim's show, and read all of his books; well, *only* if one wants to make "mad" money and thereby become "insanely" wealthy.

Boo-Yah!

Unlike the folks mentioned above, a person who is well aware that I exist, and that I am present in physical form, is my dearest friend, Dr. Vipul Chitalia, MD, PhD. He is a true friend, mentor and confidant. He is a spiritual *and* scientific guru of mine. I really would not have made it to this point without him. He has encouraged me and been a gentle, yet a true, honest, and genuine evaluator of my work, and for that I will forever remain indebted to him.

Thank you, Dr. Vipul Chitalia!

(By the way, Dr. Chitalia and the co-founders of his dynamic and very innovative Biotech firm, Dr. Ajit Bharti and Dr. Daniel Prabakaran, are working on gene-based treatments for Lung Cancer, Liver Cancer and Leukemia. Also, they are in the process of discovering a similar genetic treatment for the HIV/AIDS virus! So, you might hear his and his co-founders' names a lot in the news, in the near future.)

I also feel a great deal of gratitude for the Universe. Towards Mr. Universe, himself. Not the final winner of an intergalactic bodybuilding competition, but to the embodiment of the entire Universe. The Universe personified. Yes, I *am* talking about Mike Dooley, otherwise famously known throughout the Universe, well, *as* the Universe. By the way, if you don't know (and quite frankly, *how* can you *not* know because he is well-known in the Universe), Mike is the best, and my most favorite teacher from *The Secret*. Thank you, Mike Dooley!

I would like to express my gratitude towards the producers of the hybrid film, *What the Bleep do we (k)now!?* and all the folks featured in the film. Among them, I would like to thank Dr. Amit Goswami, especially. I consider myself a "Quantum Activist" because of his message from his book entitled *God Is Not Dead*.

Many thanks to Rhonda Byrne for revealing to me, and the rest of the world, *The Secret*. Thanks to each and every teacher featured in this world-famous documentary and book.

Thanks to my dear friend, Shailin Thakkar, the director of Aksharatit Offset Printers, Pvt. Ltd., my publisher, for having faith in this project and doing your very best to meet the needs of the same. This book is a physical reality because of your efforts. Thanks to Dharmesh and Kalpa Joshi, the creators of the artwork for the covers of my book - they took my vision and made it a reality. Kudos to you, and thank you for putting up with me and my fussiness, and of course, doing such a great job with the covers. Thanks to Rapid Publishing for employing their services.

I owe an immense debt of gratitude to Deb Weigert, my editor and dear friend for her support and encouragement, and for all that she has done. Thank you so much for your guidance and mentorship. Many thanks to Emily for always being so positive and supportive.

I would like to thank all of my friends and co-workers who have encouraged me to follow my heart and to boldly seek the fulfillment of my dreams, or have otherwise been influential in my life. A *few* of the notable ones are Paul Warner, Rakesh Khetarpal, Kristin Pagliuca-Britton, Devendra Patel, Sarvesh Patel, Anuj Hora, Jagdish Motiani, Ritesh Master, Mayank Mathur, Kandarp Joshi, Milan Patel, Ankur Shah, Chitrang Parikh, Toral Shah, Rupal Patel, Parini Shah, Stephanie Hennessey, Kathryn Quinlan, Rajal Patel, Allison Hallissey, Seth Grossman, Aaron Silva, Sharon Martell, Jogi and Deb Sajjan,

Praveen Reddy, Reza Aidin, Amrish and Nikki Patel, Monil and Asmita Patel, Mihir Rao, Manish Vaishnav, Saurabh Shrivastava, Aparna Arora, Mansi Tuli, Digant Shah, Christy Sherman, Deven Shah, Mohammad Shamroz, Kerry Wilkinson, Rhegina Sinozich, Dr. Doug Welpton, Dr. Marion Ross, Dr. Tracy Latz, Karen Nowicki, Rosanna Ienco Barned, Eve Bardanis, Dr. Anna Maria Prezio, Tara Lee Graham, Marie Witt, David C. Vento, and Michelle Kurcina.

I also wanted to thank *all* of my co-workers at the last place that I worked, which was, of course, the Phone Company; however, I will name a few, and they are in alphabetical order, by last name: Tom Alarie, Lorelei Alfano, Peter Andrade, John Bell, Jeff Berard, Dick Bergeron, Jay Bernier, Cathy Bienvenue, Ana Buccieri, Brian Carroll, Kim Case, Charlie Collins, Art Costa, Eileen Creegan, Jack Crook, Elaine DaCosta, Debra Daignault, Marybeth DaSilva, Tres Davis, Tom Dolan, Ann Downing, Maggie Fisher, Wes Garell, Laurie Goulet, Scott Grocott, Wendy Hendrickson, Pat Hull, Marvin Johnson, Donna Kramarz, Holly Kuznar, Russ LaFazia, Tim Lisak, Chris Lowell, Tina Luciano, Mike Mayette, Heather Merlet, Mike Metta, Steve Mohney, Ken Montgomery, Todd Montgomery, Brian Mooney, Chuck Moreira, Mike Moreira, Jacquie Murfield, Roger Norrgard, Bill O'Neil, Tom Ouellette, Tony Peixoto, Gina Perry, David Pitts, Peggy Plociak, Mark Rogers, Michelle Rogers, Patricia Rowe, Billy Russo, Paula Sadler, Kellie San Souci, Curtis Scholle, Lou Seligowski, Pradeep Sharma, Bob Shea, Jr., Dawn Souto, Linda Storey, Ann Sweeney, Rebecca Taber, Marilyn Taglianetti, Wendy Therault, and Veronica Vargas. (Would you believe that I "said" all those names in one breath?!)

I would also like to thank some of my ex-colleagues, bosses, peers, and friends; viz., Ben Summers, Melissa Archer, Ayyub Bailey, Walter Picerno, Dean Guimares, Kevin Kelly, Matt Medeiros, Sarah Santagata, Rick Gauvreau, Diane Roy, Jeff Greaves, Greg Mahdesian, John Souve, and Deb Carter.

(If I did not mention somebody's name, specifically, but if we are acquainted with each other or have ever interacted with one another, I beg you for the acceptance of my apologies for not having mentioned your name, and please consider this to be a "thank you" to you, also.)

Thanks to all the members of my *Satsang* group: I appreciate your support and encouragement very much.

Thanks to the wonderful folks at Bradley Communications Corp. - Steve and Bill Harrison - and all the awesome members of their staff, including the super-efficient and super-nice, Nancy Ippoliti, and the great communicator and organizer, Nick Summa. You guys have helped me hone in on the book that I wanted to write, and also, hopefully, helped me make it the same one that people would want to read. You have truly helped me make a "Quantum Leap" in my career as an author. (I would recommend your services to all authors!)

I would also like to take the opportunity to convey my heartfelt gratitude to each and every member of the entire Ganatra family, starting with the patriarch of the same, Jayantilal uncle, and the matriarch who is Sushila aunty. My thanks to Ashwin, Rekha, Pooja and Megha; Nilesh, Neha, and Kush; Asit, Bhavna, Shyama and Gopesh; Amit, Poonam, Avni and Shreya. They are a friend of the family; however, they have always been like family to us. I and my parents stayed with them the first three months that we were here in the U.S. I would also like to thank the related Kotecha family, Mahesh, Neeta, Hemang, Ravi and Sejal.

A special thanks is in order for my favorite cousin in the whole wide world - Monica Thakrar - thank you so much for believing in me always, and for being a rock that I could lean on at any time. And of course, thanks to her parents, Anil uncle and Neema aunty for *always* being there for us and for being the reason why I am here in the U.S.A. A special thanks to another one of my cousins, Alkesh Thakrar, for being the coolest person that I have ever known.

Thanks to my cousin Sweta and her husband, Gunjan Gandhi, a dear friend of mine, for being so supportive and for all their words of encouragement. And, "yes" is the answer to the question that he does get a lot; he actually *is* related to the Great Soul. Mahatma Gandhi was his grandfather's uncle! However, unlike me, Gunjan is very humble and so he does not like to admit that fact.

I thank my parents, Vinod and Sarla Thakrar, for bringing me into this world, and nurturing me and taking care of me. You are the best parents in the world! Well, other than me - I am a pretty good father to my son also. I thank them for always believing in me, and keeping the faith that all would turn out well.

I would like to thank all of my siblings, their spouses and their children for their support, and for being in my life. Here's a list of them, starting from my eldest sibling, and in the same order as mentioned above: Smita and Kishan Somaiya, Meghna and Chirag; Sandhya and Deepak Ravani, Ankit and Bhargav; Vishwa and Kalpesh Bhatt, Radhika and Devang; Anand and Anju Thakrar, Soumya and Chintan.

I would like to thank my wife, Meera. I would not have written this book if it weren't for her. Thanks to my son, Krish, for having come into our lives, and having brought us such joy that we could not have even imagined. I know that you had a choice, and you chose us. For that, I have dedicated this book to you!

Of course, none of this would be even possible without the Creator of the Universe. So, thank you, God!

ABOUT THE AUTHOR

Prasann V. Thakrar is the newest and the most dynamic author, coach and inspirational speaker in the "new" field of Self-Empowerment and Life-Transformation via blending modern science and non-denominational spirituality.

So far, Prasann has been on 11 radio talk-show interviews and has been invited to write articles in Pop Psychology/Self-Help print magazines such as *Going Bonkers?* and various other online magazines geared towards Self-development. Via his writing, which is very easy to understand, Prasann sheds light on the bridge - the connection - between science and spirituality in such a way that anyone can understand this connection, and then apply the principles in their own life to bring about self-empowerment and life-transformation…..easily!

It is the author's goal to have a permanent positive impact on your life. He knows that you are, very easily, capable of creating and leading the life of your dreams; and he wants exactly that for you.

Prasann is an inspirational speaker and a dynamic coach who can help transform the life of any individual or the direction of any business towards what is desired. Prasann is available for speaking engagements, and for group and one-on-one coaching in a personal or a business setting.

Also, you can get more information about him and his life-transforming seminars and workshops entitled **Quantum Leap of Faith™** via his website, **www.GodEqualsmcSquared.com** or by directly sending him an email at **Prasann@GodEqualsmcSquared.com**.

NOTES

NOTES

NOTES

NOTES

NOTES